Hostile Heartland

Hostile Heartland

Racism, Repression, and Resistance in the Midwest

BRENT M. S. CAMPNEY

UNIVERSITY OF ILLINOIS PRESS
Urbana, Chicago, and Springfield

Publication of the book made possible in part by a
grant from the University of Texas Rio Grande Valley

Cataloging information available from the
Library of Congress

ISBN 978-0-252-04249-2 (hardcover) | 978-0-252-08430-0
(paperback) | 978-0-252-05133-3 (e-book)

Contents

Acknowledgments

I thank many people and organizations for their support of this work. Among these, I owe a debt of gratitude to the librarians and archivists at the state archives at the Kansas State Historical Society in Topeka, the Special Collections Research Center of the Morris Library at Southern Illinois University, Carbondale, the State Historical Society of Missouri in Columbia, and the archives and library of the Ohio History Center in Columbus. I am especially indebted to the Kenneth Spencer Research Library at the University of Kansas for an Alyce Hunley Whayne Travel Award and to the Special Collections and University Archives at Pittsburg (Kansas) State University for a Hertlein-Whitehead Visiting Scholars Program grant, both of which helped facilitate the research for this project. I also appreciate the support of the University of Illinois Press, which has put its faith in me for a second time, and in particular the support of James Engelhardt, Jennifer L. Comeau, Jane Zanichkowsky, and Laurie Matheson. Finally, I appreciate the outstanding work of cartographer Erin Greb.

Thomas Britten, a generous friend and colleague, has been a supportive department chair and provided much-appreciated course releases at critical stages in the writing process. Walter Diaz, the dean of the College of Liberal Arts, and Ala Qubbaj, the vice provost for Faculty Affairs and Diversity, at the University of Texas Rio Grande Valley, furnished additional grants in support of the publication of *Hostile Heartland*.

Several friends, and most notably Adrian Holly, Philip Webb, Hsiu Hua Shen, and Fred Whitehead, offered their longstanding support and encouragement of my work. Many academic colleagues suggested additional research materials or provided crucial insights. These include Shawn Alexander, Amy Bailey, Bill Carrigan, Virgil Dean, Guy Lancaster, Clarence Lang, Jim Leiker, Joane Nagel, Michael Pfeifer, Jonathan Prude, Paul Mokrzycki Renfro, David Roediger, Sarah Silkey, Allen Tullos, Geoff Ward, Clive Webb, and Amy Wood.

I especially thank Yixiang Liu and her family for contributing happiness and fulfillment to my life.

I owe more than I can repay to my parents, Thomas and Ruth Campney, my sister, Carmen, her husband, Sven, and their children, Torsten and Solveig. With great love and appreciation, I dedicate this book to my grandparents, Harry Campney (1899–1969) and Katherine (Eaton) Campney (1916–2008), and Beryle Stevenson (1914–1994) and Myrtle (Hedges) Stevenson (1919–2018).

Hostile Heartland

Introduction

On June 6, 1903, a white lynch mob invaded the lockup in Belleville, Illinois, and seized David Wyatt, a black teacher accused of shooting a white school official in a workplace dispute. After dragging him outside, members of the mob hanged, mutilated, and burned him as hundreds of men, women, and children cheered them on. Following the burning, whites ousted many black residents from the town, some of whom headed for Danville, a fast-growing railroad and mining town located some 220 miles to the north and east. A month later, mobs assaulted blacks and destroyed their property in a days-long race riot in Evansville, Indiana, driving out many blacks, some of whom also headed to Danville, 170 miles north. Neither stream of refugees would find peace. With so many new arrivals pouring into Danville at once, whites there worried that these were an advance guard for an influx of midwestern blacks who had decided to make Danville "a nigger Paradise."[1]

Shortly thereafter, whites in Danville demonstrated that the town would be a hell rather than a paradise for the newcomers. On July 25 they too burned a prisoner, pointedly targeting one of the newcomers, John D. Mayfield. "The negro killed and burned last night, had lived at Evansville for the last two years and was a recent refugee from that city," reported the *Chicago Daily Tribune*. "Relations between the races became critical with the [arrival] two weeks ago of a number of negroes from Evansville."[2] The *Daily Review* maintained that "the bad nigger from Evansville . . . started all this trouble."[3] After the burning, the fugitives from Belleville and Evansville again scattered, joined now by local blacks. "There is an exodus of negroes from Danville," the paper observed. "Since the Belleville and Evansville riots Danville seems to have become the Mecca for negroes from these places, and it is estimated that 300 blacks came to this city during the past few weeks. Many . . . are now leaving."[4]

These interrelated lynchings, riots, and expulsions in Illinois and Indiana over a six-week period in mid-1903 provide a disturbing glimpse into the history of racism and repression in the Midwest. They show the inhumanity of lynch mobs that hanged, shot, and burned blacks, and of rioters who invaded, looted, and destroyed black-owned property. They demonstrate the pitiless efficacy of stories, created and disseminated by whites, that defamed the reputations of black people, legitimized violence against them, and pursued them relentlessly from town to town and from state to state. These attacks also reveal the routine deployment of white violence against the same black people over time and space. Nonetheless, they all occurred in the Midwest, a region often described in adulatory terms by journalists, politicians, academics, and the public at large as the meritocratic heartland of America.

Hostile Heartland challenges these deep-rooted assumptions about the Midwest as a pastoral meritocracy antithetical to the systemic racist practices and antiblack violence that defined other sections of the United States, most notably the South. Building on *This Is Not Dixie*, my study of racist violence in Kansas, it demonstrates that whites in the Midwest—typified here by Ohio, Indiana, Illinois, Missouri, and Kansas—pursued repressive practices against blacks from the 1830s through the 1940s and that they enforced their will through acts of violence that included rape, whipping, arson, murder, and much in between. It also demonstrates that black midwesterners responded to repression and violence not with the often imagined meek deference and cringing accommodation but with steadfast opposition and unbending resolve, taking up arms against mobs, standing together as family units and passing traditions of resistance from one generation to the next, and assembling local, state, and national civil rights organizations that could contest white domination through black publications, public protests, and court challenges.

Hostile Heartland is influenced in structure and organization by an analogy put forth by the historian Bernard Bailyn, who encouraged his readers to "imagine a satellite circling the globe," a satellite "equipped with a camera of perfect accuracy, a camera capable of scanning vast areas in a single sweep and yet of focusing on the smallest region or community at any point of time."[5] In its exploration of racist violence by whites against blacks in the Midwest from 1835 to 1945, this book hovers over its subject like Bailyn's satellite, capturing both the broad regional trends and the evocative local events and then placing them into conversation with each other and with the trends and events associated more generally with such violence in the United States during this period.

Over the course of the past three decades, historians, sociologists, and other scholars have studied lynching in detail, exploring its geographical and temporal patterns, its perpetrators and victims, and its relation to economics, modernity, and the criminal justice system. They have also examined race riots, particularly the largest and most lethal ones. More recently, a growing number have argued that the study of *racist violence* should involve the entire spectrum of violence, encompassing exceptional events like lynchings and riots and more routine ones like homicides, beatings, floggings, sexual assaults, killings by police, and house burnings.

Many of these scholars have focused on what they call the "lynching era," approximately the period between 1880 and 1930. They have posited that lynching increased after Reconstruction, soared in frequency and savagery through the turn of the century, declined in the early twentieth century, spiked again during and immediately after World War I, and then went into a more or less permanent decline. More recently, some have demonstrated that lynching was as prolific—perhaps *more* prolific—in the 1860s and 1870s as it was during the supposed lynching era. Others have argued that lynching was actually practiced in the South during the antebellum period, thereby upending the prevailing assumption that for economic reasons white masters would not permit mobs to lynch their slaves.

Often academics consider the period after World War I in the context of a declension narrative that suggests, in brief but sweeping assertions, that lynching naturally and inevitably faded away as ever more urban whites came to regard it as wrong and inconsistent with contemporary democratic values. Accordingly, their studies tend to reflect this approach, compressing decades into paragraphs and relying on a handful of vignettes as evidence. The exceptions are a few case studies that address well-known lynchings after World War II, such as the killings of two black couples in Georgia in 1946, the murder of Emmett Till in 1955, and the execution of Mack Charles Parker in 1959. Yet these case studies reinforce the declension narrative because they are predicated on the supposedly shocking and aberrant nature of violence that was supposedly archaic by that period.

Nonetheless, some studies do focus directly on the nature, character, and transformation of lynchings from the 1930s to the 1960s, the period when influential whites clearly recognized that lynchings were an unacceptable liability for the community and when working-class and rural whites regularly concealed their continued use. "As terrorists, the perpe-trators of white violence . . . in the early sixties fall far short of their racist forefathers," wrote Charles M. Payne. Although there were a few cases where the perpetrators operated openly, he concluded that "most of the people involved took care not to be seen. . . . The days were past when whites would, in broad daylight, boldly stride into the home of any Black who had offended custom and drag that person out."[6] Similarly, Tameka Bradley Hobbs found that whites in Florida during the 1940s recognized that "they would not be able to continue to lynch blacks with impunity without risking detection, arrest, and prosecution." At the same time, she observed, influential whites became increasingly concerned that the press coverage of lynchings would injure the reputation of their town or state, depress investment, and deter new settlement. Furthermore, "communi-ties were not eager to have their townships associated with the sadism that accompanied lynching because outbursts of violence colored white residents with the taint of bestiality."[7]

Many scholars of lynching have limited their interpretation of the term *victims* to mean those who died at the hands of mobs. Of late, others have conceptualized *victims* more broadly to include individuals close to the person lynched, including relatives and friends. Within that framework they have examined the multigenerational effects suffered by these vic-tims, including traumatic memories, profound humiliation, exacerbated poverty, forced exile, and other struggles inherent in the loss of someone to unpunished mob violence.

Many academics have portrayed lynch mobs as antimodern forces—"a backwoods remnant of an archaic and barbaric impulse," as the historian Amy Louise Wood describes them. In a persuasive critique of this view, she demonstrates that mob violence was fundamentally modern. She argues that many of the "most spectacular lynchings took place not in the countryside but in . . . newly urbanizing places, where mobs hanged their victims from telegraph and telephone poles and where streetcars and railroads brought crowds to witness the violence. Even the smallest towns were undergoing an urbanization process of sorts."[8] Lynching was modern, she explains, because both lynching and the movement against it mobilized modernity—newspapers, photographs, trains, and telegrams—in order to shape the violence or the resistance.

In recent years scholars have established the significance of sundown towns, defined traditionally as all- or nearly all-white municipalities that prohibited blacks from residing in them or, in some cases, from even passing through them. James W. Loewen observed that these towns were located primarily outside the South and particularly in the Midwest and that many of them were spawned by a wave of antiblack expulsions that took place around the turn of the century and in the decades immediately thereafter.[9] Since the publication of his groundbreaking work, others have shown how whites in Arkansas and southwest Missouri uprooted blacks through violence and permanently banished them. In *This Is Not Dixie*, I showed that, as early as the Civil War, white Kansans established sundown towns—often founding them as such—and accelerated their creation in subsequent decades.[10]

As a consequence of these more recent investigations, scholars have begun to unravel the mythology of a "lynching era." They assert that lynching did not really increase in terms of the numbers of incidents or victims during the 1880s and 1890s and that it may actually have declined. Nonetheless, they acknowledge that lynching received much greater publicity at that time as a result of the growth of an increasingly dynamic national news market, the proliferation of editorial and opinion pieces on mob violence, the acceptability of graphic and widely circulated lynching postcards, and the development of a burgeoning social science literature. In response to this welter of sensationalized and violent racism and an almost pornographic public discourse about lynching, contemporaries and later generations of scholars gained the distinct *impression* that the behavior then identified as lynching was increasing. In a well-known example of this response, the *Chicago Tribune* began cataloging lynchings in 1882, reinforcing these contemporary views.

If researchers agree on anything, they now agree that the term *lynching* is impossible to define in an entirely satisfactory way. Many have accepted and still use some variation of the definition outlined by W. Fitzhugh Brundage. "On December 11, 1940, a group of prominent antilynching leaders met to settle a debate that had raged among them over the definition of lynching," he wrote. "The gathering finally agreed upon a definition, stipulating that 'there must be legal evidence that a person has been killed, and that he met his death illegally at the hands of a group acting under the pretext of service to justice, race, or tradition.'"[11] Christopher Waldrep disputed such a definition, which he simply identified as the "NAACP definition" because of the prominent role of that organization in the 1940 conference. "Some scholars claim to rely on something called the 'NAACP definition' of lynching," he wrote. "In fact, there was no 'NAACP definition' of lynching. The papers of the NAACP in the Library of Congress document staff debates, confusions, and disagreements—but no consensus—over the meaning of lynching."[12]

Waldrep made a significant intervention into the debate when he charted the history of the term *lynching* in the United States and identified the various practices associated with it. He evaluated the sensational hanging of five white men in Vicksburg, Mississippi, in 1835—dubbed a lynching by contemporaries—and then explored the spread of the story by means of river travel and the national press thereafter. He determined that the term—used across the southern and western United States in the late eighteenth and nineteenth centuries—had until the 1830s usually connoted *nonlethal* rather than lethal violence against those accused of violating social norms. He also established that the term assumed a singularly lethal connotation around the time of the Civil War and largely retained it thereafter. As a result of his investigation, Waldrep concluded that no definition of lynching could ever be sufficiently elastic to encompass every meaning assigned to it during its history. Scholars must, therefore, recognize that a definition applicable in one situation may not be appropriate in another; instead they must relentlessly contextualize its use, as I have endeavored to do in this book.

Building on the work of Waldrep, Lisa Arellano urges scholars to interrogate the narratives developed by lynch mobs and their supporters in an effort to legitimize their acts of violence by portraying the lynching victim as a lawbreaking villain and his or her executioners as good, sturdy folks. In investigating the generation and dissemination of these heroic lynching narratives over a range of temporal and spatial contexts, Arellano came to "understand lynching itself as a set of violent practices made recognizable by a constellation of formulaic narrative practices. In other words, it is by virtue of *claiming* that a given act of violence is 'enacted against a criminal' and is 'a punishment' that a given act of violence becomes a lynching."[13] I have incorporated Arellano's insight into my own thinking and have applied it as apposite in *Hostile Heartland*.

Until recently, many scholars have portrayed blacks as passive victims of white aggression or have focused on their most subtle forms of resistance. Yet "by conceptualizing resistance as any response by African Americans, especially deference and dissemblance," argues Sundiata Keita Cha-Jua, they have undermined the concept of resistance altogether. "When combined with the eighties generation's scholarship, the 1990s historians' emphasis on deference and dissemblance threatened to resurrect the 'Old Negro,' a racist stereotype. This is most certainly subconscious, but nonetheless, it is the logical consequence of their paradigm."[14] Some pointed to World War I as the pivotal period when armed blacks and national organizations such as the National Association for the Advancement of

Colored People (NAACP) mobilized to make the world safe for democracy and, recognizing the gap between American wartime rhetoric and their Jim Crow lot, decided to make their own country safe for democracy as well. While some scholars have identified illustrative vignettes of black resistance in earlier periods, most have implied by omission that, when blacks were faced with the prospect of the lynching of a fellow black in those years, they usually fled, making little effort to protect the victim or to punish his murderers.

In recent years others have postulated a more aggressive response by blacks. Focusing on the Afro-American League, Shawn Leigh Alexander shows that blacks began organizing national civil rights groups in the 1880s, a full generation before the emergence of the NAACP. In works about the South and the Midwest, others have demonstrated that before World War I blacks had been organizing jailhouse defenses for decades, arming themselves and collecting at jails at the first sign of mob violence and, more often than not, dispersing mobs before they could fully mobilize. "African Americans did not resort to new strategies to create the Florida movement of 1919–1920," Paul Ortiz writes. "They called on pre-existing institutions to mobilize a statewide campaign for social change." Based on these findings, he concludes that the evidence of "persistent resistance to white supremacy in Florida calls into question the thesis of the 'New Negro' or a younger—largely male—generation dramatically appearing on the stage in the 1920s to fight white supremacy."[15]

Many scholars of lynching have assumed that law enforcement officials invariably colluded with mobs. As they have done with regard to black resistance, they have usually implied collusion by omission. In this case they have done so because for methodological purposes they focused on completed lynchings, which resulted in the death of the intended victims, rather than on threatened lynchings, which by definition were derailed at some point, becoming prevented lynchings. In *This Is Not Dixie* I challenged this approach. By evaluating threatened lynchings as well as completed ones, I found that, although many officers did collude, they more often than not fulfilled their duty in protecting black lives—at least by the twentieth century. Because I also investigated killings by police, I determined as well that police officers simultaneously assumed the role of the mob by gunning down blacks, often in public and always with impunity. With my focus on both black and official resistance, I demonstrated that lynch mobs were more common but less successful than scholars had previously assumed.[16]

With the exception of forays into Virginia and Kentucky, scholars have traditionally focused on the Deep South, where for economic,

demographic, and historical reasons there were comparatively high numbers of lynchings. In so doing they have produced impressive substan-
tive, methodological, and historiographical insights, but they have rarely
applied them to other regions of the United States. When they have turned
their attention to the Midwest, they have focused largely on case studies
about well-documented, large-scale, or especially brutal incidents.

More recently, scholars have shifted their efforts from the South to the
Midwest and from case studies to more wide-ranging studies of violence
occurring over longer periods and across larger areas. In so doing, they
have made two significant contributions. First, they have added to and
benefited from the concurrent development of a vibrant field of midwestern studies to rival the established fields of southern and western studies.
As Paul Mokrzycki Renfro writes, "To be sure, scholars still research and
write about people and places within the Midwest, but generally they
do not explore the region in the same way that studies focused on, say,
Atlanta situate that city firmly within the South. . . . Few—if any—academic institutions in the Midwest train their students to think critically
about the region in which they live."[17] Second, they have challenged the
familiar narratives associated with the Midwest. In my previous work, for
example, I demonstrated that white contemporaries concealed their own
racism by portraying the Midwest as a land of bucolic virtue and racial
justice compared to the South, a place defined nationally by racism. I
then posited that, unwittingly or not, some scholars embraced that narrative: "Scholars have frequently accepted the depiction of the Midwest
as a land of pastoral virtue—a 'Garden of Eden'—where racist violence
was anomalous."[18]

Because the Midwest is essentially an idea, few scholars or laypersons
agree completely about what constitutes it. Most tend to define the region
in physical terms by geographical location, fertile soil, moderate climate,
and flat to rolling topography. In historical terms, people often differ with
regard to the number of states included within the region, particularly
in discussing states on the periphery. Generally, they tend to include the
states that extend westward from Ohio to Kansas and northward to the
Canadian border. In his study *The Middle West*, however, the geographer
James R. Shortridge cautions that the "more one thinks about the Middle
West, the more muddled the regional identity seems to become." As one
example he cited Missouri, a place that, although reckoned midwestern by
many observers, is still "not totally at ease with any regional label today."[19]

In *Hostile Heartland* I build on these areas of knowledge. Focusing
on racist violence, I examine actions of many types to build a broader

and more capacious model for better explaining the efforts by whites to inscribe and maintain their dominance over blacks. Nonetheless, I focus considerable attention on lynching and its transformation as a practice and an idea because this particular type of violence has provided the most widely documented historical trail and has garnered by far the greatest attention in the historiography. In doing so, I stretch the notion of the lynching era at both the front and the back end of the usual 1880–1930 periodization, showing that lynch mobs targeted blacks for vengeance from the mid-1830s through the 1940s.

With my focus on lynching from the 1830s to the Civil War, I demonstrate two new findings. First, I show that lynch mobs in the antebellum period practiced nonlethal violence as frequently as lethal violence and that the popular understanding of the term *lynching* was tied not to the death of the victim but instead to his or her perceived punishment by a crowd of outraged people. Second, I show that, whether or not white mobs in the slave states lynched enslaved persons from the 1830s to the 1850s, white mobs in the Midwest most certainly lynched free blacks and fugitive slaves. With my focus on the period between the world wars, I demonstrate that, during what I call the "late lynching period," mobs continued to prowl, particularly in rural and all-white towns, but they acted much more surreptitiously and considerably less frequently. For these changes in approach and frequency, I show that the perpetrators were moved more by their fears about the potential impact of mob violence on their economic and political interests than they were by some popular shift toward racial tolerance or justice.

In this book I use a broad interpretation of the term *victim* to include both the direct targets of racist violence and those subjected to the fear generated by such violence or to the often attendant mass expulsions or community-wide antiblack curfews that made victimization a communal experience. In particular, I focus on the ways in which whites targeted *specific black families* repeatedly over time and space, sometimes killing family members, sometimes expelling them, and sometimes undermining their economic success. In so doing, I highlight the generational theft that resulted from this violence and that has continuing relevance today.

Building on the work of Amy Wood, I confirm that racist violence—along with the struggle against it—was a fundamentally modern phenomenon that drew on a wide array of new technologies including newspapers, photographs, automobiles, and telephones. I show, for example, that whites used newspapers to spread malicious and untrue information about black people as a group, to create and sustain racist views through the use of stereotypes and character assassination, and to sensationalize and justify white supremacist violence; as they developed their own newspapers, blacks used them to challenge white versions of events and to present black-authored alternatives, to shame the white population for its hypocrisy and brutality, and, above all, to promote black resistance and protest against white supremacy in a wide range of ways. Throughout this book I explain how modernity influenced the content and character of racist violence and shaped both white actions and black responses throughout the century or so under investigation.

In several ways I contribute to the growing literature concerning sundown towns. I challenge the popular definition of such towns. Although most observers regard them as *all*-white or *virtually all*-white places, I demonstrate instead that some sundown towns allowed some blacks—sometimes hundreds—to live in town but under ruthlessly subordinated and highly segregated conditions. I also show that other such towns allowed small numbers of black newcomers to accumulate over a period of months or years before expelling them in a sudden burst of hatred and paranoia, a denouement that in some places simply signaled the beginning of another similar cycle.

In *Hostile Heartland* I place blacks at the center of the story and, while I recognize and document their victimization, I also regard them as central actors in the events under consideration. I am careful to recognize the vast power differences often at play in interracial relations, but I find no evidence to support the prevailing supposition that nineteenth-century blacks largely suffered injustices with timid silence. I do identify subtle forms of resistance including deference and dissemblance. Nonetheless, I also uncover as early as the 1830s unflinching resistance, documenting examples of armed blacks across the Midwest—alone or in groups—often confronting larger and better-armed mobs of whites bent on wreaking racist vengeance. In addition, I explore the development of more formal civil rights organizations at the local, regional, and national levels, particularly in the early-to-mid-twentieth century.

Finally, I consider the concerns of certain white midwesterners, particularly those of the middle and upper classes located primarily in urban areas. I explain that they privileged economic development over all else, including racial justice for blacks. To that end, I show that they sought an end to mob violence, although they were no less wedded to white supremacy than were other whites. I also show that they supported a police force that increasingly challenged white mobs, often protected their would-be black victims, and yet killed an ever-increasing number of blacks under often dubious circumstances, provoking fear and rage in the black community and eliciting smug, often vocal, satisfaction among whites.

In this book I have utilized newspapers as critical primary sources because they are often the only extant records that document particular acts of racist violence, offer substantial insight into the perpetrators and the victims, and indicate the motivations for and consequences of this violence. I have supplemented these sources with a wide range of other evidence, including turn-of-the-twentieth-century county histories, legislative reports, the collected papers and correspondence of several midwestern governors, papers of the NAACP, raw and published census materials, the works of black-authored fiction about the Midwest, and other archival collections.

The eight chapters in this book grapple with the themes and issues outlined above in the context of the Midwest generally and, more specifically, the five states that constitute its southern tier from Ohio to Kansas. Like the image of the circling satellite proffered by Bailyn, *Hostile Heartland* scans large areas in a single sweep in chapters on racism, repression, and resistance within states and across states. Yet it focuses on the "smallest region or community at any point of time" with case studies on specific incidents in places like Cairo, Illinois, and Lawrence County, Ohio. Admittedly, however, it is by no means a "camera of perfect accuracy."

1 The Antebellum Old Northwest

"For the white man, and the white man only"

"As two respectable ladies were returning home, they were stopped on the road by two negroes and grossly insulted," reported the *Clinton County Whig* of events in neighboring Warren County, Ohio, in 1839. Whether the white women were really insulted or whether they initiated the interaction for their own purposes is unclear but, either way, they promised to meet the men at the same location at sundown. When the women went home, they told one of their brothers about the exchange; he assembled a posse of twenty men to defend his sisters' virtue. The posse dressed two male youths in women's clothing and dispatched them to the meeting place. When the blacks arrived and mistook the cross-dressing boys for the women, the other whites "rushed upon them, tied them to trees, and castrated them."[1] Designated by newspapers across the country as a "Lynching," this event, reckoned the *Whig*, "equals any thing we have heard of for a long time."[2]

This incident in Warren County poses two challenges to prevailing assumptions about antiblack mob violence—that lynching emerged during or after the U.S. Civil War and that it was inherently lethal. This chapter examines lynching in its nonlethal *and* lethal forms in the Old Northwest during the quarter century before the Civil War, situates lynching within a broader tapestry of antiblack violence, investigates the underlying motivations of whites for lynchings specifically and racist violence generally, and finally ruminates on the significance of its findings.

Lynching is a notoriously elusive term and one on which few scholars fully agree. For the purposes of this chapter it constitutes an act of white-on-black vigilante violence perpetrated by a mob against targets accused of criminal infractions, violations of established racial etiquette, or both. This term generally connoted an act of justifiable force that represented the self-righteous anger and moral outrage of the white majority, and either overtly or covertly received its endorsement. As scholars have argued, however, lynching had (and has) no essential meaning outside the assumptions and expectations of the beholder; quite literally, it was *whatever contemporaries identified as lynching* in any particular time and place. As a consequence, its definition was always contested, molded by the users' political, economic, and social perspectives on race and simultaneously molding those views.

Today many historians agree that there can be no satisfactory or comprehensive definition of *lynching* because the term reflects rhetoric and practices that were inherently malleable, constantly evolving, inextricably interconnected, and essentially subjective.[3] This book does not address the issue of definition, but it does advance the work of Christopher Waldrep and Michael J. Pfeifer in charting the transformation of the term and the evolution of the behaviors associated with it during its formative period. Most significant, it demonstrates that in the antebellum period the term was just as likely to connote acts of nonlethal violence as lethal violence, a point that a handful of historians have noted with respect to white-on-white lynchings.[4]

Across the Old Northwest whites enforced so-called Black Laws aimed at preventing the settlement of blacks and instilling perpetual fear in those who did settle there. White Ohioans provided a useful example because their policies and practices—draconian as they were—constituted a more liberal approach than those taken in Indiana and Illinois. At the constitutional convention of 1802 white delegates—including many racial conservatives—opposed the adoption of strict limitations on the rights of black people because they feared that Congress might reject Ohio's bid for statehood. When the Indiana legislature's passage of an antiblack law in 1803 provoked no rebuke, however, Ohio legislators felt emboldened to follow suit. In 1804, therefore, they passed a law requiring that blacks furnish proof of freedom before entering the state. Three years later, in response to continued black population growth, legislators barred free blacks from settling "unless they posted a $500 bond to guarantee their good behavior and self-support," according to the historian Eugene H. Berwanger. He added that this law revealed that "exclusion of the free Negro rather than restriction of his civil rights became the prime concern" in Ohio and in the other states of the Old Northwest.[5]

Because of their constant advocacy of abolitionist sentiment and their vocal demands for equal rights, black activists and white liberals eventually succeeded in achieving the repeal of several of the Black Laws in 1849.[6] Nevertheless, white racial conservatives, the majority, clamored for new and more stringent laws. At the constitutional convention held in 1850 they presented petitions in support of an exclusion clause, and they cited the intentions of the framers of the 1802 constitution that the state be "for the white man, and the white man only."[7] Although the liberals prevented the adoption of the exclusion clause, conservative politicians made three attempts to establish a ban on black settlement in the decade after the 1849 repeal. Observers rightly predicted that the "repealed law would still be practically enforced" in the most densely populated black areas of the state.[8]

Ordinary whites certainly endorsed the antiblack laws with mob violence well before 1835, the rough starting point for this study. In *The History of Darke County, Ohio*, W. H. McIntosh recalled that a magistrate there had inclined toward violence when he inflicted a harsh penalty on a man convicted of petty theft in 1812. "The negro was required to submit to one of two penalties, at his own option," McIntosh wrote in 1880: "to bear the infliction of the Mosaic forty lashes, save one, or be stripped stark naked and climb a thorny honey locust."[9] Vigilantes drove out blacks who in 1818 attempted to settle in Mercer County.[10] In 1829 whites rioted against a growing black population in Cincinnati.[11]

During his 1831 tour of the Old Northwest, the French traveler Alexis de Tocqueville wrote that the specifics of the Black Laws—practically speaking—were superfluous when ordinary whites could freely abuse blacks. "The gates of Heaven are not closed against these unhappy beings; but their inferiority is continued to the very confines of the other world; when the negro is defunct, his bones are cast aside, and the distinction of condition prevails even in the equality of death," he observed. "The negro is free, but he can share neither the rights, nor the pleasures, nor the labour, nor the afflictions, nor the tomb of him whose equal he has been declared to be; and he cannot meet him upon fair terms in life or in death."[12]

In many of the lynching incidents that occurred in the Old Northwest in the twenty-five years before the Civil War, whites used nonlethal violence to torture and humiliate those accused of violating the criminal law or social order. "A negro by the name of Chesam was lately lynched at Nauvoo, Ill.," a journalist reported in 1844. The members of a posse allegedly found stolen goods in his possession and, "in order to make him reveal the names of the robbers," took him into the woods and subjected him to "Inquisitional Torture."[13] Although the newspaper article failed to identify the method employed by the Nauvoo mob, it likely selected, alone or in combination, whipping, beating, or stoning—all of which were popular punishments at the time. In 1845 a mob in Columbus, Ohio, lynched a man following a chase. After subduing him with a beating, some of the vigilantes held the victim on his feet with his arms pinned behind his back. At that point one of the men threw rocks at him. He had good aim, because he hit the semiconscious man in the head, "cutting it to the skull, (some say fracturing the skull . . .)." Still not satisfied with their handiwork, the mob members whipped the victim with a wagon crop.[14]

Reporting the whipping and castration of two black men in Huron County in 1839, whites in Ohio and across the North seemed to agree that this constituted a "Lynching." The *Canton (OH) Repository* wrote that "two negroes were arrested on a charge of committing a rape on a German woman. On examination, one was committed, the other released. The one released was taken by a mob, whipped and emasculated in such a manner as to cause his death. And all the negroes in the town [were] notified to leave in a few hours."[15] The *Huron Reflector*, a local paper, denied that any such incident had occurred, although it conceded that a white woman had been raped and that a black man had been jailed. The *Reflector* nonetheless agreed that such an attack, had it occurred, could rightly be called "*Lynching Law.*"[16]

On at least five occasions lynchers killed blacks. In 1845 two hundred whites in Indianapolis beat one John Tucker to death. As those most actively involved bathed themselves in his blood, those on the outer fringes cheered them on, "multitudinous voices exclaiming at the time, 'Kill the d——d nigger, kill him.' *They beat him after he was dead.*"[17] In 1856 a mob from Manchester, Ohio, conveyed a prisoner named Bill Terry to an islet in the Ohio River, hanged him from a tree limb, and then buried him there. The *Adams County Democrat* provided a report that was long and lurid but recognized the possible implications of the incident for the reputation of the area, calling it an act that "for the last few years, is parallelled [*sic*] only in California and Kansas."[18] More than four decades later, in *A History of Adams County, Ohio*, Nelson W. Evans and Emmons B. Stivers recalled that Terry's body "was cut down and buried at the foot of the tree from which he was hanged, but it is said the remains were exhumed by medical students that night."[19]

In an incredibly vicious execution in Golconda, Illinois, a mob lynched a stranger (a "runaway negro from Kentucky") accused of the rape of a white woman in 1856. Seizing the accused man from the custody of Pope County officials, members of the mob marched him—now a condemned man—to a tree outside town and tied him firmly to it. Producing a sword, they furnished the alleged rape victim with the weapon, which she used to slash and—the newspaper account makes clear—to castrate the prisoner. Some of the men, relatives of the woman, then "shot the negro six or seven times in different parts of his body" in an effort, presumably, to extend as long as possible his suffering. Finally, they shot him in the head, scalped him, and pitched his corpse into a ditch.[20]

After the lynching in Columbus in 1845, the *Weekly Ohio Statesman* reported a rumor that the victim had died but could not confirm the report. Considering how violent some of these so-called nonlethal lynchings were, more than a few victims likely crawled off to die, their deaths little known or reported.[21] In fact, in two of the five lethal lynchings, mobs evidently killed blacks whom they intended only to injure. In Vienna, Illinois, a mob "accidentally" killed a man in 1846 after inflicting more torture than he could withstand by tying him up and whipping him. In *A History of Johnson County, Illinois*, an author identified only as Mrs. P. T. Chapman recalled this incident quite faithfully in 1925. After a traveler accused "a colored boy who did the chores around the hotel" of stealing his property, "a company of citizens took him out, drove him from place to place, beating him with switches, hanging him up by the thumbs at intervals to make him tell where the money was." When the youth maintained his innocence, the mob kept up its assault. "This continued until the negro finally dropped dead on the street, just south of where the library now stands. It is said the wife of Doctor Gerry later confessed to taking the money, establishing the innocence of the negro."[22] In Cairo, Illinois, a mob murdered one Joseph Spencer in a lynching planned to "give him a coat of tar and feathers and run him out of the place."[23] The mob misjudged its victim and the outcome, as explained in chapter 2.

In some incidents the fragmentary available documentation suggests several possible outcomes. This conundrum is evident in the various reports published about the abuse inflicted on a black man in Indianapolis in 1840. One observer claimed that the mob merely rid Indianapolis of the man, causing him to flee.[24] Another rumor, circulated by the *New-Albany Argus*, suggested that whites had killed him: "Divers[e] and sundry individuals collected, and the negro has not been heard of since. A hole cut through the ice on the canal, pretty clearly accounts for his absence."[25] Corroborating this version by omission, the city's *Indiana Democrat* did not report the event but made no effort to repudiate the report in the

Argus. In his version of the event in *Greater Indianapolis*, city historian Jacob Piatt Dunn claimed in 1910 that the black man "was given a ride on a rail and warned to leave town, which he promptly did."[26] Like the reports about the incident in Columbus, those concerning the 1840 one in Indianapolis conflicted with respect to its lethality.

Whether nonlethal or lethal, lynchings often were didactic enactments of social relations for those who witnessed them. They reinforced the social order, reasserting the power and authority of those who had them, undermining both for those who did not, and teaching everyone the difference. The 1845 lynching of Tucker in Indianapolis is instructive. "The poor fellow was murdered . . . in the presence of *two hundred people*," one observer reported. A mob member shouted that he could "'kill a nigger'" as easily as he could an ox. Another declared that he wished that "every [black] was shot, and the Abolitionists too.'"[27] The mob also killed Tucker on a symbolic day. The "horrible spectacle," observed the *Indiana State Sentinel*, was "doubly horrible" because it occurred "on the 4th of July, a day which of all others should be consecrated to purposes far different from a display of angry and vindictive passion and brutality."[28]

Like the members of the Indianapolis mob, whites often chose symbolic days for their exhibitions. Slavecatchers in pursuit of a group of Missouri runaways "desecrated the anniversary of American Independence by hunting down fugitive slaves, and shooting dead one poor fellow for the crime of choosing freedom!" reported the *Wooster Republican* after pursuers killed one of the fugitives near Nashville, Illinois, in 1857. As proof that they had killed him, the slavecatchers decapitated the corpse and placed the head in a container of liquor to preserve it so that, they claimed, they could return it to the slave's master for compensation.[29] Whites carried out attacks on Independence Day for decades to come, suggesting that they understood in their own way the words of former slave and famed abolitionist Frederick Douglass, who in 1852 asked, "What, to the American slave, is *your* Fourth of July?" The Fourth, he told his white audience, "is *yours*, not *mine*. *You* may rejoice, I must mourn."[30]

Whites threatened far more blacks than they lynched. Yet with their racist slogans and boisterous demonstrations they terrorized would-be victims and blacks generally. In Bloomington, Illinois, a mob attempted to take Josiah Brown from custody as officers hurried him along the street in 1858. "The crowd rushed along pell-mell—some before, some behind, and some abreast of the Marshals and their prisoner—and the exclamations which came from them were not calculated to have a quieting effect upon Brown's nerves," noted the *Daily Pantagraph*. As the officers and Brown hustled toward the jail amid cries of "Lynch the scoundrel!" the mob made a rush and "one man attempted to throw a rope around [Brown's] neck." The officers succeeded in keeping back the mob, although Brown did not escape unscathed: "While Brown was going up the steps of the jail, he received a powerful blow, from a powerful man, on the side of his head,—but he paid no attention to it: the only effect, if any, which it had, was to increase his speed a little."[31]

As the police demonstrated with their efforts to protect Josiah Brown, the authorities—usually the police forces—stood up to mobs on occasion. They were particularly likely to challenge mobs in the larger cities, where they were better organized and where influential people were more insistent on the protection of their interests. Officials in Cincinnati, for example, prevented an 1847 lynching with the assistance of their counterparts in Kentucky. A mob stormed the jail, seized a prisoner, and hustled him across the Ohio River to Covington, where there "was a scaffold erected and ropes provided . . . for hanging him." As the mob began its work there, the "mayor of Covington with a police posse appeared on the ground, cut the ropes, and commanded the crowd to disperse, assuring them that if they would proceed in their work of violence they must go back to Cincinnati for that purpose." When the mob returned to the legal jurisdiction, Cincinnati officers rushed the crowd, recaptured the prisoner, and spirited him back to his cell. "They were pursued on their way by the excited and noisy crowd," reported the *Cincinnati Gazette*, "hurling stones at the officers.—The police maintained their ground and committed the negro man to jail."[32]

On some occasions the residents and the press all got involved to protect their varied interests, to deflect the blame from themselves, or to signal their displeasure or pleasure with police efforts. When a mob threatened a prisoner in Jefferson County, Illinois, in 1843, "some wanted to burn him, others to hang him, and it was only by the utmost exertions of the more law-abiding citizens that he was not lynched," as reported in the *History of Jefferson County*, published forty years later.[33] During an episode in Cincinnati in 1841 the *Cincinnati Daily Enquirer* assigned fault for the mayhem not to local residents but to their slave state neighbors, "some of the Kentuckians."[34] After the Columbus lynching and riot in 1845, the *Weekly Ohio Statesman* expressed the views of influential whites there when it bemoaned the inability of city authorities—who had no well-structured police department and few law enforcement personnel of any kind—to quell the prolonged violence: "Said a bystander, 'two resolute old women, with broom sticks, would have dispersed them.'"[35]

It did not add that, since Columbus was the state capital, local authorities—including the governor—had access to a state militia that could have checked the mob had they desired to deploy it. In Bloomington the *Daily Pantagraph* praised the police officers for their work in 1858. They "were *determined* to protect Brown," it declared, and they "made a noble stand" and "succeeded in gaining the inside of the jail with their charge."[36]

Not infrequently, armed blacks challenged mobs. In the 1841 Cincinnati race riot they fought back vigorously. "Shots were discharged into the crowd, wounding indiscriminately the peaceful with the riotous," reported the *Cincinnati Daily Enquirer* on "a defence by the negroes of their houses, and their lives." Its reporter watched as "fifty infuriated blacks, with shouts and curses, armed to the teeth with guns and other deadly weapons, sallied out, pursuing the unarmed crowd down Broadway, full one hundred yards from their houses, and discharging their pieces."[37] In Vanderburgh County, Indiana, whites attacked a home in 1857 but, because the blacks had been warned "and had armed themselves with guns and knives, . . . the whites were badly worsted."[38] An avowed opponent of any black presence in Indiana, the *Evansville Enquirer* had to concede that justice prevailed. "The negroes defended themselves nobly and the would-be murderers of negroes, became vanquished by negroes, and we repeat, they were rightly served."[39]

In 1840 blacks confronted a posse conducting a raid on "the negro huts" in Clarksville, Indiana. In the course of the event a black resident struggled with whites who had invaded his residence. Needing help, he "called another black man . . . to bring a gun and assist him. The other negro brought a gun and fired it among the assailants," killing a white man. In this instance the whites threatened to lynch the shooter, now jailed, but chose not to follow through. The *Louisville Advertiser* interpreted their reticence charitably. "At first the excitement against the blacks was so great that it was feared the prisoner would be taken out by force and burned alive," it reported, describing the worst outcome in an apparent effort to put the best face on an embarrassing rebuff. "The good sense of the majority of the citizens of Jeffersonville, however, prevailed, and a meeting was called and resolutions passed that justice should be left in the hands of the law." In fact, whites may have demurred because they suspected that blacks were organizing to defend the prisoner. Whatever prompted them to abandon the threatened lynching, they did not abandon their view that "the negro race and the [A]nglo Saxon race cannot live together as equals."[40]

In defending themselves blacks risked more violence, as those in Clarksville had feared. In 1841 blacks in Dayton, Ohio, learned that lesson when a group of them defended themselves against a white mob that attempted to storm their house, killing a white man and wounding several other rioters. Outraged, "an armed mob repaired to that part of the town occupied by the blacks, and deliberately set fire to, and burned to the ground, three houses occupied by these unfortunate creatures." The blacks, "fearful of further injury, are selling their property at a great sacrifice, and preparing to leave the City."[41] In his *History of the City of Dayton and Montgomery County, Ohio,* published seven decades later, A. W. Drury confirmed the rout of the blacks.[42]

Indeed, with wholesale racist violence of this sort taking place over the course of many decades and across many states, whites prevented blacks from ever accumulating wealth and property, and, therefore, from passing this wealth and property down through the generations, as whites did. In this sense, white mobs perpetrated generational theft against their black neighbors, giving the violence of the past real and continuing meaning in the present. The *Evansville Daily Enquirer* recognized this fact in 1857 when it reported that white vigilantes had chased black farmers from a nearby township: "And now, while we are writing, these men are riding up and down Union township in squads of ten and twenty, with guns on their shoulders, while the shrewd ones are buying the crops of the half scared-to-death negroes at about one-fourth their value and thus cheating the negro and the negro's creditors out of what is rightly, and by all law, their own."[43]

On occasion, mob members themselves curbed a lynching when a majority decided that the would-be victim was a sympathetic figure because of age, infirmity, or former good conduct. For example, in an incident in Gallatin County in 1842, recollected forty-five years later in the *History of Gallatin, Saline, Hamilton, Franklin and Williamson Counties, Illinois,* "several regulators went to the house of an old and inoffensive negro for the purpose of 'regulating him,' that is, of whipping and terrifying him." Most of "the 'boys'" who went along, on seeing the would-be victim, decided that "it would be a shame to whip the old man and left without doing so," notwithstanding the fact that one of the white men remained "strongly in favor of the proceeding."[44]

The lynchings in the Old Northwest occurred against a backdrop of racist violence generally, one that makes black resistance seem that much more remarkable. Yet this backdrop was somewhat different in urban areas than in rural ones. In the larger urban centers where blacks accumulated in greater numbers and concentrated in specific locations, rioters attacked them in more intense assaults and perpetrated more extensive property damage. Furthermore, the white press located in these larger centers magnified the effectiveness of the mobs' actions by widely publicizing and more often than not supporting them. In 1841 a mob in New Albany, Indiana, swarmed a black church-school and set it aflame, destroying in one stroke two institutions. Even the more liberal whites who had previously promised to do all in their power "to promote the interests of the church, were heard to say, that nothing had gladdened their hearts more than the news of the destruction of the only house of worship and instruction belonging to their oppressed fellow citizens!" reported an observer. "Having such backers, the mob grew bold, and threatened to demolish any house in which the destitute school should be again started. Having ascertained that there was not virtue enough in the community to prevent such a catastrophe . . . the school was given up."[45]

In that same year whites in Cincinnati, Ohio, undertook a large-scale race riot that underscored the unrestrained violence of such events. "A crowd, numbering about seven or eight hundred, assembled . . . with the avowed purpose of attacking the negro houses, and driving that class of people from the city," reported the *Cincinnati Daily Enquirer*. Because of stiff resistance, it added, "the fight was kept up for several hours, in a manner defying all description, during which the crowd procured a cannon, and discharged it, loaded with slugs, three times, into the negro quarters." In the absence of "any accurate information of the extent of the injury and loss of life," it determined that "at least two white men [were] killed and several badly wounded. Several negroes [also were] killed, and wounded—but the extent not known."[46]

On more than one occasion lynchings mutated into race riots. After a man and his son affronted popular opinion in some manner in Carlyle, Illinois, in 1852, whites first lynched them and a handful of other blacks and then took vengeance on the rest of the population. "The citizens took the negroes who had first offended, tied them up and whipped them," observed the *New York Times*. "Three other negroes, who had somehow signalized themselves in the difficulty, were served in like manner."[47] Frenzied, the whites "resolved to chase [all of] the negroes out of town." Consequently, "the cannon was . . . brought out and leveled in front of one of the negro houses, and was so ranged as to have blown negroes, houses, and all up, but some person raised it so as to graze the roof, scaring the 'colored individuals' so bad that they made their hasty *dis*-appearance with the greatest imaginable *gust*-O!"[48]

As the riots in Cincinnati and Carlyle suggest, antebellum mobs involved cannon in their acts of violence with surprising regularity. Although none of the sources identified where the mob secured these weapons of war, whites in all likelihood seized them from armories established for the local militia. When a mob decided to wreak vengeance on a black man in Cleveland in 1837, a resident of that city explained that the cannon functioned as a means of recruiting whites. "A mob collected near the courthouse, and was much increased by the firing of cannon," he told the *New-York Commercial Advertiser*. Once it reached sufficient size, the mob marched on his house, smashing it and destroying his belongings. After reciting the damage that followed the cannon blast, the resident wondered: "How long are such [mobs] destined to sway our civil institutions?"[49] As subsequent chapters show, white midwesterners continued to ask themselves this question for the next hundred years, although they evidently retired the use of cannon by the Civil War period.

In order to advance their objectives, whites organized into self-styled regulator bands similar to the one operating in Gallatin County, Illinois, in 1842. The *Shawneetown Republican* reported that the crisis had "arisen from the organization of a body of men called Regulators, whose avowed object is to force all negroes, without respect to age, sex, condition, or character, to leave the country."[50] Before long the regulators rode into Shawneetown. "The poor negroes heard of the coming of the corps in time, and soon were as scarce as squirrels on a windy day," according to the *History of Gallatin, Saline, Hamilton, Franklin and Williamson Counties, Illinois*. "Not a single woolly head was anywhere to be seen."[51] On other occasions vigilantes acting alone or in small numbers simply attacked black victims. In 1841 two such vigilantes beat a laborer in Ripley, Ohio, putting "into practice the spirit of hatred to colored people so prevalent among many of the better class of society." The assailants, an observer opined, were "but a looking glass in which many respectable people may see a picture of their own hearts."[52]

Driven by the desire for profit, slave hunters seized blacks irrespective of their legal status as fugitive slaves or freed men. In several such cases they murdered those who resisted. In 1854 three men beat a prisoner near Cedarville, Ohio, stuffed him into a wagon, and hurried him toward Cincinnati for eventual sale in Kentucky. "We had not gone over two or three miles before the negro died," one of the killers recalled.[53] In 1857 a white woman assisted slave hunters in ferreting out their quarry in Adams County, Illinois, as the *Chicago Tribune* chronicled. "A negro woman fleeing from Missouri, with her three children" took refuge in some woods. With a thousand-dollar reward posted for her capture, white men in Adams County turned out "in force armed with their guns, and aided by the deceit and treachery of a white democratic sister, seize[d] the poor mother and hurr[ied] her back into bondage."[54]

Slave hunting was so common that stories about it litter the county histories produced in the late nineteenth and early twentieth centuries. "Arrests of fugitive slaves in this county were not unfrequent [sic]," wrote Andrew W. Young in his *History of Wayne County, Indiana*, published in 1872. Although Young professed sympathy for some fugitives, he demonstrated little concern for the one who, as he recollected, had escaped to Wayne County from Mississippi in 1844. When townspeople found the fugitive hidden in a wooden crate furnished with air holes,

> the whole city was excited by the news of this discovery. It being Sunday, congregations in some of the churches were either greatly *thinned*, or their meeting prevented. It was proposed to put the negro back into the box and throw him into the river. Others said, "Nail him in the box, and bury him alive." He was at length handcuffed and placed in the calaboose, and his master notified of his attempted escape.[55]

The author of *Baird's History of Clark County, Indiana* (1909) delighted in recalling the terror that blacks endured there during the antebellum years. Slaveholders in Kentucky and antiblack zealots in Indiana conspired to circulate stories that Clark County was "a dangerous place for a black face to be seen in, and that if a negro valued his life he had better keep away from it." Without a hint of regret even half a century later, he explained that the "owners of slaves, for protection to that old-time property, instilled into the young darkies' minds that we were not only poor white trash, but that we would steal them and sell them to cotton planters down South, and the young darkies believed that as firmly as ever a white child believed in old Santa Claus."[56]

In what was perhaps the most common type of racist violence but the most difficult to identify, whites confronted blacks—residents or visitors—at the edge of town or in town, if they got that far, and then expelled them by peppering them with threats and, when necessary, with projectiles. In 1848, for instance, a black man and a white woman, denied the right to wed in Indianapolis, went to Boone County, where they found a justice to marry them. On the groom's return to the capital, "he met a warm reception—eggs were plenty and the boys [knew] how to throw them. He left for parts unknown."[57] In other confrontations whites initiated rough-and-tumble brawls that claimed black lives and probably white ones. In

1838, for example, white and black men warred in the ironically named New Harmony, Indiana. Officials did little to investigate, and observers made deft use of the passive voice to deflect responsibility for the incident. One claimed that amid the fighting, which left a white man wounded, one of the blacks "was instantly killed by three stabs in different parts of the body."[58] Another argued that the "negro having received three stabs, it was impossible for the Coroner, according to the evidence, to identify the guilty."[59]

Although equally difficult to document and certainly inconsistent with the prevailing narrative, white men regularly practiced sexual assaults against black women. After the 1841 Cincinnati race riot, blacks and their white allies claimed that a group of white men had gang raped a black woman. Predictably, the *Cincinnati Daily Enquirer* was skeptical because the charges were based on what it considered untrustworthy testimony. "If true, the [rape] was inexcusable and shocking.—But what is the evidence of its truth? The *statements of negroes*." It countered these charges with accusations of an alleged black-on-white rape at some unspecified time and place. "More we will not say, except that this matter rests upon the statement of a WHITE person, and was of recent occurrence. It could find no place however, with the negro sympathizers—the chaunters of black martyrdom."[60]

In 1841 race riots erupted across Ohio, most notably in Dayton, Cleveland, and Cincinnati. In addition, they seemed to spread across the region like a contagion from one city to the next and to cross state borders. An observer identified the connection between the number of incidents and the timing between them. "The persecution of the colored people is extending all along the Ohio river," he concluded. First, it hit

> Indiana and Ohio. And now we hear, that in Kentucky the same devilish spirit is abroad. At Louisville the free people of color have been warned out of the State. In Lexington they were charged as incendiaries. At Maysville they have been mobbed, and their church has been burnt. . . . Will the God of the oppressed permit these acts of cruelty to pass unpunished?[61]

The *Evansville Journal*, located down the Ohio River in the extreme southwest of Indiana, volunteered an answer of sorts. The white residents of that town had decided to rid themselves of a recent influx of black fugitives. "Owing to the recent expulsion[s] of the free negroes" elsewhere, it reported, "there has been within the last month or two, an extraordinary influx of this sort of population into our town." Since many whites there bitterly hated blacks, it continued, "we regret to say that an attempt was last week made by some individuals to abate it by violence. To obviate the necessity of such a procedure hereafter, as well as to get rid of the evil, the citizens generally have taken the matter in hand, and adopted such measures as will, we are confident, produce the effect desired. The meeting on Monday evening was one of the largest ever held in the place."[62]

As indicated by the well-known killing of abolitionist Elijah Lovejoy in Alton, Illinois, in 1837, racist mobs sometimes pursued their objectives by means of attacks on whites who were working on behalf of equal rights, including abolitionists in more than a few cases. After the 1845 lynching in Indianapolis the mob assaulted Henry W. De Puy, the editor of the *Indiana Freeman* and a man unpopular with white conservatives for his views. When he remonstrated with the mob, an onlooker told him that "he must leave the street or he would be murdered. De Puy expostulated, but the reply of the man was, 'You have no friends here.' De Puy escaped, and it was well he did, as the mob made diligent search for him, for an hour afterwards." A supporter of De Puy implored him to resist, saying, "He has friends out of Indianapolis, if he has none in it."[63]

In many of the small towns and rural areas that constituted most of the Old Northwest, whites refused residence to any blacks at all. In 1846, for example, whites expelled a group of settlers from Mercer County, Ohio. "After being driven from Mercer," noted the *Anti-Slavery Bugle*, the blacks bought land in Shelby County, provoking new hostility. "One hundred men assembled around the negro camp" and drove them out. Again, the blacks scattered.[64] The *New York Daily Tribune* condemned the vigilantes, noting, "The people of Mercer County, after selling the land with the knowledge that the Negroes were to be the occupants of it, and taking from them an exorbitant price for it, have turned out with arms in their hands against an unarmed people and driven them from the soil which by every right is theirs." After the blacks fled to Shelby County, they were again "foiled, being persecuted, maltreated and driven from the attempt as if they carried with them a pestilence."[65]

The following year blacks faced similar obstacles in other western Ohio counties. Some purchased land in Darke County, but mob violence drove them out. Others faced the same reception in Miami County. Shortly after they had built their cabins, whites leveled them. The blacks rebuilt them, but "no sooner was this accomplished than a second attempt was made to destroy the fruits of their labor."[66] In this area of Ohio antiblack sentiment was so strong that white supporters of the black settlers abandoned the plan, "stating that 'it would be useless to attempt to settle them in a community where the Judges and Ministers rise up in opposition.'"[67] Even Quakers organized to drive blacks from Miami County in 1847. The area, lamented the *Cincinnati Herald*, "is settled chiefly by members of the Society of Friends—a class of persons who have in all time professed to be the friends of this degraded part of the human family. It might, therefore, be expected that these despised negroes would find a shelter from the persecuting intolerant spirit which abounds elsewhere. Not so. Facts show that they cannot live without molestation even in that neighborhood."[68]

Driven from the small municipalities, blacks continued to concentrate in the handful of urban centers scattered across the region. Responding with fear, whites lashed out with lynchings and other attacks. As noted, they lynched blacks in the capitals of Ohio and Indiana within a few months of each other in 1845. In Indianapolis they left little doubt as to their objective. Documenting the killing there, a witness wrote that many in the mob—participants and spectators alike—agreed that "the niggers are gitting [*sic*] too cursed thick, and they ought to be thinned out."[69] With lynchings in 1840 and 1845, the Indiana capital became a regional capital of racist violence. Writing of Indianapolis in this period, the historian Jacob Piatt Dunn wrote that "there was no apparent favor for [the Negro]. Abolitionism was at a discount and anything like association on terms of equality was not considered by any one." Detailing three attacks on blacks that occurred between 1840 and 1848, he erroneously concluded that, "notwithstanding the general development of feeling on the negro question through political agitation, there is no record of any further serious mistreatment of negroes in Indianapolis before the Civil War."[70]

On the eve of the Civil War whites in municipalities of all sizes expelled blacks. The authorities in New Albany, Indiana, appropriated money to "remove the free negroes from that town who are residing there contrary to the State law."[71] In Xenia, Ohio, whites hoped to "banish" blacks by withholding employment "and thus bringing upon them starvation."[72] Explaining the intent, the *Xenia Torch Light* declared: "Men swear about them, (the negroes) and then sell to them—talk about a 'ruined community,['] and then trade with them and seek their trade. Now let us stop the traffic, and thus put an end to the influx, or stop the talk and hide the inconsistency. We prefer the former."[73] Although blacks would return to New Albany and Xenia, those driven from smaller towns often abandoned them permanently (or were banished) and migrated to larger cities, swelling the populations there and, in turn, stimulating renewed violence. "Other Cities and Towns in Indiana are expelling the Negroes from among them and owing to the laxity exhibited by our authorities and citizens generally, Evansville is being overrun and cursed by the worst class of this lazy, worthless, drunken and thieving race," declared vigilantes in that city in 1860. Henceforth, they warned, "every negro, of either sex, who is not by Law entitled to a residence among us must not be found in the city, else he will be dealt with in a summary manner."[74]

Regardless of the particular type of violence used, whites could always draw on a range of motivations to justify its use. At the most basic level they aimed to keep blacks in their place, to deny them prestige or property, to remind them starkly of their appointed position at the bottom of society. After the riot in Cincinnati in 1841 the *Enquirer* expressed a widespread anger among whites against blacks who did not exhibit what they regarded as appropriate deference and who, therefore, required a lesson in racial etiquette. "We [are] overrun with negroes," it raged. Before the riot "they took the inside of the pavement [sidewalks] upon all occasions,—swelled and swaggered, and obtruded their miscreated visages, like Milton's devils, where they had no business. A couple of them enter a private enclosure for blackberries—a German, having charge of it, orders them out—they refuse."[75]

Often, whites sought to protest politically against the periodic efforts of blacks, abolitionists, and other more liberally inclined groups to advance the cause of blacks. In January 1841 abolitionists in Ohio's House of Representatives enraged many whites by attempting to place black children with white ones in the schools in Brown County. "I never saw such a *nigger-ridden* body as the House of Representatives," raged one critic.[76] Presciently, another predicted that black and white abolitionists and their white race-traitor allies in Columbus could not "be blind to the fact, that the negroes must suffer for all their folly."[77]

Taking their cues from politicians and editors, and infuriated by the possibility of integration, mobs took to the streets of Dayton in a series of riots in late January and early February. Also in February another mob attacked a black-owned house in Cleveland, assaulting the inhabitants and smashing the structure. The *Ohio Statesman* drew the connection between the proposed legislation and the violence. "It is folly for the abolitionists to expect to peaceably carry their designs into effect," it roared. "The excitement since the conduct of our Legislature, is higher than we ever witnessed it in Ohio."[78] Swept up in the hatred, whites in Ripley assaulted a black laborer in May.[79] In Cincinnati whites rioted on a grand scale in September. After the riot the *Cincinnati Daily Enquirer* attributed the cause of the violence to the vote in the previous winter "to incorporate a school in Brown county, where negroes and whites were notoriously classed and taught together."[80]

Furthermore, whites tried to curtail sexual relations between black men and white women, a practice that, they feared, would produce mixed babies, upend white supremacy, and weaken white male dominance. In 1837 a report by a resident of just such a relationship prompted—as mentioned above—the firing of the cannon in Cleveland and the violence which followed.[81] In 1841 rioters in Cleveland again targeted a black man. "A gang of rowdies made a systematic and outrageous attack upon a house . . . in which resides a mulatto man who is said to have a white . . . wife," observed the *Cleveland Herald*. The man was "caught, and every thing tangible was used by the mob in beating the poor fellow. Pots and kettles, spiders, pails, table, shovels and tongs, and all the furniture of the house was thrown at him, until he was left for dead."[82]

In addition to beating the "mulatto," the Cleveland mob attacked the white woman, leaving her apparently alive in the wreckage of the residence. Other white women who challenged the racial-sexual order, thereby rejecting white male protection, found themselves similarly victimized and humiliated by their would-be guardians. After learning of a mixed-race relationship in Indianapolis in 1840, white men quickly rid themselves of the black man. They focused their time and energy, however, on humiliating the white woman. According to a correspondent, they "dragged the young woman from her bed in one of the coldest nights of this winter, put her on horseback nearly naked, and rode her about the town, as I was told, for three hours, during which they insulted and abused her as if they had been demons from below rather than men."[83] Reporting an 1850 act of "linch law" in New Albany, Indiana, where a mob whipped two black men for living with two white women, the *Louisville Democrat* expressed its view that the mob was too lenient: "the women should be branded as well as the men, and then run out of town."[84]

During the 1841 attack on the black man and the white woman in Cleveland, the lynch mob demonstrated its racist hatred generally by assaulting a black woman who had the misfortune of being inside the house. "The doors were forced, the windows demolished, and the gang filled the house," reported the *Cleveland Herald*. "A shovel full of live coals was thrown upon the head of the colored woman, and she was knocked down with the shovel." The *Herald* noted that the mob had forced the black woman from the house, beat her, and left her unconscious, but it did not report her ultimate fate.[85]

When they could, whites identified sexual relations between black men and white women as rape. They regarded black men as rapacious beasts and at least some of their alleged victims as despoiled flowers suffering "a fate worse than death."[86] After the arrest of a black youth in Columbus for the sexual assault of a young white woman in 1845, a mob rained blows on a black bystander who defended the youth by implying that any contact that may have occurred was consensual. When he defended himself, the mob increased in size and ferocity. When he fled, the attackers chased him, caught him, and in the vernacular of the day, lynched him. After the lynching, rioters marched "through the streets unmolested by the police, beating peaceable blacks and stoning their houses."[87] Whites were so obsessed with interracial relationships that, in the absence of evidence to the contrary, they sometimes assumed that rape was the cause of anti-black violence. The *Logansport Telegraph*, for example, concluded after the lynching in Indianapolis in 1845: "Causes of the mob not given—perhaps from the fact that a negro man had a few days before assaulted a lady."[88]

Frequently, white women and their families used the charge of rape to deny illicit liaisons once exposed. A woman in Xenia may have selected this option in 1859. She became "the mother of an African child, greatly to the amazement and horror of her relatives and friends, who had never doubted her purity for a moment," reported the *Cincinnati Enquirer*. Needing an explanation, she "told, with the deepest sense of shame, and in a perfect agony of mind, that ten months before . . . she was approached by a stalwart negro" who "most brutally violated her person!" Although the *Enquirer* betrayed some doubt about the story, her relatives and friends believed her—or pretended to. "The negro, it appears, had left Xenia a few days before his crime had become known, or the people of that vicinity, with all their morbid sympathy with the colored race, would have lynched him on the spot. A number of persons are now in pursuit of [him], and will, if they capture him, hang the black villain, as he richly deserves." The baby, it added without elaboration, "fortunately, lived but a single hour."[89]

Lynch mobs underscored their sexual anxieties with the castration of alleged rapists. They did so in the Warren County incident that opened this chapter, an event involving the de-sexing of two black men by a white mob that, in an interesting twist, included two cross-dressed white men. In the Golconda lynching, the alleged victim of rape castrated the man that she had accused of the crime. After the mob attempted to seize Josiah Brown, an accused rapist, in Bloomington in 1858, the *Daily Pantagraph* suggested just how common castration may have been in its casual reference to it after the prevented lynching. "If there had been a *leader* for the excited crowd," it asserted, "Brown would certainly have been hung or mutilated." After all, the men were determined "to seize Brown and either hang him or subject him to some other kind of violence."[90]

After the beginning of the Civil War, and in 1862 particularly, whites attempted to offset the profound economic changes and demographic shifts that resulted by exerting more rigorous control over blacks. According to the *Huntington (IN) Democrat,* for example, dockworkers "visited their vengeance upon every nigger in Toledo; visiting negro quarters and assailing all who came within their reach."[91] In that same year a mob in Peoria, Illinois, nearly beat a black man to death. "A crowd went to the calaboose with the avowed intention of breaking it open," reported the *Peoria Union.* By a stroke of luck the victim survived. "[He] was dragged out amid the cries of the excited crowd, who fell upon him and pounded him severely. They would probably have killed him, but the confined space and darkness prevented them from knowing friend from foe, and by some means the negro escaped."[92]

In the South, confederate newspapers gleefully reported the riots. "The negroes appear to be in very bad odor at the North," declared the *Fayetteville Observer,* a newspaper in North Carolina. "At Toledo and Cincinnati, Ohio, furious riots have occurred in consequence of the negroes presuming to want work, whereby white laborers were thrown out of employment. At Chicago, an excited crowd refused to allow two darkeys to ride in an omnibus, and even the sheriff, who took their part, was unable to protect them from a foot race to escape from the crowd." The newspaper predicted that "the Yankees and the blacks will [soon] have enough of one another. We wish them joy of their happy association."[93] Suggesting that its prediction was correct, and that blacks and whites had in fact had "enough of one another," a race riot erupted in New Albany that same year, prompting the *New Albany Ledger* to proclaim "a perfect exodus of the colored population from [the] city."[94]

White midwesterners used the same types of racist violence and justified their violence in the same ways in the antebellum period as did their counterparts in the postbellum period. In addition to serving their overarching objective of maintaining or expanding white supremacy, they used violence, like lynching, murder, and rape, to articulate anger about political developments considered overly generous to blacks, interracial sexual relations deemed immoral, and the profound changes attendant on the war. As they would for generations thereafter, white midwesterners often attempted to place the blame for this violence on the white southerners among them or in neighboring states.

Violent and boisterous mobs threatened more lynchings than they actually perpetrated. Nonetheless, by taking over streets or public grounds and by demonstrating their desire to whip, hang, or burn a black person, mobs reinforced white domination in countless but so far mostly undocumented incidents. In response, white authorities took steps to secure victims who were in the custody of mobs, to defuse mobs by removing prisoners to more secure locations, or to increase the number of guards at the jails. In addition, black residents frequently confronted mobs with armed force. Both groups sought to curb mob violence, but they did so for divergent reasons. The authorities opposed violent action of any kind—racist or not—because they reflected the nascent concerns of a small but increasingly influential group of middle-class and elite whites that wanted to stabilize a social order dominated by themselves and to prevent mob violence, which was inimical to the reputation of the community and the development of its economy. For their part, blacks did not oppose *mob* violence as a rule, but they did oppose *racist* mob violence because they recognized its role in enforcing and expanding white supremacy.[95]

As an initial foray into the study of antiblack violence in the antebellum Old Northwest, this chapter must be considered tentative until other practitioners turn their focus to this book's expanded time frame and geographical area as well. Nevertheless, the five lethal lynchings identified do supplement the more well-known 1840 incident in which a white mob killed a black laborer named Nathaniel Morgan in Dubuque, Iowa.[96] In addition, some of these findings, such as the Vienna incident, corroborate those exemplified in Dubuque, where vigilantes killed their victim by whipping him until his body could no longer stand the abuse. These examples show that several of the mobs in the Old Northwest killed blacks accidentally through a wanton disregard for their fates rather than through clearly murderous *intentions*. This distinction is significant in the context of the sharp definitional shift that occurred after the Civil War, when suddenly the death of the victim determined whether a *lynching* had or had not occurred.

White men responded aggressively to situations where white women cried rape because they could then avenge them by disciplining black suspects, thereby enabling them to present themselves as saviors of white women and in the process to assert control over black people deemed uncivilized and white women dependent on their protection. When some white women refused to cooperate by openly engaging in interracial relationships, white men were more than willing to punish these betrayers as harshly as they punished blacks. In Cleveland and Indianapolis mobs assaulted such women. Furthermore, they silenced whites who opposed racist violence, such as the abolitionists Lovejoy and De Puy. In this sense mobs came to represent all whites. As the historian Noel Ignatiev recognized, although mobs accounted for only a small fraction of the white population, that "organized force of hundreds was able to batter those [whites] who opposed it, or even those who held back, into silence and submission, so that in time it came to speak for the entire community."[97]

In punishing black "rapists," antebellum mobs sometimes resorted to castration. In fact, when the local newspaper asserted that the would-be victim in Bloomington would certainly have been hung *or* mutilated, it implied that mobs may have regarded this practice as a punishment that obviated the need for a killing. Given the reticence of whites to record such punishment, historians have found it difficult to determine its frequency in the postbellum period. Nevertheless, contemporaries hinted that vigilantes continued to castrate blacks after the war. Following an 1880 lynching in Indiana, the *Indianapolis News* did not report castration—but endorsed it. "What shall be said for the hanging of the negro at Brazil for rape?" it asked. "Imprisonment is what the law says shall be the portion of a ravisher. Outraged humanity says death is the proper portion, and it says so with such unfailing regularity that it must be pur[e] blindness on the part of the legislators which permits this grave offense to go unpunished except by imprisonment." At the least, it added, "emasculation should be the portion of every ravisher, whether the prison or the gallows await him after that."[98]

These findings raise a question about the applicability of some of the assumptions developed in the literature focused on the South. The influential work by the historian Martha Hodes found that sex between black men and white women did not alarm many whites prior to the Civil War unless the woman enjoyed high status or the couple acted in a manner deemed publicly provocative. She concluded that after the war, however, when racial status replaced slavery as the principle around which society was organized, whites responded to such relations with violence.[99] This study finds instead that whites in the Midwest—where slavery did not exist and racial categories, along with free labor, were already established principles around which society was organized—responded with habitual violence to interracial sex well before the end of slavery and as early as the 1830s, if not before. Although additional research is required, this study suggests that white northerners were targeting blacks for alleged sexual crimes decades before their southern brethren began to do the same.

This book is part of a wave of scholarship that contests the tenet that lynching emerged during or after the Civil War and that lynching was inherently lethal.[100] Building on previous studies, this one pushes the timetable back by another quarter century and as a consequence raises several historiographical questions. It suggests that by the mid-1830s the term *lynching* usually applied to a nonlethal act but could apply to a lethal one, as exemplified by the hanging of Bill Terry in Adams County. It also indicates that the antebellum idea of lynching was not the lethality of the outcome but the enactment of a punishment rendered outside the bounds of the law, supported by a majority of whites, and targeted at the correction of some perceived wrongdoing, whether a crime or merely a violation of racial etiquette. Hence, this book builds on the work of Waldrep and Pfeifer, who independently interrogated the meaning of *lynching* as it was used from the 1830s to the 1860s. They agreed that the term came to be used nationally after the widely publicized hanging of some white men in Mississippi in 1835, an event that revealed and exacerbated an unresolved division within the term lynching between nonlethal and lethal violence, both of which were embraced by a term with an elusive meaning until ordinary usage and an objective uptick in the number of killings eventually resolved the matter in favor of its lethal definition.[101]

In identifying the relatively frequent lethal and nonlethal lynchings in the Old Northwest, this study builds on the work of Pfeifer, who questioned the conventional wisdom which said that lynching was uncommon in the slave states because influential whites would not tolerate the destruction by a mob of their human property. His study identified fifty-six examples of lynched slaves across the South and in the Border States, and on the basis of that evidence he speculated that many others await rediscovery in the archives.[102] This book applies Pfeifer's insights to the Old Northwest in the antebellum period and finds that, despite the relatively small black population there, the number of incidents was higher than scholars had previously imagined. Yet by applying his insights about the South to the Old Northwest, it also challenges his assumptions about the trajectory of lynching there. Reviewing lynchings in New York, Michigan, and Wisconsin in the 1860s, his study concluded that these were firsts in the North because the mob members involved were "in a sense, innovators, as they were among the first white Americans to lynch free blacks in a society organized around principles of free labor."[103] This one shows that the mobs in the Old Northwest of the 1860s were not innovators; they were instead imitators following in the footsteps of their fathers, who—at least as early as the 1830s—lynched free blacks in a society theoretically organized around the principles of free labor.

2 Illinois and the Legacy of Antebellum Racist Violence

"The peculiar climate of this region"

"Perhaps some of our readers may remember a tragical affair that occurred in the mudwalled 'city' of Cairo, Illinois, in the autumn of 1854," wrote Edward Willett nearly a decade after the fact. "I refer to the lynching of a negro named Joseph Spencer." In the lengthy article that followed, Willett, a lawyer and a participant in the events he described, provided what he called a "truthful account" of events that had garnered national attention when they took place.[1] Because of the location of this small but growing Illinois town at the confluence of the Mississippi and Ohio Rivers, witnesses carried reports of the events in Cairo along these waterways, as well as by rail, to newspaper editors throughout Illinois and in larger regional centers like St. Louis, Louisville, and Cincinnati.[2]

With minor variations, newspapers reported that on or about November 27, 1854, authorities pressed a charge of trespassing against Joseph Spencer, a well-known black resident who operated a hotel in the cabin of his boat. When summoned to court, Spencer arrived armed with a pistol and a keg of gunpowder. "He entered the little room, took a chair, drew a six-shooter, deliberately knocked in the head of the keg, cocked his pistol, and inserted the barrel in the gleaming black powder," reported Willett, "announcing that if justice was not done him he would blow them all to hell."[3] Not surprisingly, Spencer succeeded in persuading the judge to postpone the hearing; a commentator reported that "the court wisely took time to 'consult,' and adjourned in hot haste."[4] Spencer's threat enraged whites. "This outrageous affair soon got wind," Willett related, "and the excitement against the negro became intence [*sic*], and propositions to lynch him were received with general favor."[5]

Well aware of the fury that his actions had unleashed, Spencer retreated to his boat and locked himself in the cabin, a mob hot on his heels. When whites threatened to storm the boat, Spencer placed the muzzle of his gun into the keg and threatened to kill anyone who approached. For a time, the whites contented themselves with cries of "Kill the d——d nigger!" With three hundred whites assembled, snipers stationed themselves around the boat waiting for Spencer to make his appearance. When he refused to leave his cabin, whites boarded the ship, only to be driven back by a fusillade from their quarry. Five of the whites, including Willett, sustained gunshot wounds and retreated onto the wharf. At that point mob members determined to burn the boat. In order to prevent other vessels from catching fire, they cut Spencer's boat away from its mooring and set it aflame.[6] "While all this was going forward," Willett wrote, "several shots were exchanged between the crowd and the negro, who had previously supplied himself with two double barreled shot guns and a revolver."[7]

The mob, however, was not satisfied with letting Spencer take his chances on his fiery barge. "The river around the burning boat was soon dotted with skiffs and other boats, many containing armed men, waiting to shoot the doomed negro, if he should attempt to escape," Willett continued. Once Spencer had endured the flames for as long as possible, he appeared on deck "with a weight of some kind tied around his neck. He gave vent to some undistinguishable exclamation, cast himself into the river, and sank to rise no more. The boat burned to the water's edge, and grounded on the Kentucky shore, and thus ended what was known in the West as the Joe Spencer tragedy."[8] Given that Spencer took his own life to thwart an execution, his death should be regarded as a circumstantial suicide, one that he would not have undertaken but for the imminent mortal threat posed by the mob. Under these circumstances, his suicide does not preclude the classification of the event as a lynching.

Three objectives drive this chapter. The first is to analyze the lynching of Joe Spencer, as reported by Willett and the contemporary press, in order to gauge white attitudes toward blacks in Cairo in 1854. The second is to situate the Spencer lynching within the larger historical context of race relations and racist violence in Illinois—and more particularly in the southern Illinois region known as Egypt—in the 1840s and 1850s. The last is to speculate on the implications of the Cairo lynching and its context for the historiography of Illinois and of mob violence more generally.

Most of the existing accounts of the Cairo lynching—invariably written by whites—portrayed Joe Spencer as a reprobate and a gambler, a man deserving of his terrible fate. The *Missouri Republican* reported that Spencer "had become very offensive to the citizens on account of various misdemeanors he had lately committed."[9] In a dig at Spencer and at the lawlessness of the city in which he died, the *St. Louis Intelligencer* declared that he had "been for years the terror of Cario [*sic*], which alone tells his character."[10] Nearly three decades after the event, H. C. Bradsby painted an especially unflattering portrait of the victim:

> Joe Spencer was nothing but a wretched, desperate, ignorant and brutal negro, whose life was a constant menace to all. Nothing is clearer than that it was the right way, the high and solemn duty of the people of Cairo to either drive off or kill the dangerous, bad negro. They should have done this long before they did, and if it was necessary to kill him in order to get rid of him, he was entitled to no more consideration than a snake or a rabid dog.[11]

Nevertheless, the evidence suggests that whites despised Spencer not because he was the terror of Cairo or some rabid dog but because he refused to abide by the stifling expectations of the white supremacist society in which he lived. First, Spencer had achieved significant success as a businessman and, perhaps, a gambler, creating resentment within the white community. "It cannot be denied that Joe kept, for the place and the time, a good hotel," acknowledged Willett. "As a natural consequence of his location and lack of competition he . . . was making money." With surprising frankness he elaborated: "A feeling had been for some time growing up against [Spencer], on the part of some of the people. Some were embittered against him by feelings of envy on account of his prosperity; others because he had been too successful in playing his favorite game of poker with them."[12] In short, Spencer, like so many of those who would be lynched over the course of the following century, aroused white enmity because he outshined them. "For many poor whites, seeing blacks do well was an intolerable, even perverse, inversion of the social structure," conclude the sociologists Stewart E. Tolnay and E. M. Beck. "As a result, 'Every prosperous negro who *shows his prosperity in a way to be seen by the whites* is a focus for hatred.'"[13]

Second, Spencer exuded strength and dignity and refused to show whites the cringing deference that they expected. As Willett put it, some "thought he did not treat white men with proper respect." Not only was he "generally acknowledged to be 'smarter' than many among the whites"; being a large and stalwart man, he was abundantly capable of pummeling anyone who tried to make him show respect for whites. In addition to demanding that white men treat *him* with the proper respect, Spencer was proud of his blackness. Although Willett claimed that Spencer's final remark could not be understood, the *Louisville Courier* deciphered it— "the negro . . . clapped his hand on his breast, swore he was king of the black race, and would die like a man."[14] Given his prosperity and pride, Spencer was likely a man of influence in the local black community or, as one critic put it in a disparaging play on his final words, "the 'king of [the] darkeys.'"[15] By killing Spencer, whites intimidated the black population more generally.

Finally, given his demand for respect, Spencer was—as the facts illustrate—unwilling to accede to whites' efforts to fetter him. "He appreciated the disadvantages of his position, as a negro," noted Willett, and watched with mounting anger the campaign to destroy him. "Joe . . . had become impressed with the idea that there was an intention on the part of the people to mob him, if they could find an occasion. Perhaps he was not far wrong; at all events he believed it, and acted upon the belief." As a result, when he received the summons for trespassing, he saw it as an act of provocation. "It was a small matter," insisted Willett, but Spencer regarded it as part of a widespread effort to undermine him.[16] As a testament to his determination to resist, he conceived and executed his plot knowing that it would precipitate violence against him. Indeed, given his stockpile of weapons, it is likely that Spencer knew how dangerous such a confrontation might be.

The account by H. C. Bradsby of the Spencer lynching in the 1883 *History of Alexander, Union and Pulaski Counties, Illinois* provides insight into how subsequent commentators could reshape the narrative of a lynching to suit their purposes. In a version that scarcely resembled the somewhat harsh contemporary newspaper accounts or Willett's more measured 1863 version, the *History* presented a much more exaggerated account that recharacterized Spencer and the nature of his alleged crimes, transforming him from a gambler, trespasser, or reprobate into a serial murderer. Possessing a "wicked eye," Spencer had a hotel boat where "crimes of the deepest cast had long been going on," it claimed. "Strangers had been known to repeatedly stop there and were never seen or heard of again after going to bed." Confronted with such a monster, the *History* explained, the frightened but overly indulgent whites offered a generous compromise: "Spencer was waited upon by a few representative citizens and informed of the determination of the people, and at the same time he was assured that he should be safely conveyed across the river."[17]

After agreeing to the terms proffered by these courteous white citizens, the *History* continued, Spencer reneged on his promises, outraging the slow-to-anger whites. "Spencer not only declined to go, but mocked and defied the people he had so signally outraged. An hour's time was given him for preparation to leave—then another hour; but instead of employing the time for such an end, he used it in preparing himself for resistance." The crowd now grew quite incensed and rushed the boat, only to be driven back by Spencer's gunshots. Although contemporary reports and Willett's account claimed that the shots killed no one, the *History* insisted that they had—although, conveniently, the author could "find no one now able to recall the name of this man, he being almost an entire stranger." Only at this point, the author remembered, did the crowd become a mob, chasing the fiery barge into the river and emptying their guns into it. Nonetheless, the book still insisted that Spencer was responsible for his own death. As the boat burned,

> many had concluded [that] the wretched creature had perished in the flames, and as they were about to turn from the sickening sight there was a crash of glass heard in the great bulk of flame. In an instant afterward Spencer appeared upon the stern in full view of the great crowd . . . and, looking defiantly at all, he placed his hand upon his breast and leaped headlong into what he then must have considered the "friendly waters of the Ohio." Long and anxiously the crowd looked for his appearance to the surface, but the waters had closed over him once and forever. Thus, calling destruction on his own head, perished the desperate negro, Joseph Spencer.[18]

In the final part of its reconstruction, the *History* bemoaned the earlier coverage, which, in the author's view, assassinated the character of the white population and elevated Spencer to the position of oppressed hero. Mustering as much sarcasm as possible, it claimed—with little evidence— that the national press had created a story that had Spencer "conducting a prayer meeting on his boat" when a white mob "without premeditation . . . assembled shortly after dark on the morning of the bloody day for the hellish and authorized purpose."[19] However far-fetched its version of the events, it became (if it had not already become) the standard version of the event among whites. In a history of Cairo written in the early twentieth century, John M. Lansden declined to address the incident at all, simply referring interested readers to the 1883 account.[20]

With its insistence on refashioning the story, the *History* demonstrated the significance of narrative to lynch mobs and their supporters. The tome's indifference to facts indicated its author's recognition that the legitimacy of lynching—indeed, the right to claim that an act of violence was a lynching at all—required that the black victim be a lawbreaking villain and that his white executioners be good, sturdy, wholesome folks. In this sense, this book underscores the argument of Lisa Arellano that lynching should be understood as "a set of violent practices made recognizable by a constellation of formulaic narrative practices" and that it "was by virtue of *claiming* that a given act of violence is 'enacted against a criminal' and is 'a punishment' that a given act of violence becomes a lynching."[21]

For decades the Illinois Country had permitted slavery, introduced originally by French settlers and retained under Virginia law after 1776. Because Article 6 of the Northwest Ordinance of 1787 forbade slavery north of the Ohio River, Illinois failed to attract the large influx of slave-holders that its climate, soil, and proximity to the Upper South might otherwise have enticed. The influential pro-slavery faction pushed hard to repeal the antislavery provisions of Article 6 in the late eighteenth and early nineteenth centuries but could not overcome the resistance of antislavery settlers who slowly and steadily entered the state during this period. When Illinois entered the Union as a free state in 1818, however, it allowed for a vague system of involuntary servitude as a balm for the fraternity of slaveholders who had been among its earliest white settlers. During the Panic of 1819 the state again experienced a bitter debate about slavery when its advocates insisted that a system of human bondage would lead to economic growth. The voters resolved this skirmish in favor of freedom with a constitutional referendum in 1824.[22]

Before the referendum, most white residents, whether of southern or northern origin, opposed slavery because they feared that it would establish a tyrannical elite, depress manufacturing, and restrict opportunity for free white men. They did not, however, view slavery as immoral, and they did not seek its demise in the American South. They considered blacks untrustworthy, immoral, and ignorant, and they certainly feared the implications of having a large population of free blacks for their ultimate objective of an all-white state. "Both this distrust of what were considered innate characteristics of the Negro race and the assumption that the Ohio River states were becoming a dumping ground for penniless former slaves brought demands to curb free Negro immigration," writes the historian Eugene H. Berwanger. "And the demands to place limits upon free Negroes became stronger as antislavery sentiment crystallized."[23]

In the late eighteenth and early nineteenth centuries, when racist inden-tured servitude existed in Illinois, slave masters from Virginia migrated to southern Illinois, where they used violence to maintain their authority. A local historian described this violence in his 1883 *History of Effingham County, Illinois*. Planters who brought their slaves with them would offer the enslaved "a chance to choose freedom or years of service and bondage for their children till they should become thirty years of age. If they chose freedom they must leave the State in sixty days or be sold as fugitives." He added that "servants were whipped for offenses for which white men are fined. Each lash paid forty cents of the fine. A negro ten miles from home without a pass was whipped."[24]

Whites' rancor toward blacks expressed itself in the very names assigned to places early in the nineteenth century. For example, in his collected papers John Willis Allen, the southern Illinois historian and archivist, detailed the origins of the name Black Bottom in Pope County: "Some say that it was because a number of Negroes settled in that region. Others claim that it was because of the black soil." The latter explanation, he mused, "seems to be the better one even though several families of Negroes resided in that area."[25] This book asserts that the former is actually more likely. Elsewhere in Egypt, whites thoroughly isolated the scattered settlements of blacks. Writing of Oskaloosa Township, the local historian who produced the *History of Wayne and Clay Counties, Illinois* in 1884 noted that a small colony founded in Clay County in 1835 "has ever since been known as the 'Nigger settlement.'"[26]

In the 1820s and 1830s whites codified their animosity toward blacks in statutes that banned blacks from the militia, denied them voting rights, prohibited them from testifying against whites in court, and required proof of freedom and a thousand-dollar bond on their entry into the state. In "Negroes in Jackson County, 1850–1910," Johnetta L. Jones chronicles other methods of racial control practiced by white citizens of Illinois in the 1840s. She writes, "Negroes who wandered into Jackson County on their own were running a tremendous risk of being re-enslaved," and quotes at length from the diary of resident James Green:

> I remember that Uncle John came to see us several times when we lived at Brownsville. He never came when Father was at home, for Father said that he didn't want any thing to do with a man that bought and sold human beings like they were a cow or a horse. Father said that there were several Negro slaves that would run away from the South and come up the Mississippi River. Uncle John would catch them and either sell them to a slave trader or return them back to their owner. Father said that is where he made most of his money, and he never stopped until his wife threatened to leave him if he didn't quit.[27]

As anxiety about competition for work and interracial sexuality continued to grow, whites intensified their antipathy toward blacks. When legislators wrote a new constitution in 1847, they further tightened restrictions on blacks by proposing an exclusion provision. The following year, according to the historian Leon F. Litwack, "voters indorsed the Illinois constitutional clause barring the further admission of Negroes by a margin of more than two to one."[28] Despite its approval legislators did not move to enforce exclusion until 1853, when a lawmaker introduced "An Act to Prevent the Immigration of Free Negroes into This State." Within days, legislators passed the measure.[29] Berwanger observed that the statute,

> undoubtedly the most severe anti-Negro measure passed by a free state, stipulated that any person bringing a Negro or mulatto into Illinois, other than someone traveling through with his slaves, was liable to a fine of from $100 to $500 and a one-year prison sentence. Moreover, the act required the governor, if such a person was not a resident, to request his extradition to face charges and trial. Negroes entering and remaining in the state for ten days were to be tried for high misdemeanor. Conviction meant a fine of $50, payable immediately. If the fine could not be paid, the Negro's labor was to be publicly auctioned; the period of service was determined at the time of purchase. Any Negro punished under the act was to be apprehended again if he did not leave the state within ten days after his service ended. The fine was increased $50 for each subsequent offense.[30]

The 1853 Illinois Black Law was so draconian that many whites who supported its intent recoiled at its severity. In fact, it prompted the editor of the *Ottawa Free Trader*, an ardent opponent of any black presence in the state, to write, "We should like to see the man that would mount the auctioneer's block in this town and sell a freeman to the highest bidder, and we should like to see the bidder." Because it was not strenuously enforced, the law proved to be largely ineffective, as demonstrated by the fact that the black population of Illinois grew from 5,436 to 7,628 from 1850 to 1860.[31] Nevertheless, it functioned as a ubiquitous means of intimidation and could be dusted off when necessary to punish those who got out of line or to rob them of their hard-earned property.

"Our readers are all no doubt aware of the law . . . which sells a free negro into slavery if he presumes to immigrate and settle in Illinois," noted the *Daily Illinois State Journal* in 1857. It related how some whites in Washington County had manipulated the law to their own advantage.

> A poor old nigger, long in a state of bondage, finally, through the indulgence of a generous master, succeeded in purchasing himself and family, and, thinking to find a home where he might be permitted to earn his bread undisturbed, he come [sic] to Illinois, was induced to purchase a piece of

land, and paid the granter of the land to build a house upon it. In so doing, he expended nearly all of his hard savings. Unfortunately, however, he was too hasty; for, being somewhat illiterate, he was not acquainted with the fact that he had no legal right to settle in this State, and no one was kind enough to warn him of his danger. About the time his money was all expended, he was informed, by some one, in relation to the law. He then tried to induce the man of whom he purchased the property to take it back and restore the money. This was refused. Finally, as he *must* leave, and was without means, he borrowed a sum of money equal to but a moiety of the amount he paid for the property, pledged the whole of the property for its payment, and departed for some more charitable locality."[32]

Few editors overtly endorsed the law, and "public opinion seemed to be running clearly in opposition to it," found the historian Roger Biles. Nonetheless, whites endorsed it by keeping it on the books until the Civil War had begun. "No effective movement for repeal came until 1864," wrote Biles, and the climate for the small black population—which constituted less than one percent of the state's population—"remained decidedly inhospitable."[33]

"Little Egypt," or simply "Egypt," was and is a vaguely defined region that includes the bottom third of the state and largely consists of a rolling and fertile landscape. White yeomen from the Upper South initially settled the area, bringing with them a highly evolved hostility toward slaveholding white aristocrats and black people generally. "Southern pioneers concentrated in Egypt" and in some areas farther north, notes the historian Richard J. Jensen, "leaving to the Yankees the challenge of taming the prairies" in the central and northern stretches of the state.[34] Because many of the initial slaveholding colonists living in Illinois in the 1700s settled in southern Illinois, as previously noted, they and their progeny made that region more amenable than the rest of the state to human bondage well into the nineteenth century.[35]

White "Egyptians" were vociferous advocates of the exclusion provision of 1847. Delegates from the region argued that "their constituents had left the South to escape the evil effects of slavery and the Negro. Southern Illinoisans, they maintained, preferred the society of white men and settled in the free states 'to get rid of this intolerable nuisance.'" One warned that, if legislators failed to act, "the people in his section of the state [would] 'take matters into their hands, and commence a war of extermination.'" Consumed with fear, they claimed that they were being overrun. When they approved the exclusion provision in 1848, one editor acknowledged their role in pushing the cause: "Sound the Loud trumpet 'oer [*sic*] Egypt's dark sea, The people have spoken,—and Egypt is free!" Five years later a newspaper suggested that the fear of blacks rather than the growth in their numbers was really the driving force behind whites' actions.[36] "The Alton (Illinois), *Courier* proves, by actual statistics, that the negro population of Southern Illinois is decreasing," noted the *New York Evangelist* in 1853. "The *Courier* argues from this, that all [the] alarm about the increase of free negroes is unfounded."[37] In her study of Jackson County more than a century later, Johnetta L. Jones reached similar conclusions, writing, "[white] Egyptians . . . viewed the spectre of wholesale Negro immigration as a calamity to be avoided at all costs. Most of them believed that their area would be the only section of the state harmed because of its proximity to the surrounding slave states."[38]

Egyptians sometimes decried what they viewed as the efforts of whites in central and northern Illinois to scapegoat them as uniquely racist bigots whose animosity for blacks exceeded that of whites elsewhere in the state. The *Jonesboro Gazette* denounced one such characterization in 1857: "We have noticed upon several occasions like slurs emanating from the northern portions of the State." Fuming, it charged that those who wrote such slurs "never remain [here] long enough to acquire [any] knowledge of the people, though they generally make ample amends for ignorance by great proficiency in the refined art of lying about us."[39] Egyptians had cause for complaint because their neighbors to the north routinely portrayed them as the state's backward problem population. "The emergence of a Yankee-dominated, more urban, modern northern Illinois polarized the state along north-south lines," writes Jensen. "Economic development was far more rapid in the north, while the central region was slow to catch up, and Egypt lagged far behind."[40] Nevertheless, while it rightly resented efforts to foist all racial sins on Egypt, the *Gazette* freely conceded "the peculiar climate of this region."[41]

In order to discourage black settlers, drive out those who were already there, and enforce white supremacy over those who remained, whites in Egypt regularly employed violence. The *Alton Weekly Courier* recognized that the Cairo lynching was no aberration. In 1852 it observed that there was "considerable excitement throughout the more Southern parts of the State, between the whites and colored people. We notice accounts of rows, and hostile movements quite often, in our exchanges from that quarter."[42] In 1857 the *Mound City Emporium* made a similar point. "At this particular time the white and free colored population of Southern Illinois . . . seem to be at serious loggerheads." Using these "violent outbreaks" as an index to public opinion, it concluded: *"Really in these times we are almost persuaded that a negro had no business to be a negro."*[43]

In some cases such outbreaks took the form of mob violence. The most well-known episode—and one of the most notable such incidents in ante-bellum America—was the killing of Elijah Lovejoy, a white abolitionist, in Alton in 1837. The violence underscored the racist attitudes of many whites in the region, occurring as it did during an assault by an anti-abolitionist mob intent on destroying his printing press and silencing his views. As Lovejoy attempted to protect his press, the mob opened fire. Ironically, Lovejoy had fled to Alton from St. Louis, Missouri, after whites there burned a black man in 1836 and menaced Lovejoy. In 1838 a lawyer in Springfield, Illinois, registered his concern about the recent outbreak of mob violence across the American West. Recalling the "horror-striking scene at St. Louis," Abraham Lincoln lamented: "Such are the effects of mob law; and such . . . scenes, [are] becoming more and more frequent in this land so lately famed for love of law and order."[44]

The Spencer lynching was not even an aberration in Cairo. In July 1857 a number of whites kidnapped two black men, beat them, and transported them to Missouri for sale into slavery. One of the blacks escaped and swam back across the Mississippi to Cairo, "naked as the day he was born, and horribly mangled about the head."[45] Slave catchers had, of course, long pursued fugitive slaves (and free blacks alleged to be fugitives) into Illinois, but the recent *Dred Scott* decision by the U.S. Supreme Court and a recent and very brutal incident elsewhere in Egypt gave the issue tremendous import in the summer of 1857. In March of that year Chief Justice Roger B. Taney had declared that blacks "had no rights which the white man was bound to respect."[46] Then, just weeks prior to the kidnapping in Cairo, slave hunters cornered three fugitives in Nashville, Illinois, the seat of Washington County. When one of the fugitives purportedly fought back, they shot him and then severed his head for delivery back to Missouri. "Even when dead," declared a disgusted *Illinois State Chronicle*, "[black] bodies are not to be respected, but must be mutilated and their heads taken to a sister State as a trophy."[47] An observer linked the *Dred Scott* decision to the Nashville incident, arguing that the slave catchers "desecrated the anniversary of American Independence by hunting down fugitive slaves, and shooting dead one poor fellow for the crime of choosing freedom! The two companions of the slave made their escape from the white blood-hounds hissed on by Taney."[48]

Following the botched kidnapping of the man who escaped the slave catchers and swam back to the city, whites in Cairo vented their anger on blacks, assaulting them openly in the streets and shooting at them from hiding places. The *Cairo Times and Delta* objected not to their stated purpose but to their more sinister one, writing, "The proposed object of the attacking party has been, to run the negroes out of town, a thing well enough if done in a legal manner; but their real object is said to be to kidnap negroes and sell them in slave States."[49] Fueled by both racism and a pecuniary motive, the vigilantes escalated their lawlessness. On July 25 they visited the homes of all the blacks in the city and ordered them to leave town. When the blacks failed to do so, the whites surged into the black quarters in the early hours of July 26. They targeted a house, smashing the doors and windows, driving out the residents, and setting it ablaze. "There was an instant stampede of the blacks from all parts of the city," the *Cincinnati Times* reported, "and they were pursued, and in some instances fired at."[50]

Many whites in Cairo supported the rioters. "Some of our citizens have taken the matter up strongly, and insist that the rioters were right," noted the *Times and Delta*, because they were merely acting under the provisions of the "law providing for the expulsion of free negroes not raised in the State."[51] On the following day "many called for the expulsion of all the free negroes from the town; and two were arrested under the 'Black Law,'" reported the *Chicago Tribune*. "They were both fined, one $25, and the other $50, paid their fines and left town." Seeing the law enforced against these men, "the [other] free negroes then took the alarm and fled precipitately." Whites in Cairo thereby succeeded in ridding themselves of blacks for a short time. Before long, however, blacks returned, driven from even more hostile rural areas or lured by the prospect of jobs and the (very) relative safety of numbers.[52]

Municipal authorities and business leaders in Cairo dispatched a hastily organized army of deputies to quell the violence and arrest the rioters. They were not primarily concerned with protecting the blacks, of course, but with mitigating the bad publicity that the incident would bring upon their city, potentially damaging its reputation, deterring further settlement, and jeopardizing its economic prospects. One of them identified the stakes. "Strangers who have arrived here within the last day or two, leave by the first conveyance," he wrote. "They are afraid to stop, and I do not wonder at it. God only knows how long this reign of terror is to last." Although some critics of the rioters expressed genuine sympathy for the blacks, most shared the racist sentiments of the rioters. "I regret to say that some of our merchants sympathize with the rioters," stated one observer. Another expressed his view that, "law or no law, every nigger should leave Cairo."[53]

At the end of the Civil War whites in Cairo—aided and abetted by Union soldiers posted there—unleashed still more violence against the local black population. In the fall of 1865 they were aggressive, indeed. A few miles outside of town a mob attacked an elderly man in an effort to force him to admit to recent thefts. "The neighbors—none too intelligent, perhaps, and with deep rooted prejudices against his race, attempted to make him confess the theft, but he persisted in stoutly denying it," reported the *Cairo Daily Democrat*. "Finally, they resorted to extreme measures to force him into confession, actually suspending him in mid-air, from the limb of a tree, taking care, however, to let him down before life was extinct."[54] Union soldiers and veterans clashed repeatedly with blacks. In one instance white members of the Sixth Illinois Cavalry engaged in another race riot. "They got drunk and attacked every negro they could find with brickbats and stones. Several were badly cut and bruised." Their officers, in turn, made no effort to curb the rioting.[55]

In the aftermath of the war blacks in Illinois, like those elsewhere in the Midwest and across the North, experienced a brief period of hope that their social position would improve measurably. In Illinois legislators repealed the Black Laws. In Washington, DC, members of Congress passed the Thirteenth, Fourteenth, and Fifteenth Amendments abolishing slavery, assuring the freed people their citizenship, and affording black men the right to vote. In so doing, state and national leaders ensured in theory that blacks would enjoy unfettered the freedom and opportunity so long denied to them.

In practice, however, whites in Illinois, like those across the country, crushed the aspirations of blacks by their refusal to abide by the letter or the spirit of these laws. They started their retreat from racial Reconstruction shortly after the war. Then, amid the economic devastation of the mid-1870s and the mounting pressure for sectional reconciliation, they accelerated that retreat, sealing it with the Compromise of 1877, in which the Republican North agreed to the withdrawal of federal troops from the former Confederate States—in effect, placing black southerners at the mercy of their white counterparts—in exchange for the acceptance by the Democratic South of the ascension of Rutherford B. Hayes to the presidency after the disputed election of 1876. White northerners finalized their retreat in 1883 when the Supreme Court declared unconstitutional most of the provisions of the Civil Rights Act of 1875, a finding that encouraged whites, northern and southern alike, to impose the ever more discriminatory practices and laws that would soon come to be known as Jim Crow.[56]

By the turn of the century, blacks in Illinois found themselves in circumstances only marginally better than those endured in the antebellum years. "After the Civil War, despite the repeal of the Black Laws and the passage of the Thirteenth, Fourteenth, and Fifteenth Amendments, a relatively small number of black expatriates from the South chose to resettle in the Land of Lincoln," writes Biles. Those who did "enjoyed few civil rights. The 1870 Constitution guaranteed all males the right to vote, but because of their limited numbers, blacks exercised little political power."[57] In addition, blacks lost their right to equal education because of the imposition of segregated schools and faced acrimonious competition with desperate European immigrants for jobs and housing. "African Americans too often occupied substandard housing, paid higher rents, were forced to accept the lowest-paying jobs, and received little aid from social service agencies," notes the historian Wanda A. Hendricks. "Many Republican leaders hesitated to pursue racial equality too strenuously for fear of making Illinois a haven for African Americans fleeing harsher treatment in the post-Reconstruction South," according to Biles. Indeed, changes sweeping across Illinois in the decades after the war "created few opportunities for the state's modest African American population."[58]

Although scholars have devoted little attention to antiblack lynching in the antebellum North, this chapter, like chapter 1, suggests that they might do so profitably. This work suggests, albeit tentatively, that whites in the Old Northwest, like those in the slave states, probably lynched blacks far more often than previously imagined in order to enforce white supremacy prior to the Civil War.[59] At the least, it should encourage others to explore the possibility and to account for the frequent "hostile movements" mentioned in the *Alton Weekly Courier*.

In the years immediately following the Spencer lynching (and despite the evidence presented by the race riot), contemporary prognosticators questioned the likelihood of a similar event. "While here," wrote a correspondent to the *St. Louis Intelligencer* in his dispatch from the scene of the lynching, "we witnessed a scene characteristic of the past history of Cairo, but probably the last of the kind that will make the town famous."[60] In his 1863 reminiscences Willett confidently predicted that racist violence of that sort was a vestige of the past. In his final line he asserted that "there is no danger of a negro being lynched in Cairo now."[61] To those familiar with the subsequent history of race relations in Cairo, those predictions now seem like some form of macabre humor.

In one of the most infamous lynchings in U.S. history, a mob of thousands in Cairo hanged one William James in November 1909. The mob members hanged him from a steel arch that towered over a downtown intersection. "Someone had the ingenious idea to turn on the electric lights that illuminated the arch, and for a moment the crowd was treated to a surreal tableau of a large, slowly strangulating black man profiled against the dusk sky and festive bulbs of the arch," writes Philip Dray. When the rope broke and James fell to the street, white men unloaded on him indiscriminately, riddling him with bullets. "A huge bonfire was built and the rest of the corpse was burned, once the heart and other organs were removed to be sold as keepsakes."[62]

In the twenty-first century the lynching of James has received attention from writers and scholars such as Dray and James W. Loewen. Photographs from the affair were featured in a collection of lynching photographs titled *Without Sanctuary* (2000) and in the touring exhibit of the same name. Given the horror of the incident, the attention that it received in the contemporary press, and the subsequent role that it played in poisoning race relations in the city in the twentieth century, it has come to represent in the minds of many the starting point for both the racial unrest that reached a climax in ugly race riots in 1967 and the series of interracial clashes that occurred over the course of the next six years—all of which contributed greatly to the city's subsequent decline. The historian Joanne Wheeler advanced this view. Between the Civil War and the turn of the century, she argued, Cairo enjoyed relatively serene, if deteriorating, race relations. The 1909 lynching, however, represented a clear rupture; it "ushered in a second stage in Cairo's racial history," she declared, and "Jim Crow appeared in the region of Egypt."[63]

In fact, the roots of the city's agonizing racial tensions are embedded not in the early twentieth century but in the early nineteenth. The conviction that Cairo was an inhospitable place for blacks was expressed by the *St. Louis Democrat*, which harshly criticized the city after the legal execution of convicted murderer William Campbell in 1873, observing, "They hung a negro lately in Cairo. It was a severe death, but what a relief to get out of Cairo."[64] The riot in 1857 and the lynching of Spencer in 1854 place the origin at mid-century, yet the *St. Louis Intelligencer* hinted that the Spencer lynching was an incident consistent with its past, just one of many over the decades. Indeed, the violence of the 1850s belies the image of Cairo so familiar to the readers of Mark Twain's *Huckleberry Finn* as the safe haven sought by the fugitive slave Jim as he and Finn drifted down the Mississippi. "We talked about Cairo, and wondered whether we would know it when we got to it," Finn recounted. "There warn't nothing to do now but to look out sharp for the town, and not pass it without seeing it. [Jim] said he'd be mighty sure to see it, because he'd be a free man the minute he seen it."[65]

Just as observers have wrongly attributed the origins of racist violence in Cairo to the 1909 lynching of James, so too have they mistakenly assigned the origins of racist violence across Illinois more generally to the same period. "The last years of the nineteenth century witnessed an increase in violence against blacks," writes Biles. "Heightened racial violence along with unrest in the factories and on the farms underscored the rapid changes sweeping across Illinois in the post–Civil War years and the difficulties experienced by the state's people in adjusting to these alterations." Hendricks arrives at a similar conclusion. "During the first decade of the twentieth century, the heightened racial tensions between African Americans and whites led to an alarming increase in violent attacks against blacks," she claims. "The quality of life for African Americans in the state deteriorated. At least twelve lynchings took place, and the number of racially motivated incidents continued to climb."[66]

Racist violence unquestionably raged throughout Illinois at the turn of the twentieth century: after an outbreak in Eldorado in 1902, the *Springfield (MA) Daily Republican* noted that the "situation regarding the colored race in southern Illinois . . . continues to be a crying disgrace to the commonwealth of Abraham Lincoln."[67] Furthermore, despite Dray's claim that "there was never another lynching recorded in the state of Illinois" after 1909, lynch mobs killed several more victims.[68] In 1915 a mob killed Zack Phillips in Taylorville. "It is frankly admitted," said the *Daily Journal-Gazette*, "that Phillips was shot after he had thrown away his gun and put up his hands."[69] The coroner did not seek to press charges, deferring to "the general opinion that no one could offer testimony sufficient to prove that any certain person fired the f[a]tal shot[s]."[70] In 1924 the *Chicago Daily Tribune* reported that "lynch law was applied in Chicago last night." Outside a jazz bar on Maxwell Street "one man, wielding a baseball bat," struck a black man over the head. "The blow appeared to stun him and he fell. The crowd, constantly growing, stormed around him. Blows and kicks were aimed at him and some of the men in the crowd trampled on him as he lay on the ground."[71]

Without disputing the prevalence or ferocity of racist violence in Illinois at the turn of the century—for such a thing could not be disputed—this chapter *does* challenge the assumption that this was a new development. Indeed, it asserts that the lynchings, race riots, and mass expulsions of the 1840s and 1850s, such as the grisly Golconda incident detailed in chapter 1, differed little from those that convulsed Cairo half a century later except in the extent and the sensationalism of the coverage.

If this chapter demonstrates that racist violence was rampant in Egypt *before* the Civil War as well as *after* 1900, common sense—along with substantial evidence—suggests that it was rampant in the intervening period as well. In 1867 a mob in Venice secured custody of a black prisoner, tied him by means of a noose to the back of a wagon, and dragged him to his death. In 1870 another mob there hanged and shot to death another black man.[72] In 1874, five hundred white men hanged a black prisoner in Mt. Carbon. The state's chief executive made little effort to respond to the hanging. "We do not much blame the Governor," noted the *Cairo Bulletin*. "[He] is human, and cannot be expected to be very energetic in an effort to punish the summary executors of justice on a negro [accused] of the rape and murder of a white woman."[73] In 1883 white men raided the jail in Mound City, beat and shot a black prisoner to death, and then hanged his mangled body on a tree limb. "Howard deserved hanging, there is no question about that at all," declared the *Cairo Daily Bulletin*, "but he was in the hands of the law and ought to have been hung . . . after a trial and conviction."[74]

In 1945 an elderly white woman identified only as Mrs. Modglin agreed to talk to an interviewer about her memories of an 1882 lynching in Elizabethtown. After the arrest of a young black man for the rape of a local white woman—a story that seems to have been suspect—a mob marched into town and seized the prisoner from the jail without the slightest interference from the local authorities. "At a little store next door to the jail," Mrs. Modglin stated, "the men had stopped and secured a length of rope. This was knotted about the negros [*sic*] neck and they proceeded toward the edge of town." The witness, a small girl at the time, saw the mob marching by her house. She remembered how the mob, including about a dozen white men, often pushed the youth to the ground and dragged him by the rope or pistol-whipped him and ordered that he rise again to his feet. The mob members eventually led him to the cemetery, where it hanged him on an oak tree. Many whites seemed to know that the youth had committed no crime, and some even argued with the mob before it killed the prisoner. According to Mrs. Modglin, however, a mob leader simply replied, "If this ain[']t [the] right ~~negro~~ nigger—we'll get the right one." At the bottom of the typed manuscript, the interviewer added that other subjects supported this view: "People best acquainted with the . . . facts and situation as it existed then are of the decided opinion that the young man lynched was not guilty."[75]

As the incidents described herein attest, whites in Egypt always subscribed to extremely racist notions of white supremacy and demanded harsh legislative and extralegal remedies to deal with what they viewed as a troublesome population. As they demonstrated with the lynching of Joseph Spencer, they were intolerant of blacks who achieved prosperity, projected strength, demanded respect, and willfully ignored white authority. Quite simply, they viewed blacks such as Spencer as mortal threats to their belief in natural white superiority. Whites in Egypt may have held racial attitudes that on the whole were more conservative than those of other Illinoisans, but this chapter does not suggest that Egyptians were singular in their racism or their use of violence. As the avalanche of support for the 1848 referendum clearly indicated, most whites across the entire state favored exclusion.[76] Furthermore, as the succession of lynchings and riots that took place in the central and northern regions of the state in the late nineteenth and early twentieth centuries indicate, whites in the southern part of the state were not the only ones susceptible to violent racist impulses.

In *A History of the City of Cairo, Illinois*, published in 1910, John M. Lansden exemplified the vituperative animosity for blacks so vividly exhibited in the lynching of William James a year earlier. Reflecting on "the dangers white women were in from the debased negroes of the town," he declared that "the fact that the victim was a young white woman and the assailant and murderer a black brute of the city would have put a strain upon any community." Curiously, Lansden concluded that the lynching "was the first occurrence of the kind in the city of Cairo. The Joe Spencer affair . . . could not be called a lynching in any sense of the word."[77] The latter statement is odd in two ways. First, it marked the only reference in his book to the spectacular events of November 1854, events that might typically have merited extensive discussion in a local history of this type. Second, it made a strong, strange, and unexplained claim that the lynching of one black man bore little relation to the lynching of another. Why was the killing of Joe Spencer omitted from Lansden's book? And, why would it not be called a lynching?

The answers are not difficult to identify. Although whites succeeded in lynching Spencer, they never exerted the mastery over him that was customary in such incidents. Within the terrifying bounds of the events unfolding around him, Spencer died on his terms—at least within the confines of the terrifying circumstances in which he found himself. Unwilling to surrender to the mob, he held it at bay for a lengthy period and gunned down five of its members before apparently deciding that, if he was going to die, he would at least decide how. As he stumbled onto the deck, Spencer signaled this understanding with his words and with his gestures. "Although conscious of his fate, [he] beat his breast and cried out that he had a true heart and that all Cairo could not take him alive," declared the *St. Louis Intelligencer*. "At length as the flames reached him, and having loaded himself with iron, he plunged over board and sank at once."[78] In this sense, Lansden may not have viewed the Spencer incident as a lynching because, quite simply, the story is as much about unflinching black resistance as it is about white power. At a time when whites undoubtedly feared reprisals by blacks for the James lynching, Lansden may also have worried that the Spencer affair might resuscitate a historical model and hero for black residents. After all, in death Spencer had continued to be the terror of white Cairo throughout the 1850s because, as Willett noted, "for a long time it was supposed that Cairo was haunted by the ghost of Joe Spencer." Furthermore, the martyred Spencer may also have inspired clandestine reprisals against whites by other blacks. Willett suggested as much when he reported that "a number of fires that occurred mysteriously are attributed to the incendiary influences of his ghostship."[79] White fear about the empowering meaning of the Spencer lynching for blacks may help explain why Lansden consciously suppressed the story—and why the episode is so important to the history of the city, the state, and the nation.

3 Indiana during Reconstruction

"This negro elephant *is getting to be a pretty large sized animal"*

"A gentleman just from below," the *Crisis* of Columbus, Ohio, reported in 1862, "says that a few days ago a large number of freed negroes were on the Kentucky side of the Ohio, trying to cross over into Indiana, when a regiment of Indiana Union soldiers was about to fire on them if they attempted to cross, threatening to kill every one of them, [and] declaring that they did not enlist in the war to fill their State with free negroes. . . . There was very great excitement, and it was not safe for any white man to interfere on behalf of the negroes." As the actions of the soldiers suggest, white Indianans were becoming bitter about the growing number of black fugitives fleeing into their state during the Civil War. In an oddly evocative phrase, the *Crisis* captured their concern: "This negro *elephant* is getting to be a pretty large sized animal."[1]

Few scholars have explored the response of white Indianans to the influx of blacks from the South and their concentration within the state during the Civil War and Reconstruction. This chapter augments that study in four ways. First, it examines white efforts to subordinate blacks, drawing attention to the surges of racist violence that marked the beginning and end of this period. Second, it explores some of the motivations for this violence but focuses on its overtly political nature during the Exodus of 1879–1880, when a large number of southern blacks entered the state. Third, it analyzes the geographical patterns associated with this violence. Finally, it assesses the implications of the violence for the subsequent history of Indiana and situates it in the historiography of racist violence in the Midwest more generally. Before proceeding, the chapter briefly addresses the nature of white-black relations in Indiana prior to the Civil War.

From the earliest days of white settlement most white Indianans manifested a strong disdain for slavery—not from humanitarian concern for blacks but from self-interest. Many early settlers were white "upland southerners who had not been slaveholders [in their states of origin] but who had witnessed the expansion of slavery from the lowland into the upland South," according to the geographer Gregory S. Rose. "They had experienced the deleterious impact of cheaper slave labor on the value and competitiveness of the products of their own free labor and had migrated to Indiana in part to escape the economic effects of slavery."[2]

Although they opposed slavery, these whites vigorously opposed an influx of free blacks into the state and were determined to prevent such an outcome. "Most Indianans regarded slavery as a violation of the laws of God and man," the historian James H. Madison summarized. "But few whites in pioneer Indiana believed in the equality of the races or made efforts to improve the unfortunate lot of many black Americans, slave or free."[3] In the 1820s a traveler marveled that the residents of Indiana possessed "a most unparalleled prejudice" against blacks.[4] In 1850 an Indianan declared that "it would be better to kill [blacks] off at once, if there is no other way to get rid of them."[5] In 1857 the *Evansville Daily Enquirer* opined that, "if we had our own way there should not be one [black person] tolerated any place except in Canada or in a slave State; we would not tolerate one in the State of Indiana. Out of slavery a negro is a nuisance."[6]

Contemporary politicians enshrined these prejudices in law. In 1818 legislators prohibited blacks from testifying in court; thirteen years later, they required newly arrived blacks to "post a bond of five hundred dollars as security against becoming public charges." Delegates to the constitutional conventions in both 1816 and 1851 passed provisions prohibiting blacks from voting. Lawmakers also outlawed interracial marriage, fearing that the unlimited immigration of free blacks would result in sexual relations between black men and white women, spawning racially mixed children and challenging white male control over these two subordinate groups.[7] The *History of Pike and Dubois Counties*, published in 1885, expressed the view that the lawmakers of the 1850s were so consumed with their antipathy for blacks and their concomitant need for restrictions on them that

> they were very busy. They had to pass all sorts of regulations concerning the negro. They had to protect a good many white people from marrying negroes. And as they didn't need any labor in the State, if it was "colored," they had to make regulations to shut out all of that kind of labor, and to take steps to put out all that unfortunately got in, and they didn't have time to consider [any other] scheme.[8]

By limiting the size of the black population, whites hoped to prevent competition for jobs. The historian Eugene H. Berwanger speculated that one of the principal reasons for the "increase in racial enmity" in the mid-nineteenth century was the "economic rivalry between unskilled Negro and white laborers in midwestern urban areas."[9] At the Indiana Constitutional Convention of 1851, delegates debated a measure to exclude blacks altogether. During this debate many expressed concern about a large influx of blacks. One delegate warned: "When we are overrun with them—as we most assuredly will be unless we adopt some stringent measures to prevent it—there will be commenced a war which will end only in extermination of one race or the other." Eventually, the delegates approved by a decisive vote "Article XIII, declaring that 'No Negro or mulatto shall come into or settle in the State.'" They also decided to submit this provision to the voters, who embraced it by a vote of 113,828 to 21,873.[10] In addition, ordinary whites often directed their antipathy for the blacks among them with violence. Despite the considerable control exercised by whites over them, however, the freed people were not reticent about defending themselves and did so on several well-documented occasions in the antebellum period.

Given the history of racism in Indiana before the Civil War, it is not surprising that whites there responded defensively once the sectional hostilities significantly increased the number of blacks fleeing the slave states for the relative safety of the Hoosier State. Concerned that they were being overrun, as they had long feared, whites rioted in New Albany in 1862, beating or shooting any blacks they found, killing at least one, and temporarily ridding the town of its black population.[11]

As the war ended in April 1865, more fugitives headed north. The *Baltimore Sun* noted that free blacks were entering Indiana from Kentucky in large numbers.[12] The *Cleveland Plain Dealer* announced, "Every train and boat . . . brings large re-inforcements of these swarthy blacks, who, in a few months will become a burden to the tax-payers and a pest to the communities upon which they force themselves."[13] Between 1860 and 1870 the number of blacks in Indiana increased from 11,428 to 24,560.[14] A hostile contemporary mused that the blacks were "led to believe, if they come north, [that] they will find freedom, easy times, plenty of employment, and social and political equality." With well-founded skepticism he predicted that they would be quite disappointed.[15]

In the summer of 1865 whites expressed their hostility in a series of incidents that took place along the Ohio River, the area most immediately affected by the black migration. In Evansville they smashed into the jail, took out two black men and, "after beating them to death, shot them, and then hung them up to lamp posts." At that point rioters drove other blacks from the town. The lynching, declared the *Jasper Weekly Courier*, "is one of the fruits of letting the much loved 'freedmen' of the South settle in the State, and those localities which permit it may expect more of such occurrences."[16] The *Vincennes Sun* declared that the Evansville violence constituted "a warning to niggers in this part of the State [to] keep their place, and keep it well, or they will be exterminated."[17]

To the east whites dislodged blacks from Boonville. "The darkies from Kentucky are pouring into this portion of Indiana, and our population is becoming considerably mixed," worried the *Boonville Enquirer*.[18] Confronted by a significantly different demographic reality than the one that they had left, returning veterans took action. Initially, they expelled only a few blacks. Weeks later, as the *Vincennes Sun* chronicled, they expanded their operations, ordering all blacks to leave. The newspaper added that the veterans had vowed "to proceed in a forcible and illegal manner to eject this class" if the blacks did not heed their warning.[19]

Further to the east white youths stoned two black men in New Albany. When one of the two reciprocated, injuring a white man, "the negro was beaten by some white men or boys, who endeavored to balance the account in that way."[20] In nearby Jeffersonville "the feeling of the citizens, as well [as] white soldiers, against the negro regiment stationed there is intense." An unknown vigilante (or vigilantes) expressed his feeling by bayonetting a black soldier, leaving the "gun sticking in his body, the bayonet extending through the body into the ground." The next day unknown parties murdered another black soldier, leaving his body on the road.[21]

In addition to the violence committed along the Ohio River, white Indianans attacked blacks elsewhere. In Sullivan County, further north, they gave "the 'niggers notice to leave,'" reported the *Vincennes Sun*. The *Sullivan Democrat* did not deny the *Sun*'s charge. In fact, it volunteered that "we have heard various rumors as to the purpose of our people to 'run off' all the niggers in the county—next Saturday being the time fixed by rumor for the consummation of the act."[22]

By the end of 1865 whites had established a template that they followed thereafter. In 1866 they organized in Martin County, posting inflammatory handbills that notified "the 'faithful' who may think 'themselves as good, or better than the *nigger*'" to attend a meeting to devise some means of keeping blacks down and, if possible, out of the county. An attendee joked that one of the local politicians who spoke "used the word 'nigger' just forty-nine times—no more nor less—in every speech."[23] The next year a mob near Seymour killed one Bob O'Neal, a former Kentucky slave and

Union veteran "hung merely because he was a nigger."[24] Lone vigilantes
mowed down blacks without fear of repercussions. On July 4, 1868, a
white named James Janes killed a man in Eureka and then "proceeded to
the grove where the picnic was being held, got upon a bench, [and] told
the people what he had done."[25] Boasting of his deed, he declared that "all
negroes ought to be killed, and that now was as good a time as any."[26]

Juries routinely endorsed the view expressed by Janes with their
acquittals of such vigilantes. A jury in Indianapolis did so in 1869 when
it released George Davidson, who had killed a black man "almost without
provocation." The *Cincinnati Daily Gazette* attributed the acquittal to the
fact that "Davidson [had] friends and money, and [was] a white man."[27]
Published in 1885, the *History of Warrick, Spencer and Perry Counties,
Indiana*, recollected another such injustice that had occurred in Warrick
County about a decade earlier: "John Bell and Mr. Frame were prosecuted
for killing a negro. The evidence is said to have been rather strong against
the defendants, but notwithstanding this, they were declared not guilty
by a jury of twelve men."[28]

In the 1870s whites perpetrated several exceptionally gruesome exhibitions. In 1871 a mob took three men from the Charlestown jail to the
woods, stripping one naked and using torches to torture him and coerce a
confession to a homicide, after which it hanged all three. "It was a ghastly
sight," the *New Albany Daily Standard* lamented, "to see the ugly carcasses
of the three murdered negroes dangling from the limbs of the trees, . . . but
it was a more disgusting sight to witness the rude boys of the town hanging like vultures over their lifeless remains and then indulging in remarks
unbecoming barbarians."[29] In 1878 a mob raided the jail in Mount Vernon
and seized four black men, whom they hanged. As whites massed beneath
the swinging corpses, they learned that the mob had killed a fifth man
in the jail, dismembering him and throwing his severed head, limbs, and
torso into the facility's outhouse.[30] The *Jasper Weekly Courier* added that
"the negroes are fleeing from the place in large numbers, terror stricken."[31]

Whites carried out several major riots. On Election Day in 1876 a mob
in Indianapolis targeted black voters, killing one.[32] Two years later, a mob
attacked blacks in Coal Creek, "shooting negroes on sight" and killing
three.[33] Whites there terrorized blacks for the next two months, climaxing
in a second disturbance that claimed a fourth black life. Before long, they
compelled blacks to sleep in the woods for fear of attack. A black woman
told a journalist that she had not slept well since the previous April. The
reporter painted a vivid scene: "About 50 negroes, men and women, went
down with us from Covington, whence they had fled, and our march up

the hill looked like a march in the south during the war, with the refugees bringing up the rear."[34] In 1880 a mob assaulted blacks in Rockport, cheering, "Run the d——d nigger out of here." After beating several, it killed one. "His death must be attributed to . . . the unreasoning fury of men who allowed their hatred of the negro race to run away with every better instinct of humanity," declared the *Rockport Journal*.[35]

Against the odds, blacks continued to defend themselves. In Jeffersonville, for instance, black soldiers killed two white men in 1865. At the inquest for one of these men, the coroner's jury articulated white anger, rendering "a verdict that the deceased came to his death from the effects of a gun-shot wound, inflicted by a d——d black s—n of a b——h (verbatim)."[36] The press followed suit, sympathizing with whites and assailing blacks: "The feeling of the white soldiers and citizens is said to be intense against the negro regiment quartered there," reported the Washington, DC, *Daily Constitutional Union*. "Murders of the most diabolical character are charged to have been committed by the negro soldiers."[37] Black civilians likewise defended themselves. Amid the tensions in Indianapolis in 1876, for example, "the colored men, seeing themselves thus pursued, and about to be assailed . . . looked about them for such weapons as they could find, to be used in their legitimate self-defense."[38]

In late 1879 and throughout 1880, an estimated two thousand black North Carolinians migrated to Indiana as part of the Exodus, a movement of thousands of blacks from the South to Kansas and, to a lesser degree, to the Hoosier State. According to the historian William Cohen, "In 1870, there were 1,354 blacks who had been born in North Carolina living in Indiana. In 1880 . . . the number rose to 3,167."[39] Although the number of blacks arriving in Indiana was considerably smaller than the number that reached Kansas, the Indiana press sensationalized the Exodus and persuaded fearful whites that they would be overwhelmed. An Illinois newspaper remarked that "mob law . . . is threatened in Indiana, if the negro exodus continues in that direction."[40]

As they had in 1865, white Indianans did respond with mob law. In some cases they acted before the newcomers set foot in town. Learning that a trainload of blacks from North Carolina was en route to Shelbyville in 1879, a crowd descended on the railroad depot "with the declared intention of preventing any negroes from getting off [there]. It is said they filled their pockets with stones and threatened to use violence against the emigrants if [they] landed." When the train arrived, the crowd surrounded it and "noisily informed the darkies that they must move further on. It seems they were all ticketed through to Indianapolis, and none of them intended to stop here, otherwise there can be little doubt that there would have been mob violence."[41]

Throughout 1880 mobs terrorized blacks. A group of vigilantes in Shelbyville engaged in a "Negro Hunt," pursuing a fugitive who, evidence suggests, was guilty only of quarreling with a white man. They soon captured him. "The fellow was badly scared, and looked worn out and weary," noted the *Cincinnati Daily Gazette*. "He had been shot once in the thigh of the left leg, the ball being still embedded. The ball entered in front, showing that he was facing the person who did the shooting." He evidently survived his wound.[42] In Brazil members of another mob lynched a black prisoner. "About 2 o'clock yesterday morning, when the citizens of our quiet little city were in the midst of their slumbers, Judge Lynch convened his supreme tribunal at our County Jail," noted a correspondent to the *Fort Wayne Weekly Sentinel*. Over a hundred men raided the jail, seized one George Scott, "a saddle colored negro[,] . . . and conveyed him to a beech tree, 100 yards away and hung him to a limb."[43]

Thus relatively few Exodusters went to Indiana—and many of those who did soon left. A southern newspaper came to that conclusion in 1880 when it reported the views of a black woman attempting to return to North Carolina after her experience in the Hoosier State. "In reply to an inquiry as to how the emigrants were treated, she said that they were treated like dogs," reported the *Alexandria Gazette*. "The emigrants cannot procure work, and are dying from cold and starvation."[44] Cohen drew the same conclusion, writing that "the figures suggest that after the migration of 1880 many migrants returned home or went elsewhere and that migration from North Carolina slowed to a crawl." Had the "conditions in Indiana been . . . attractive to blacks," he added, that "would not have happened and the statistics would have been quite different."[45]

In order to justify their use of violence, white Indianans used a number of familiar motives. They had, for example, long feared interracial sexual relations and used mob violence to curb the practice. They now continued that campaign at a quickened pace. Again, however, they framed it, when possible, not as a consensual union between black men and white women but as rape. In fact, they made this claim in lynchings involving a number of victims that occurred between 1865 and 1880. A quarter of a century after the lynching of two purported rapists in Evansville, Robert M. Evans, in his *History of Vanderburgh County, Indiana, from the Earliest Times to the Present*, hinted that this charge had been a mere pretext and that they had died for "an alleged offense of which one of them at least was, after his death, admitted to have been innocent by his accuser."[46] Whites in Posey

County cited rape as a motivating factor behind their quintuple lynching. "On Monday a party of seven negroes outraged four white women near Mount Vernon," reported the *Indianapolis News*. "Last night Deputy Sheriff Oscar Thomas, in attempting to arrest them, was shot and killed," it added, prompting a mob to murder "the ravishers."[47]

Because discrimination effectively locked blacks out of the industrial sector, whites did not feel compelled in most areas of the economy to intimidate black labor. They did respond violently in mining districts when company executives imported black "scabs" to crush strikes. Unable to lash out at their managers, white miners vented their fury instead on scabs who were even more exploited than they. "A difficulty occurred with the negro imported laborers from Virginia," a reporter from Knightsville attested in 1873. "The affair gave impetus to the embittered feeling of the miners and puddlers here who are on a strike, and soon the whole town was engaged in the general melee."[48] Similarly, those who rioted in Coal Creek in 1878 were members of "a militia company, composed of miners" who had been involved in a strike there in 1877.[49] Recalling that the miners had lost that strike, the *Inter Ocean* concluded that the riot represented the release of "all the pent-up passions of hatred and revenge which had smoldered for half a year."[50]

In areas with a sufficient number of blacks to tip the scales for the Republican Party in closely contested elections, white Democrats employed violence to keep blacks from the polls. Shortly before the 1876 Indianapolis race riot mentioned above, the Democrats charged that Republicans had inflated their voting base by importing blacks just before the election and that these black voters intended to cast multiple ballots. White Democrats also resented the recent hiring of seven black officers for the city police force. For a week before the election, reported the *Chicago Daily Tribune*, Democratic leaders made "incendiary remarks" that "boded ill."[51] Then, on Election Day, they assaulted black voters. The beleaguered blacks were chased, asserted the *Cincinnati Daily Times*, "by a police force that already knew that its days were numbered, and a mob of heated and angry Democrats . . . armed . . . for the fatal work to which they had been urged."[52]

At the time of the Exodus, Democrats had even greater incentive for such politically motivated attacks. Before the migration Democrats and Republicans enjoyed roughly comparable electoral strength in Indiana. For partisan purposes, therefore, both parties targeted in different ways the Exodusters, who were arriving in search of freedom and opportunity. The Democrats feared that the black newcomers, likely to be Republican in their political allegiance, could hand victory to the GOP in 1880. They also charged—correctly—that the Republicans were exploiting the Exodus for electoral advantage. "The original [black] impulse toward colonization," Cohen argued, "was distorted into a politically manufactured migration whose sole purpose [from the perspective of these cynical GOP operatives] was to strengthen the Republican party in the election of 1880." He continued: "Indiana had gone Democratic by a narrow margin in 1876, and three years later it seemed possible that the in-migration of a few thousand Republican voters might tilt the state in the opposite direction."[53]

In order to minimize the possibility of such a tilt, Democrats undertook a campaign of violence against the Exodusters and blacks generally in the lead-up to the 1880 election. In June Democrats in Bartholomew County declared that "no dam niggers" could "lay around here . . . and vote the republican ticket, the exa dust hed quarters [sic] must be abolished."[54] In August they followed through, attacking the home of a black man, threatening to hang him, and ordering him to leave Columbus. They also advertised their intention "to 'clean out all the g—d d——n niggers in the county before the election.'"[55] An observer (and Republican partisan, of course) claimed that "'the niggers must go' is the war cry of the Democrats in certain parts of Indiana."[56] When Democrats learned that unknown blacks had been spotted in Shelbyville in September, they warned that "little doubt is entertained that these 'coons' are a portion of the Republican army of occupation which is at present settling down on Indiana in dark clouds preparatory to the [November] election. But it will not be healthy for any unacclimated negroes to vote here."[57]

Democrats articulated their concerns in spectacular fashion in Rockport in October. Following a Democratic rally, revelers-turned-rioters attacked blacks, shouting "Kill them, kill them" and unleashing "a cloud of brick-bats" against their fleeing targets. After beating several, the members of the mob focused on a certain Uriah Webb, pelting him with brickbats and chasing him along the sidewalk. As Webb broke away and darted into the street, a rioter drew a pistol and fired. The Rockport Journal—ardently Republican, it should be noted—claimed that Democratic rioters crowded around the dying man and explicitly mingled their political and anti-black objectives: "One fellow cried out: 'One vote less'; others lifted their caps and hurrahed for [Democratic presidential candidate Winfield S.] Hancock."[58]

White Indianans practiced racist violence most commonly in the southernmost counties along the Ohio River, where many of the state's blacks were concentrated. The Louisville Democrat recognized this during the spate of attacks in 1865. "Within the past two months," it asserted, violence

Map 1. Racist Violence against Blacks in Indiana

"in the border counties of Kentucky and Indiana [has] been of frequent occurrence, and so intense [have] been the feelings of the [white] citizens against this class of persons [blacks], that many of them have been compelled to leave their houses to escape summary punishment, for if they had been captured they would no doubt have been hung on the first tree."[59] That this area of the state was the one most heavily settled by white southerners is *not*, however, necessarily evidence that they were more racist than white Indianans of northern descent, even if that might appear to be the case initially.[60]

Whites elsewhere in the state also resorted to violence when "provoked," most commonly by the arrival of a small number of blacks. In 1867 whites in Pierceton demonstrated this phenomenon when they interpreted the arrival of a handful of blacks as an effort to achieve "the Africanization of [Kosciusko] county."[61] When policemen arrested a black man for an alleged felony, "he was brought back to Pierceton, where he was met by an excited mob, [which] immediately fell upon him, and shot, beat, and stabbed him, until he was dead. A rope was then placed around his neck, and his body was dragged through the streets and finally, left lying in the road."[62] This violence, a resident declared, demonstrated "the necessity for a removal of the negroes out of the country. To-day, at Pierceton there would be a unanimous vote for the measure."[63]

Clearly, whites were targeting blacks in the locales where they concentrated, however few they were. "After the Civil War most of the [black] newcomers settled in cities and towns," the historian Emma Lou Thornbrough observed. "Older residents also left rural areas and headed for the cities."[64] In either case blacks privileged the security and employment that urban centers offered. They headed in large numbers to Indianapolis. Remarking on the bloody outbreak of 1865 in the southeastern counties, a reporter left no doubt that the capital, too, pulsated with the predictable tension attendant on this demographic reality. "Already there are indications of a demonstration in this regard [in Indianapolis]," he proclaimed, "and from Evansville the [n]ews comes of continued disturbances."[65]

In an unknown number of sparsely populated rural districts, whites enforced their will with loosely organized vigilante groups dedicated to the intimidation and expulsion of the black population. They also policed all-black agricultural colonies such as the Beech settlement, established by black migrants to Rush County in the 1830s. In 1875 a mob lynched William Keemer, a resident of the colony, in Greenfield. "The wagon was drawn from under the ravisher's feet, and he was left to die," the *Indianapolis Journal* reported. "The rope was a new one, and, with the heavy weight attached, stretched until Keemer's great feet touched the earth, but the ground was scooped out by a dozen willing hands in less time than it takes to tell it." After hanging Keemer, mob members affixed to his corpse a note declaring that his lynching was the unanimous "verdict of 160 men from Hancock, Shelby and Rush [counties]."[66]

As the Keemer execution illustrates, participants and spectators from across a wide area could ensure that a single lynching spectacle would have an outsized impact and thus enforce white supremacy not only in the municipality where it occurred but throughout the region. A mob achieved a similar result with the lynching of a black prisoner in 1872 that attracted spectators from far and wide. The *Sullivan Democrat* maintained that "the scene of the tragedy was visited on Sunday by hundreds of people from Orleans, Mitchell and the surrounding country. The hanging took place in Lawrence county, just outside of the boundaries of Orange."[67]

After the Civil War (and probably before it), whites established sundown towns and counties. In 1867 they ensured the all-white composition of Salem when Alexander White, the last black to live there, was murdered. Warder W. Stevens recalled in his 1916 *Centennial History of Washington County* that "two young men, somewhat intoxicated, Robert Cline and Harvey Zink, were seen trailing after him and were heard to threaten his life if he didn't leave Salem." Whites failed to punish the killers, who "fled the country. Zink was finally arrested, tried and acquitted. Cline made good his escape."[68]

During the Exodus the residents of sundown towns like Aurora felt obliged to reaffirm their intolerance. When two black barbers arrived there in 1879, the antiblack residents ensured their expeditious departure by explaining to them the ugly "history of Aurora on the negro question." The hometown paper gave notice that "Aurora is no nigger town."[69] In 1880 residents engaged in more of "this 'nigger business,'" menacing temporary laborers there. In so doing, they distinguished Aurora as among the best-known antiblack towns in the state.[70] "Unreasonable persecutions of colored men continue in Indiana towns, especially at Aurora and Shelbyville," noted an observer at the time. "All colored folks are driven from Aurora."[71]

Sundown jurisdictions like Salem and Aurora were not limited to southern Indiana but were situated elsewhere in the state, including its northern stretches. "Within the last year or two a few negroes have found their way to Bluffton," stated the *Indianapolis Journal* in 1880. They were not there for long because whites drove them out with "regular ku-klux methods."[72] With acts of this sort the residents of Bluffton and surrounding Wells

County established reputations that long persisted. In 1900 the *Louisville Courier-Journal* reported that no blacks lived in Wells. When a black man "strays along that way," it reported, "he is frightened by a recital of stories of what happened to those who were in the county in years gone by."[73] Taking the advice offered, he often made himself scarce thereafter. In 1922 Wells still claimed "no negro population."[74]

Unlike the jurisdictions located adjacent to or en route from the sources of the migrations of freed people and Exodusters into Indiana, those that were further north probably had a better opportunity to exclude black migrants outright simply because they were more distant from those sources. Nonetheless, those northern jurisdictions may also have exhibited an even greater intolerance for *any* black presence whatsoever. After all, if the whites in southern Indiana were more oppressive than those elsewhere in the state, why would the blacks have chosen to remain there rather than migrate to more welcoming areas?

The census data confirm that blacks were present in extremely small numbers throughout much of Indiana. In nineteen of the ninety-two counties they accounted for twenty-five or fewer residents—an arbitrary but very low number—in 1860, 1870, and 1880, and in many of these jurisdictions they did not approach that modest upper limit. For instance, in 1860 and 1880 no blacks at all resided in Brown County, one of the nineteen counties referenced above; in 1870 there was only one. Despite their significant increases in numbers after the Civil War and during the Exodus, blacks also declined steadily in absolute numbers in five additional counties, falling below the threshold of twenty-five in three of them by 1880. Between 1860 and 1880 the black population had declined from 103 to 12 in Franklin County, from 52 to 22 in Martin County, and from 187 to just 3 in Washington County. Each of these twenty-two counties was probably a sundown county, given that anecdotal evidence clearly indicated that some of them banned blacks. Furthermore, fully sixteen of the nineteen counties with fewer than twenty-five blacks in all three censuses were located in northern Indiana. Finally, individual sundown towns surely existed in many counties, whether or not they claimed more than twenty-five black residents.[75]

Because of the hostility of whites in Indiana, blacks tended to congregate more and more in a relatively small number of comparatively large urban centers. In 1860 only 12.2 percent of all black Indianans lived in the three cities that claimed more than 250 blacks. By 1870, 30.9 percent of them lived in the seven cities that had reached this population threshold; by 1880, 36.6 percent lived in the nine cities with 250 or more blacks.[76] As a result, whites were able to target blacks in these centers and terrorize a large proportion of them with a relatively modest number of violent incidents. An observer was prescient when he speculated, following a notorious Depression-era Indiana hanging, that the "only reason there are more lynchings in the South than in the balance of the country is because there are more negroes in the South."[77]

This chapter has implications for the subsequent history of racism in the state. In the late nineteenth and early twentieth centuries whites built Jim Crow on the foundation of the violence that scarred Indiana during the Civil War and Reconstruction. Despite the Thirteenth, Fourteenth, and Fifteenth Amendments, they ensured that blacks would continue to occupy the bottom rung of the social ladder. "Perhaps the major challenge facing black families was earning a living wage," Madison noted. "Black men usually could find employment only as unskilled laborers—janitors, waiters, hod carriers, teamsters." Although Jim Crow was largely enforced by practices rather than by laws, the system was very much in place by the turn of the century, as evidenced by the fact that "restaurants, hotels, theaters, and barber shops often refused service to blacks."[78]

In order to implement and enforce Jim Crow, whites resorted to violence. In *Following the Color Line*, published in 1908, Ray Stannard Baker identified the relation between discrimination and unlawful violence. "In Indianapolis the Negro comes in contact with the 'bungaloo gangs,'" he noted, "crowds of rough and lawless white boys who set upon Negroes and beat them frightfully, often wholly without provocation. Although no law prevents Negroes from entering any park in Indianapolis, they are practically excluded from at least one of them by the danger of being assaulted by these gangs."[79] Here again, whites not infrequently required spectacular types of violence to impose their discriminatory practices on a resistant black population.

In 1886 a mob lynched a black prisoner in Vincennes. "Holly Epps, the foul murderer . . . has expiated his terrible crime at the hands of Judge Lynch, and his worthless black carcass hangs suspended in the Court-house yard at this hour, 2 o'clock," a correspondent wrote from the scene to the *Indiana State Sentinel*. "The court-yard by the time the lynching bee was over was full to overflowing with spectators. Scores came from every direction, and as soon as the vigilantes dispersed the crowd rushed forward for bits of rope and pieces of Epps' clothing."[80] In 1890 vigilantes killed Eli Ladd in Blountville. A West Virginia paper chuckled over what it saw as Hoosier hypocrisy. "This infamous outrage occurred in the banner

Republican county of Indiana," reported the *Wheeling Register*. "Had it
occurred down South the uproar raised by the bloody shirt howlers would
be deafening."[81]

At the turn of the century white mobs rampaged, lynching blacks in
towns such as Rockport, Terre Haute, and Sullivan, and rioting against
(and expelling) blacks in Evansville. "Cities and towns along the Ohio
river have begun a crusade against the negroes," the *Indianapolis Sentinel*
noted. "The entire trouble dates back to the lynching of the negroes at
Rockport and Booneville [*sic*]." Vigilantes also expelled blacks from towns
like Grand View, Enterprise, Newburgh, and Tell City.[82] Across the state
whites expanded the number of sundown towns. "Up in Scott county
colored people are not welcome," an observer bluntly stated.[83] The *Marion
Chronicle* expressed its discomfort with sundown towns despite under-
estimating the total. "The people of Elwood, Tipton, Gas City, Bluffton,
Decatur and fifteen or twenty other small places in Indiana," it declared,
"are violating the fourteenth and fifteenth amendments to the constitution
every day in the year by proscribing races."[84] For decades thereafter, whites
found novel ways of showing their aversion to the presence of blacks. A
northern Indiana town expressed its strong antipathy thus: "Stone pil-
lars, flanking the northern entrance to this town now warn the Negro he
is barred from it," noted a 1925 report on Hobart. "On eight sides of the
posts is the inscription, 'TNT—Travel, Negro, Travel.'"[85]

It is not surprising that white Indianans would subscribe to the com-
fortable fiction that they did not perpetrate the kinds of crimes that they
were happy to condemn when perpetrated by white southerners. In fact,
when mob members hanged the three black men in Boonville and Rockport over a period of several days in 1900, they adopted fictive southern
identities in an elaborate sort of intraracial and intersectional minstrel
show: "The mob is said to have come from Spencer county [Indiana], but
all inquiries as to the place from which the men came received the same
laconic reply, Kentucky. Kentucky is a convenient place to come from on
such an occasion," the *Evansville Courier* joked. After the killings, "the
mob, the strangers, the 'Kentuckians,' dispersed as quietly as they had
come."[86] The mob members were, in other words, eager to foist their own
racist sins on white southern scapegoats already popularly—and quite
fairly—associated with antiblack racism and violence.

In some respects, Indiana historians have addressed antiblack racism
in the same way, foisting responsibility for it on the state's white southern settlers and their progeny. In so doing, they have received an obvious assist from the incontrovertible fact that acts of racist violence were

much more frequent in southern Indiana, an area "entirely dominated" by upland southerners.[87] Even when they acknowledge that anti-black sentiment was a statewide issue, they still lapse into this conventional wisdom, exemplified by Madison, who wrote: "Some small towns and rural areas, particularly in southern Indiana, developed reputations for special hostility and intimidation."[88]

This chapter affirms that white southerners in southern Indiana were deeply racist and that they frequently deployed racist violence. Nevertheless, it challenges the corollary that the whites who migrated from New York, Pennsylvania, and Ohio, and who settled in central and northern Indiana, played a peripheral role in this history of racist brutality.[89] It is true, for instance, that white voters in southern Indiana approved the 1851 exclusion measure by more than 90 percent; however, it is also true that whites across the entire state approved it by nearly 84 percent, suggesting a very high level of antiblack sentiment everywhere.[90] In addition, it is true that whites in southern Indiana tended to use violence to control relatively small black populations; yet it is also true that whites in central and particularly in northern areas tended to exclude blacks altogether, using violence as a means to expel black migrants who ventured into the area or to establish a reputation that would deter others from coming later. In this sense it is probably more accurate to say that white "southerners" and "northerners" in Indiana responded to black populations *differently* rather than to suggest that one group was more or less receptive to blacks.

As they had always done, blacks vigorously defended themselves. Black miners, for example, did so in the coal mines around Evansville in 1899 when, as they had done in Knightsville in 1873 and Coal Creek in 1878, striking white miners and their families menaced black strikebreakers. "The Non-Union Negroes Arm Themselves with Winchester Rifles and Prepare for a Battle," screamed the *Evansville Courier*, downplaying reports of rock-throwing intimidation by the strikers and foregrounding what it viewed as the illegitimate acts of blacks. "The scene was one that one can never forget," the paper declared. "One word, one careless act, one unwise move would have [cost] dozens of lives. Not only would the miners who are fighting for what they call right, would have fallen victims. Women and little defens[eless] children would have been slaughtered."[91] In this way black Indianans again took up arms against their oppressors as they had done in the antebellum period—noted in chapter 1—and would do throughout the nineteenth century, despite the views of those who insist that blacks did not adopt these tactics until well into the twentieth.

This chapter also has important implications for the history of the Midwest more generally. First, it shows that white Indianans met the influx of blacks during the Civil War with a surge of violence in an effort to control that fast-growing population. This finding is consistent with earlier findings regarding Kansas, where whites targeted blacks with all types of violence, including the lynching of twenty-six blacks in fifteen incidents between 1864 and 1870.[92] Together, these studies begin to illuminate an apparent but heretofore unrecognized reality: the Midwest experienced a dramatic outbreak of racist violence at the moment that many scholars associate with the triumph of enlightened racial "radicalism."

Contemporaries did recognize this reality. Following the 1862 New Albany riot, the Baltimore *Sun* placed the event in a larger Midwestern context. "The ill-feeling between the whites and blacks which has lately been exhibited in Toledo, Columbus and Cincinnati, Ohio, and Chicago, Illinois, has also begun to ripen in Indiana."[93] Another affirmed the point in an 1865 editorial on, among other topics, the recent Evansville lynching. "The 'inevitable nig' is creating trouble wherever he is found," mused the *New Hampshire Patriot and Gazette*. "The negroes are becoming intolerably insolent, and the result is constant riots." These difficulties, the paper predicted, "are but indications, we fear, of what is to come" from Emancipation, "the 'first fruits of the experiment of negro 'freedom.'"[94]

Second, this investigation finds that whites in Indiana initially met the Exodus of 1879–1880 in much the same way as did their counterparts in Kansas, the other major destination for Exodusters. Both targeted the black newcomers fleeing the post-Reconstruction South with a surge of violence intended to subordinate them and curb further migration. The political parties in the two states responded quite differently, however.[95] Many Indianans were Democrats who feared an influx of black Republicans and mobilized to beat back both a racial and a political challenge. Conversely, many white Kansans were Republicans like the black newcomers. Although they feared blacks on a *racial* level, they could take solace "in the knowledge that they shared the Republican political allegiance of their black adversaries, profiting from their votes while denying them meaningful participation in the party."[96] Many white Indianans saw no such silver lining. In 1879–1880, therefore, they employed a level of *politically* inspired racist violence more similar in character to that employed in the highly Democratic former slave states, where whites had recently crushed black and Republican power, than to that employed in Kansas.

Third, this chapter demonstrates that white Midwesterners for decades successfully concealed or obfuscated their anti-black proclivities—and preserved the image of the Midwest as a bucolic land of racially neutral meritocracy—by scapegoating white southerners. White Indianans, for example, eagerly condemned antiblack violence in the American South but willingly excused or camouflaged similar violence within their own state by attributing it to the southerners among them or to invaders from the border states. As I showed in *This Is Not Dixie*, white Kansans did likewise, characteristically blaming racist violence on or near the Kansas-Missouri border on Missourians eager to stir up problems or on settlers from Missouri whose attitudes were supposedly southern.

Fourth, when placed into conversation with the expanding scholarship concerning racist violence in the Midwest, this chapter challenges the notion that "Indiana was strikingly different from other states in the Old Northwest because of its considerable population of southern natives and former residents of the South."[97] As this work shows, Indiana witnessed many lynchings but was no more prolific in this regard than was the more "northern" state of Illinois, as illustrated in chapter 2. Furthermore, between 1861 and 1920 Indiana apparently had fewer recorded lynchings than did the even more "northern" state of Kansas, where blacks constituted a larger percentage of the total population and congregated in far greater numbers in the principal cities.[98] As in other midwestern states, antiblack lynching in Indiana apparently correlated more closely to the perceived threat among whites from local concentrations of blacks than it did to the sectional origins of the lynchers.

Finally, historians have often treated racist violence in the Midwest as something of an aberration. In revealing the common nature of racist violence in Indiana, however, this investigation joins several studies that have begun to establish the centrality of such violence in midwestern history.[99] Including the newly identified incidents in this volume, Michael Pfeifer and I have cumulatively identified about ninety lethal white-on-black lynchings that took place between the Civil War and the Great Depression in Illinois, Indiana, Kansas, and Ohio alone. In so doing, we have already accounted for far more than the number attributed to the *entire* Midwest by the historian W. Fitzhugh Brundage in 1997, when he wrote that in that region "79 black victims died at the hands of mobs."[100] Scholars have identified antiblack lynchings in Iowa, Michigan, Minnesota, Nebraska, North Dakota, and Wisconsin and will surely uncover more. Eventually, they will establish a more accurate inventory of these incidents of racist violence so that a more comprehensive assessment of its role in the history of the Midwest can be established.[101]

If scholars have failed to see systemic racist violence in the Midwest, contemporary white southerners recognized it. "What's the matter out there?" teased Alabama's *Mobile Register* after a rapid succession of midwestern lynchings in 1877. "Here is another negro lynched in Ohio—and then, again, another in Illinois! Won't those rebellious western men quit persecuting colored citizens?"[102] In 1878 the *Augusta (GA) Chronicle* took a similar view after the Mount Vernon lynching: "It will not do for the North any longer to hold up its hands in horror over the disposition of the South to indulge in lynch law."[103] When vigilantes in Indiana rampaged in 1880, an Ohio newspaper ceded this point by recognizing that white midwesterners paid little heed to antiblack movements within their own section but routinely condemned those in the South. Whereas midwesterners would fail to see the Indiana violence as racial terrorism, the *Cincinnati Daily Gazette* recognized that they would almost certainly see the southern variety through that lens: "South of the Ohio it would be known as the Ku Klux plan."[104]

In August 1930 a mob lynched Thomas Shipp and Abram Smith in Marion. The incident was captured on film by the local photographer Lawrence Beitler, whose image quickly achieved lasting notoriety. "If you have seen only one picture of an American lynching," the scholar Ashraf Rushdy recently observed, "it is likely that it was the one that shows a man in the [Marion] mob pointing at the two bodies hanging from a maple tree in the courthouse square. It is difficult to think of a lynching photograph that has had a more influential life than that picture." In emphasizing the impact of the Beitler photograph, Rushdy asserted that it has "become not only what the ABC news program *Compass* called the 'most famous photograph of America's era of lynching' but in fact, as Madison says, '*the* generic lynching photograph.'" He added that a portion of the photograph was used as the cover illustration for the book *At the Hands of Persons Unknown*, Philip Dray's 2002 popular history of antiblack lynching.[105]

If the Marion hanging has become *the* generic American lynching photograph, it has also become—unsurprisingly—*the* generic Indiana lynching story. Indeed, it was the subject of a gripping narrative of the terrible 1930 ordeal endured by the sole black survivor of the lynching, James Cameron, published in 1982 and titled *A Time of Terror*. It provided the storyline for two more books, as well: James H. Madison's *A Lynching in the Heartland* (2001) and Cynthia Carr's *Our Town* (2006).[106]

Although the Marion lynching is an incident of tremendous significance to the history of race relations in Indiana and the United States, the usual focus on it obscures much. Because this focus portrays the lynching as an *aberration* rather than as a dramatic and, perhaps, final episode in a long chain of lynchings, it disguises the fact that racist violence was common in the history of the Hoosier State and central to the enforcement of white supremacy.[107] As a result, it effectively places the blame for racist violence and for the social order that it sustained on a comparatively small group of white people in one town on one night rather than on all those who participated in the practice across the entire state over several generations.[108]

The focus on Marion also implies that this infamous incident was unusually brutal and for this reason merits the oversized attention that it has received. In fact, as brutal as it was, the incident was quite conventional and was certainly no more vicious than the fiery torture and hanging of the three blacks near Charlestown, the hanging of the four men and the quartering of the fifth in Mount Vernon, the hanging and burning in Terre Haute, or the double hanging in Rockport. Quite simply, the Marion lynching was an ordinary lynching made extraordinary by its immortalization in the photograph and its subsequent mass circulation. Some may find comfort in the suggestion that the Beitler photograph captured something unusually savage, but the fact is that the image captured for all intents and purposes the savagery of lynching as it manifested itself in *every* town in Indiana and in America where such events occurred.

4 Black Families and Resistance in Kansas, 1880–1905

"There is nothing like reputation"

In 1880 Ike Sneed, a black farmhand, narrowly escaped lynching by a white mob in Atchison, Kansas. Remarking on his ordeal, the *Atchison Daily Champion*, a white newspaper, conceded that his membership in the Sneed clan amplified the bloodlust: "The bad character of the Sneeds added to the sentiment against the prisoner."[1] The *Champion* doubled down after several readers visited to register their displeasure, writing, "Two young colored girls . . . called at the office to protest against The Champion's statement that the Sneed's were a family of thieves. . . . The old man is in the State prison; the old woman has been arrested for theft within the last year, and Ike, who came so near being hung . . . had, before his last offence, a well-established record as a loafer and chicken thief." Nonetheless, "if this interesting family [has] been wounded in [its] honor, The Champion will make reasonable reparation." After all, it joked, "there is nothing like reputation."[2]

The fevered desire among whites in Atchison to kill a member of this particular family, the Sneeds, underscores the underinvestigated fact that late-nineteenth and early-twentieth-century racist mobs targeted *certain* black families for disproportionate pain and suffering. Furthermore, as the *Champion* recognized, whites could attach a negative reputation to these families through their control of a press that circulated defamatory stories about them and a criminal justice system that hounded them. Using these levers in tandem, they created negative images of these families and then used them as justification for the ongoing violence against family members. With whites in control of their reputations, these embattled families rarely had the opportunity to tell their own stories or to contest the avalanche of self-righteous hatred directed at them.

This chapter turns this sort of contemporary white narrative on its head. It argues that whites targeted these beleaguered black families for an extra share of abuse not because they were of bad character but because—in their manner, their conduct, their provocation—they challenged white supremacy to an unusual extent and refused to submit to it. Based on a detailed investigation of limited and often fragmentary sources over an extensive period and across a wide geographical area, this chapter demonstrates that historians may derive alternative and far more sympathetic stories of these families, stories that may finally enable a restoration of their long-maligned reputations.

The data used here come primarily from white newspapers that, like the *Champion*, labored strenuously to denigrate these especially resistant black families and to justify the attacks on them. Despite their bias, these papers provide the most extensive biographical details about these families, the violence against them, and the defiant responses from them. Furthermore, because these papers did not coordinate their attacks against these families, they often provided contradictory details, explanations, and justifications, all of which can raise questions about the underlying narratives. In addition to these sources, some data derives from black newspapers that occasionally challenged the lampooning of these families and often contradicted the accounts of white-controlled papers.

The chapter first focuses on the campaign waged against the Godley family in southwest Missouri and southeast Kansas at the turn of the twentieth century. In order to do so, it details the acts of violence themselves and outlines the narratives by whites that explained and justified these acts to local whites and to a larger white audience predisposed to accept them. Using the lacunae and contradictions within the sources, it demonstrates that, the propaganda blitz deployed against this family notwithstanding, the Godleys were demonstrably innocent of virtually every accusation leveled against them. It next identifies the ways in which the Godley family embraced the fight against white supremacy more publicly as a response to the violence against them, affirming that their fighting spirit was really the fundamental cause of their victimization. The chapter then places the Godleys in a broader context by comparing and contrasting them with other oft-victimized families, all of whom were linked on the basis of their residency at one time or another in Kansas. Finally, it assesses the findings of the study and speculates on their significance.

On August 19 and 20, 1901, whites targeted blacks in what contemporaries called a race war in Pierce City,[3] Missouri. After Carl Wild, a white youth, discovered in a culvert the mangled body of his sister, Gisele, whites assigned the blame to an unknown black perpetrator, prompting an observer to predict that "the people are so excited they will hang the first nigger they see."[4] They focused their suspicions on William (Will) Godley, whom they promptly seized from authorities and hanged. "As the body swung to and fro, it was riddled with hundreds of bullets," reported the *Carthage Democrat*. "After Godley was hanged 350 men started toward what is known as 'Nigger town,' and riot reigns. Several houses have been set on fire and others riddled with bullets. The slogan is 'the negro must go.'"[5]

In sacking the black quarters, the mob inflicted particular suffering on the Godley family. When it stopped at the home of French Godley, his stepson, Pete Hampton, opened fire in self-defense. The mob returned fire, killing them both, and then burned the house. The next day, whites dug their charred remains out of the wreckage and hauled them downtown, where they placed them on display alongside Will's mangled corpse. A young white woman later recalled that she and her family had gone into town "to see roast negro, scared negro and a hanged negro."[6]

Shortly after these events took place, an unknown number of black refugees from Pierce City relocated to Pittsburg, Kansas, just over the state line and sixty-five miles from the conflagration. The *Pittsburg Daily Headlight* observed this influx and expressed its reservations. "Without regard to sex the Pierce City negroes, as a class, were a low[,] degraded set who would steal, murder and rob, varying the program with rapine and assaults upon white women," it declared. "It is understood that a number of them have Pittsburg and the surrounding mining camps in view as places in which to locate. A Frisco railroad man said last evening that he heard a bunch of about half a dozen of them who had fled to Joplin, talking about Pittsburg being the place to locate." These blacks were a "very hard looking lot[,] said the railroad man[,] and he thought it would be the proper treatment towards Pittsburg to warn the police and other officers and if they find a strange negro and he says he is from Pierce City they had better move him on."[7]

Among the fugitives who settled in Pittsburg were the remnants of the Godley family. Wary whites in their adopted city took note of their arrival and placed the family under scrutiny. "The Godleys came here from Peirce City at the time the citizens of that place drove the colored people from their population," the *Pittsburg Daily Headlight* later recalled. In the town of Joplin, roughly halfway between Pierce City and Pittsburg, the *Joplin Record* had expressed the widely held view that "the Godley brothers have bad reputations" and that "as soon as they showed up . . . everybody knew there would be trouble." In republishing this article, the *Headlight* signaled its agreement with the views of the *Record* and, presumably, those of its readers.[8]

Trouble came on Christmas Eve in 1902. Mumpford (also known as Montgomery), Gus, Jess, and Joe Godley, along with other members of the family, were celebrating the holiday with other blacks. Around 11 P.M. policemen jailed Mumpford for public drunkenness.[9] When he learned of the arrest, Joe hurled invective at two officers, Milton Hinkle and Tome Galer, who placed him under arrest as well. A black resident reported,

> They had walked about one third of a block, going to jail, when Joe asserted that he would not be arrested for he had not done anything. At that time, Mr. Hinkle started to hit him over the head, when a rough and tumble fight took place. Joe Godley was on the bottom; it was dark; Tome Galer drew his gun and began shooting, of which Godley was shot in the neck and Policeman Hinkle through the head. Joe Godley made his escape. At least a dozen saw the affair.[10]

Whites told a very different story. According to the *Headlight*, Joe Godley and his brothers attacked the officers: "In the melee one of the Godley boys grabbed the officer's revolver from his hand and shot him from behind. . . . The news of the murder spread like wildfire up and down the street and soon a crowd of people were assembled at the city hall." Whites carried the image "of the dying officer with blood and brain oozing from the ragged hole in his head" and "a determined desire in the[ir] breasts . . . for vengeance." At this point officers arrived at the jail with another member of the Godley family (probably Gus), whom the crowd beat until he escaped into the night. Early on Christmas morning the mob surged into the jail and threatened to lynch Jess, who had also been arrested. Finally, members of the mob seized Mumpford, although he had been in jail when Hinkle was shot. Dragging him outside, they slit his throat and hanged him.[11] Three days later, the *Topeka Daily Capital* reported Mumpford's unceremonious end: "Mont Godley was buried today in the potters' field, even his parents evidently being afraid to show enough regard for him to claim his body."[12] Following his escape, Joe fled Pittsburg for points unknown.

"There is a strong probability existing that in the lynching of Montgomery Godley . . . Christmas morning for killing Policeman Hinkle the wrong man was hanged and that while Montgomery was implicated in the trouble, he did not fire the fatal shot," reported the *Lawrence Daily Journal-World.* "If Joe Godley is captured the officers will have a hard task to protect him, as the people here insist that the same treatment will be given him as his brother received."[13] Similarly, the *Topeka Daily Capital* reported that "there is very little feeling of horror here on account of the lynching . . . even if it be ascertained that Mont was not the murderer . . . as all four of the Godleys were very aggressive in the fight in which Hinkle lost his life."[14] With the Christmas lynching the Pittsburg mob furthered the work—begun a year earlier by the Pierce City mob—of shattering the Godley family.

According to their persecutors, everybody knew that there would be trouble when the Godleys arrived because of the supposedly self-evident criminality of the family members. One newspaper report, for instance, denounced the "insulting and insolent manner" of the Godleys in general,[15] while another denounced Mumpford, for he, it growled, had "a most unsavory reputation."[16] An examination of the evidence, however, suggests that everybody knew there would be trouble because the Godley family demonstrated an unusually fierce and uncompromising disinclination to submit to the racist proscriptions of the society in which it existed and because the white residents of Pierce City and Pittsburg felt an absolute compulsion to defend the social order against a family that posed such a threat to its existence.

The strongest evidence for this explanation comes from two facts. The first is the decision of whites in both Pierce City and Pittsburg to snuff out this particular family among any number of black families. The second is the extreme ferocity of their attacks within the span of a year and a half to rectify something in the family's attitude and behavior that was unusually provocative—even maddening—to them. While cynics might argue that the single-minded determination of whites to destroy this family lends credibility to their claim about the strong criminal proclivities of the Godleys, the facts contradict this interpretation.

According to news reports written mainly by whites, the Godleys were demonstrably innocent of each offense for which they were ostensibly punished. In Pierce City, Will was plainly not responsible for the killing of Gisele Wild. The *Lawrence Chieftain* made light of this fact, joking that "it is not claimed [Will] Godley killed the young girl, but his reputation was of the worst." Confirming his innocence, "the citizens of Pierce City offered a $1,000 reward for, as the local paper states it, 'the capture of the real murderer.'"[17] French, of course, faced no charges at all, fabricated or otherwise. Furthermore, if Pete Hampton did fire on the mob, he was guilty only of defending himself and his family against it, a right that most whites would have taken for granted.

In Pittsburg whites continued to claim that Mumpford had been a party to the killing of Hinkle. The *Pittsburg Kansan* later admitted the truth, however: "Mont . . . had been imprisoned, in the city jail an hour earlier." Whites further insisted that, though they killed the *wrong* Godley, their story was essentially true, even if it had been Joe rather than Mumpford who shot the officer. Nevertheless, when captured in California and extradited to Pittsburg for trial in 1904, Joe won acquittal, an incontrovertible attestation to his innocence given the antipathy of whites and the injustice faced by blacks in the courts. In 1905 the *Kansan* seemed to support blacks' claims that the other officer shot Hinkle. "The murderer of Milton Hinkle seems likely to escape punishment," it growled. "The incident is closed."[18] Further confirming Joe's innocence, the *Headlight* ran a headline stating, "Jury Was Out But Twenty Minutes."[19] Based on this record, it is clear that, if the Godleys had an unsavory reputation, whites—eager to justify their relentless attempts to destroy them—had created it.

Furthermore, the Godleys were not silenced by the violence against them in Pierce City or in Pittsburg. Instead, they resumed the fight. Because the young men tended to be the ones perceived by whites to be most overtly defiant and dangerous, they tended to attract more violent responses. As a consequence, other family members stepped into the breach after violence against them occurred. "Widow of Man Who Was Hanged Asks $1,000 Damages," reported the *Springfield Republican* on August 7, 1902, after America Godley, the wife of Will, filed suit in Joplin for his lynching.[20] Despite the immediate danger she faced, Joe's mother, Katy Godley, aided and abetted his flight from Pittsburg after his confrontation with police and the lynching of his brother. "A physician . . . was called upon by the mother of the Godley boys to treat her son Joe for a bad gunshot wound," stated the *Salina Daily Republican-Journal*. When the doctor refused to help, Godley protected her son in another way: "The doctor . . . could not get the woman to tell where Joe was."[21] Furthermore, after Mumpford's hanging, Mr. and Mrs. Godley almost certainly refused to claim his body not because they were afraid, as the white press assumed, but because they refused to shoulder an economic burden laid on them by the whites. Subsequently, they pressed for justice in a court of law. "Because his son, Mont Godley, was hung by a mob in Pittsburg Henry Godley . . . brought suit against the city for $10,000," reported the *Pittsburg Kansan*. Yet more galling, he won a limited victory. "By a compromise effected in district court last week," the *Kansan* added, "the aged negro will receive $400 and the city will pay the costs of court."[22] By these acts of resistance, the extended Godley family reinforced the supposition of whites that it was devoted to trouble-making. For the purposes of this chapter the Godley family, and the parents in particular, demonstrated the critical role of parental influence in instilling spirited resistance into their children rather than meek submission to white supremacy.

The terror suffered by the Godleys and their capacity for resistance against their white oppressors is particularly well preserved because of the sensational nature of the violence that claimed Will, French, Pete, and Mumpford and because of the frenzy of newspaper coverage that ensued. Their experiences suggest that whites targeted for a disproportionate level of violence black families that bucked social conventions. The family's ordeal also shows that whites in Pittsburg responded negatively to the Godleys in part because they expected the same submission and deference as did their counterparts in Pierce City, and in part because they were already aware of the negative reputation of the Godleys as a consequence of their demonization in Missouri.

Other families had similar experiences in Kansas. In Lawrence members of the Vinegar family saw their name slandered in the local white press and suffered abuse at the hands of white residents. In 1882 the *Lawrence Daily Journal* published a defamatory appraisal of this family when policemen arrested Margaret ("Sis") Vinegar, a fifteen-year-old, and George Robertson and Isaac King, young men who, according to an initial report, were staying with her family, for the alleged murder of David Bausman, a white man. "This is only the culmination of a series of smaller crimes, which have been growing up in the family to which this girl belongs," the *Journal* declared. "The family it may not be possible to break up—but it would be a boon to the city to have the individuals composing it placed under other influences than those which govern it while together."[23]

The following day, white residents did find a way to break up the family. That night members of a mob stormed the jail and took therefrom Robertson and King, as well as Pete Vinegar, the aged patriarch accused of no role in the murder but arrested, it seems, on the basis of guilt by association. The vigilantes marched the men to the bridge over the Kansas River, where they placed nooses around the victims' necks and tossed them over the side to their deaths. The mob spared Margaret, who was in the lockup at the time of the lynching, but a jury subsequently sentenced her to prison, where she died of tuberculosis seven years later. The

Kansas Daily Tribune laid the blame squarely on the victims, concluding that whites in Lawrence had become exhausted with "the shocking and repulsive character of the loathsome 'Vinegar' den."[24]

Although the mob did not lynch Margaret, the press maligned her, portraying her as a prostitute and conspirator in the alleged plot to rob and kill Bausman. The blacks had learned that the white man had substantial money, claimed the *Chicago Daily Tribune*, "and got a common prostitute, the daughter of Pete Vinegar, who enticed Bausman to the vicinity" of the killing site. "While he was enjoying her embraces he was knocked [on] the head with a hammer, and killed."[25] The press continued to malign her during her trial. "Margaret (or Sis) Vinegar was to-day convicted of murder in the first degree," reported the *Topeka Daily Capital* on April 12, 1883. "Sis is a negro prostitute."[26] The historian William M. Tuttle Jr. has, quite rightly, suggested a third possibility for explaining what sparked this incident. Based on the ease with which white men could prey on young black women in this period, he speculated that Bausman might have sexually assaulted Margaret and that King and Robertson might have caught him in the act and killed him.[27]

In Salina the Adams family experienced repeated conflicts with whites. After an unknown rapist allegedly assaulted a white woman in 1893, posses rounded up suspects. They arrested Jack Adams immediately. "Jack," observed the *Salina Union*, "was the first negro to be taken before Mrs. Frost the night of the assault upon her."[28] He survived because Frost failed to identify him. His brother Dana was not so lucky. Two weeks later, amid elevated tensions resulting from the rape and several threatened lynchings, whites charged Dana with an assault on a white man, although accounts suggest that the white man initiated the affray. A few hours later members of a mob seized and hanged him. Whites also arrested and prosecuted Wade Adams Jr., Dana's brother, for the same alleged assault on the white man, although they did not lynch him. As usual, whites engaged in character assassination of the family and its individual members. The *Salina Daily Republican* declared that Dana was "a tough negro. . . . fond of flourishing his razor."[29] The "Adams boys," all young men in their late teens or early twenties, were "well known toughs," added the *Salina Herald*.[30]

Five years later vigilantes inflicted more suffering on the Adams family, this time torching the property of the patriarch, a rather significant holding for blacks at the time and one that less successful whites might have considered an affront. "Two houses belonging to a colored man named Wade Adams [Sr.] were burned . . . together with 300 bushels of wheat and some farm machinery," reported the *Topeka Daily Capital*. "The cause of the fire is unknown but is supposed to have been of incendiary origin."[31] Reporting on the efforts of the officials responsible for quelling the flames, the *Salina Daily Republican-Journal* hinted that they may have colluded with the arsonists after the fact, noting that the fire department arrived "as soon as possible" but not before the fire spread from the first to the second house.

> After they had made couplings with a water plug the hose burst and caused a delay. After removing the bursted joint of the hose and replac[ing] it with a new one the hose broke in another place. It began to look as though the large house would be a total loss. But at last a stream of water was playing on the flames which resulted in saving part of the building.[32]

The Toliver family in Tonganoxie faced similar hostility. On Christmas Eve in 1897 policemen there attempted to arrest Andy and John Toliver and their half-brother, Bill Ross. Instead, the three men defied the officers and avoided arrest. "There was a hot time in the old town the other night, and razors were flying," charged the *Tonganoxie Mirror* in a none-too-subtle vilification of this black family. "It took the entire police force to quell the riot, and even then they failed to land any prisoners in the abode provided by the city for the wicked."[33]

Officer John Evans settled the score in 1899 when he fatally shot twenty-one-year-old Andy Toliver while arresting him and Bill Ross. Evans claimed that the victim resisted arrest. In killing Andy, he precipitated unrest in town and across that area of Leavenworth County, the *Tonganoxie Mirror* reported. "A great many were present at the inquest, and many out of town people came in to hear the testimony."[34] In a subsequent dispatch on legal wrangling concerning the case, the *Mirror* observed that "the colored people in adjacent neighborhoods turned out with those in town, for they take the killing as a race affront." It added that "the white people are much more united than usual in supporting the officers in the battle with the desperate characters they had to combat."[35] After deliberating for only a few minutes, the jury acquitted Evans. The *Mirror* opined that the killing was "a tragedy that was inevitable and bound to come sooner or later." Although it groused that "an error was made in bringing [trial] and putting the county to a lot of needless expense," the paper insisted that "the influence of this shooting affray has been very wholesome in this community."[36]

In the immediate aftermath of the killing, the *Mirror* cruelly caricatured the family with its portrayal of the reunion between Bill Ross and his mother Vina, casting the woman as obnoxious and unfeminine and portraying the young man as weak and unmanly. It also conveniently shifted the blame away from the officer and onto the Tolivers: "Ross was locked up, and later when in his cell was upbraided by his mother for being the cause of the death of his half-brother."[37] In 1902 whites again threatened this family. In its report of the arrest of several blacks for an alleged assault, the *Mirror* indicated that "the Tolivers managed to get into the game in the person of Charlie."[38] There was "much excitement about the matter," added the *Leavenworth Times*, "and for a while it looked as though the matter would terminate by a lynching."[39]

Concerned, perhaps, that its readers might conclude that whites in Tonganoxie were relentlessly targeting a blameless family, the *Times* undertook to correct the record with an article depicting the Tolivers as a family of criminals deserving of the violence aimed at them. "Of three killings that have taken place in Tonganoxie, brothers of Charlie Toliver[,] who was in this assault [that prompted the threatened lynching in 1902], figured in two of them. Bill Ross, his half brother, struck another colored man named Cobb in the head with a rock and he later died from the wound. Ross served a short term in the penitentiary for it. Andy Toliver was killed while trying to use a knife on a deputy marshal." All of the young black men accused in the present assault, the *Times* added, "are[,] so it is said, tough characters and it is said Charlie Toliver is especially so."[40]

Whereas the Vinegar, Adams, and Toliver families suffered violence over time within a single municipality, the Porter family—like the Godleys—endured it across two states. In 1898 whites in Lawrence threatened to lynch two of the family's teenaged sons. Shortly after officers went to "look for two colored boys named Porter, who were wanted on the charge of attempting to assault a little white girl named Fox, they found the farmers of the neighborhood looking for the boys with ropes, and the boys would probably have suffered immediate punishment if the irate farmers had gotten hold of them."[41] The officers found them first, however, and hustled them to jail amid rumors of an imminent lynching. There the youths spent a terrifying night awaiting a mob that never materialized. The Porter brothers "are well known in criminal circles," reported the *Lawrence Daily World* in a familiar effort to denigrate an assertive black family. "Their names are Princeton [Preston] and Arthur and this makes four of that family now in the same jail. About a year ago the family came to town . . . and some of the boys have been in trouble about all of the time."[42] At some point thereafter, the Porters left Kansas.

Two years later whites again targeted the Porters, this time five hundred miles to the west. In November 1900 members of a mob in Limon,

Colorado, burned Preston at the stake, accusing him of the rape and murder of a white girl named Louise Frost (no apparent relation to the white woman allegedly assaulted in Salina). Before the lynching, it coerced a confession from the victim by threatening to lynch Arthur and their father as well.[43] After the incident, chattering townspeople in Lawrence confirmed that the mob in Limon had victimized the same family. "The burning of Preston . . . has caused considerable talk," indicated the *Lawrence Daily Journal*, "owing to the fact that the Porters claimed Lawrence as their home and the boy who was burned, had been sent [to jail] twice from here."[44] Frost's father expressed his anger that the people of Lawrence had not done what he viewed as their duty. At least "no other father will have to [go through] what I did on account of that nigger," he declared in justifying the burning of Preston, "and, as I said before, if the brute had been lynched for his first offense in Kansas, my baby would be alive to-day and our hearts would not be broken."[45]

As was the case with the Godleys, direct evidence of resistance by the Vinegar, Adams, Toliver, and Porter families before their most tragic of family events was limited because all of them were simply ordinary people trying to survive in an oppressive environment. There is, however, some such evidence. In Salina Wade Adams Sr., along with about thirty other blacks, sent a letter to a black newspaper outlining the steps that they had taken a little more than a week before the lynching of his son Dana to protect the life of John Hudson, a black youth likewise jailed and faced with mob violence. According to their letter, they met initially to discuss the advisability of dispatching armed black men to the jail to defend Hudson. Ultimately, they recommended something less confrontational—the appointment of a subcommittee to consult with the police, to demand an increase in security for the prisoner, and to engage an attorney to defend him in court.[46]

Preston Porter exhibited defiance with his extraordinary composure, refusing to buckle in fear. "For more than an hour, while preparations for his execution were in progress, he stood mute and sullen among the avengers," reported the *New York Times*. In his most poignant act, Porter attempted to shame his murderers. According to the *Times*, "the negro had, since his confession, been devoting every moment of daylight in the perusal of a Bible given him by the Denver jailer. Even while waiting for his execution he sat by a bonfire reading from the Gospel of St. Luke. Just before he was tied to the stake, upon a request for souvenirs, the boy tore the leaves from the Bible and distributed them among his executioners." When the mob had completed its preparations, "he walked to the stake with a firm step." When the mob set him ablaze, Porter struggled to remain mute. "Almost instantly the negro's trousers caught fire. Even though the flesh must have been scorched, he did not utter a sound."[47]

Pete Vinegar supposedly exhibited similar composure as his executioners prepared to hurl him off the bridge with the two younger men. "Robertson was the first victim swung over," reported the *Lawrence Daily Journal*. "Vinegar followed without a word except a protest that he was innocent."[48] A few weeks later the *Daily Kansas Tribune* grudgingly conceded that "poor old Pete Vinegar died with more heroism than [Charles] Guiteau," who broke down emotionally before his execution for the assassination of President James A. Garfield.[49] Ironically, with his murder at the hands of whites Vinegar was able to provide his family with some of the financial support denied to them in the racist society in which they lived. "Pete Vinegar's life was insured for $5,000 and his children have already put in their claim for the money," announced the *Topeka Sunday Capital*.[50]

In the context of these images of Preston Porter and Pete Vinegar as stoic and cool in their final moments, it is worth considering how such images might have justified lynching in the eyes of whites, since they were the audience for whom these lines were principally written. On one hand, such images invest the victims with a certain strength and resolve that might have struck readers—and may strike a researcher today—as noble or praiseworthy. On the other, such images coexisted on the same pages as strident assertions of white supremacy and harsh denunciations of blacks as a class and should, therefore, be seen as advancing the view of lynching itself as heroic. It seems obvious that by portraying black men as detached from and indifferent to their own lynchings, the construction of such "noble" images of black victims assuaged any doubts that whites might have entertained about perpetrating such acts of violence. In fact, the *New York Times* asserted precisely this in its discussion of Porter's stoicism: "As he had exhibited indifference to the enormity of his crime, so he seemed to lack all understanding of its terrible consequences."[51] In this sense, the noble image created what Lisa Arellano has called a narrative of lynching that would encourage and legitimate other lynchings. How, one might ask, would a white reading public have responded to these acts if the press had reported that the black victims wept or pled for their lives in their final moments?

Pete Vinegar and Wade Adams Sr. were much more successful economically than local residents were willing to concede; in fact, whites may have targeted them and their families in part on the basis of that resentment.

After all, Vinegar's possession of a five-thousand-dollar insurance policy to care for his family in the event of his death certainly suggested that he was a man of at least reasonable means. Adams's central role in the meeting of prominent black men to devise ways of protecting John Hudson and his ownership of agricultural land, a barn, and two houses suggest that he too provoked animosity by daring to outshine many whites.

During the standoff with police in Tonganoxie on Christmas Eve 1897, Andy Toliver undertook an act of open defiance that undoubtedly made him a local hero among blacks—and a marked man among whites. "When the marshal and deputy arrived," the *Tonganoxie Mirror* declared, he "defied arrest and actually disarmed the officers and told them to go home."[52] With this act he surely undermined the honor and masculinity of the officers, a humiliation that they were unlikely to forgive or forget. Fourteen months later, Officer Evans very likely remembered this humiliation when he shot and killed Toliver during an arrest and may consciously or unconsciously have desired to restore the dignity of the department.

As with the Godleys, direct evidence of the actively defiant and sustained resistance of these other families after violence claimed the lives of their family members is quite clear. Whereas the young black men in these families were the ones most likely to challenge whites or, at a minimum, attract lethal responses, their parents, siblings, and extended families were often the ones to resume the fight in the aftermath of those confrontations. This finding again lends credence to the idea that the parents must have played a role in instilling in their children the spirit to fight.

After the lynching of his son, Wade Adams Sr. resisted the demands of his persecutors. "The body of [Dana] Adams was turned over to the undertakers this morning and taken to the cemetery for burial," reported the *Salina Daily Republican*. "Adams' father refused to have anything to do with the burial and would not take possession of the body, giving as his reason that the white people had killed the boy and should bury him." As a result, the city shouldered the cost.[53] In refusing to accept responsibility for burying his son, Adams—like Henry and Katy Godley—showed that an act which many whites interpreted as a sign of *fear* was actually a sign of vigorous opposition.

Like Henry Godley, too, the senior Adams sued for damages after the lynching of his son, demanding $5,000. In so doing, he exercised his rights, fought anew his tormentors, and won a nominal victory. Yet he also enabled whites to demean his family once again. Because the case had been brought on the basis of the economic value of the dead youth to his father, and because the white townspeople regarded Dana Adams as an individual of little value whatsoever, the jury decided that Wade had suffered no real damages. Accordingly, reported the *Lawrence Daily Journal*, "in the district court the case of Adams vs. the City of Salina was concluded and the jury returned a verdict allowing $2 damages to Adams (colored) for the loss of his son."[54]

Two years after the mob murdered her father, Margaret Vinegar, still just a teenaged girl, showed composure—and a degree of honor that her persecutors would never have conceded—when she suffered more vindictiveness. "One of the rules of the [Kansas] prison is that convicts, by good behavior and dilligence [*sic*], may earn three and one-half cents a day, which sum is placed to their credit and may be used as they direct," reported the *Chicago Herald* in 1884. "'Sis' Vinegar proved a model prisoner and received the allowance daily. When she had accumulated ten or twelve dollars a butcher in Lawrence heard that she was making money, and, proceeding to the prison, he presented a bill for $8, the amount owed him by her family when the murder took place." Although she was surely dispirited by the addition of this insult to her previous injury, Margaret denied the butcher and other whites the tantrum that they may have anticipated. "The girl was a trifle surprised, but on satisfying herself that the claim was just, she gave the man an order for the money and he went his way rejoicing."[55]

The family of Andy Toliver took immediate steps to punish his killer in Tonganoxie. "Alfred Toliver, father of the young man killed," reported the *Tonganoxie Mirror*, "swore out a warrant an hour or two after the tragedy, charging John Evans with murder."[56] The Toliver family then reached out to a prominent black attorney, himself a member of a particularly resistant black family targeted for serial abuse, in nearby Leavenworth to assist them in their efforts to seek justice.[57] Shortly after the killing, "W. B. Townsend received word from Toliver's parents requesting him to come to Tonganoxie and represent them," wrote the *Leavenworth Times*. "They are determined to prosecute Evans and will do all in their power to do so."[58] Alfred Toliver acted swiftly, challenging a police officer who not only served as a representative of the power structure but also enjoyed an almost inviolable presumption of innocence. Under the circumstances the aggrieved father could not have been surprised when the jury acquitted Evans.

Whites in Missouri, Kansas, and Colorado targeted *particular* black families for especially frequent and brutal abuse, as the experiences of the Sneeds, the Godleys, the Vinegars, the Adamses, the Tolivers, and the Porters illustrate. They targeted these families because they fiercely rejected the racist social order that enveloped them, and surviving members continued to resist in the aftermath of a killing of a son or brother at the hands of law enforcement, a lynching by hanging or by fire, or the threat of such violence. In order to justify their unrelenting abuse of these families, whites generated defamatory stories about them that, as a result of newspaper accounts, telegrams, and street-corner conversations, sullied their reputations and depicted them in all cases as criminals and malcontents.

Clearly, some black families were unusually committed to bucking racist conventions and to cultivating spirited resistance in their children. In their individual struggles members of these families demonstrated uncommon courage, fearlessness, commitment, pride, and outspokenness, character strengths that they drew not only from the justness of their cause but also from the unwavering support of their families and the activist tradition imparted to them for decades. As families and as individuals, therefore, they *earned* "reputations" as troublemakers among whites who demanded their supplication and their acceptance of the status quo.

With these findings this chapter identifies near the end of the nineteenth century what historians have identified in activists in the freedom struggle of the mid-twentieth. In his study of the 1950s and 1960s, the historian Charles M. Payne identified *movement families*. Although he had started with the assumption that he would focus on individuals, "in many ways," he writes, "the more appropriate starting point is the distinction between movement families and non-movement families. Much of what drew individuals into the movement and kept them there is explicable only in the light of the nature and the history of the particular families they came from." He found that the movement drew "some of its most important members from families that had, if you will, been grooming its members for such roles." These families were the ones that instilled in their children a belief in asserting control over their own lives. "It is as if they were saying . . . that there is *some* shit we will not eat." [59]

The term *movement family* is, perhaps, inappropriate for families such as those discussed in this chapter because it requires a conscious recognition among its bearers that they were members of a movement. Living obscure small-town lives, these families were committed to resistance in their own lives but could not have conceived of themselves as participants in the kind of national movement in which their grandchildren participated because no such activity yet existed. Nevertheless, despite the obstacles and the violence that they were unable to overcome, families like these cultivated and passed along the habits of resistance that would bear fruit after World War II. In this sense the study affirms the notion of a "long" civil rights movement advanced by historians and others who place the freedom struggle of the postwar years in a temporal context stretching back into the nineteenth century.

Given his temporal focus, Payne employed extensive interviews in identifying and examining movement families. In addition, he enjoyed a plethora of documents providing the insights of blacks into the civil rights struggle. Historians investigating the late nineteenth and early twentieth centuries seldom enjoy such luxuries. Instead, they must rely primarily on material written by whites that often is infused with the most strident racist assumptions. This chapter is significant because it illustrates that, armed with material culled from limited and often fragmentary sources covering an extensive period of time and a wide expanse of territory, historians may identify some of the families who had a relatively highly evolved commitment to the pursuit of their rights, investigate their stories more critically and, ultimately, assess their impact on black resistance in the more distant past.

In so doing, historians may be able to restore the reputations of these maligned black families, an important task since, as the *Atchison Daily Champion* averred, "there is nothing like reputation." More important, they may be better equipped to support today's journalists, scholars, and others who write about these families but still rely on the rough draft of history created by the very whites who aimed to crush these people. Despite his sympathy for the victim and his recognition of the racism involved in his lynching, for example, the author of a 2005 article about the hanging of Pete Vinegar in the *Lawrence Journal-World* took nearly word for word information contained in the 1882 coverage. "Vinegar and his family had a bad reputation," he maintained. "They were dirt poor. . . . The children often walked about town begging businesses and individuals for money, food and clothes. Sometimes they resorted to stealing."[60]

It is possible that the Vinegar family was dirt poor, as were many black families in the 1880s. It is also possible that its members panhandled and committed acts of theft to survive. Finally, it is conceivable that Margaret Vinegar, George Robertson, and Isaac King did murder Bausman in the manner alleged. Nevertheless, it seems equally (if not more) plausible that whites reviled the Vinegars for reasons having little to do with criminality and that they used the Bausman murder, at least in part, as a pretext for meting out the long-desired vengeance—a supposition given credence in part by the lynching of Pete, whom all recognized to be innocent, in part by his ownership of a $5,000 life insurance policy, and in part by Tuttle's hypothesis about the possible self-defense motive behind the killing of Bausman. Modern observers, therefore, are remiss in accepting at face value the depictions in the contemporary white press of the "shocking and repulsive character" of the families who suffered relentless racism and violence in the late nineteenth and early twentieth centuries.

Similarly, writers invoking the Godleys today portray them as reprobates no less than did their counterparts in 1901–1902—except that they do not mention race. Despite the evidence that Mumpford did not kill Officer Hinkle and that the jury acquitted Joe Godley of the charge of murder, the website for the City of Pittsburg, as of this writing, continues to publicize the original story. Describing the death of Hinkle, it claims that one of the Godleys "took Officer Hinkle's sidearm and shot him from behind. The suspect, Montgomery Godley, was taken into custody and placed in the city jail. As word spread throughout the town, an angry mob of citizens stormed the jail and hanged Mr. Godley. However, it was later determined that they hanged the wrong brother, and the likely killer was Joe Godley, who was wounded during the altercation by a gunshot to the neck."[61] By *not* invoking race, which was central to the affair at the time, the website sidesteps the issue of racism by simply ignoring it.

Even historians committed to the study of racism and lynching may subscribe to the negative mythologies created about these families. In her study of lynchings and race riots in southwest Missouri, Kimberly Harper takes for granted that the criminal record attached to Will Godley and Pete Hampton was a reflection of *their* misdeeds rather than the possible result of their demonization and targeting by whites. "Both Godley and Pete Hampton had previous scrapes with the law," she writes. "Godley had been convicted of the rape of a sixty-year-old white woman. Hampton was a local criminal with a lengthy criminal record. The Peirce City Citizens Committee, in its public statement, noted that it was a commonly held belief that most crime in town was committed by African Americans, and because blacks refused to testify against one another, black criminals went unpunished."[62] Similarly, Harriet C. Frazier, who briefly examined the suffering of the Godleys in Pierce City, asserts that most lynching victims deserved their fates. "During the 25 years I researched and wrote about mob violence and capital punishment," she explains, "I reluctantly and slowly realized that the lynched were often guilty of the offense the mobs believed their victims committed."[63]

This chapter contributes to the historiography because it illustrates that, by delving deeply into the available sources, scholars may reconstruct and reinterpret the lives of the black families who were badly abused and maligned for their supposed bad character. Challenging narratives by whites, it shows that these families demonstrated an unusually robust commitment to defying their oppressors, thereby earning more—and more vicious—abuse than did other families. In this sense the chapter offers a new methodology for the study of the histories of these particularly resistant black families and contributes to the call by the historian Kidada E. Williams for a closer investigation of the effects of violence on black families. "How did families manage the horrors of lynching?" she asks. "I do not believe that lynching scholars' work is finished. However, I do believe that integrating the violence victims' families experienced into the histories produced is essential to the work that remains."[64]

In a powerful passage in *White Man's Heaven*, Kimberly Harper underscores the potential merits of investigating the experiences of the families who suffered the lynching of a loved one or who suffered extensive property loss and banishment after a riot. She offers a vignette that affirms that some black families suffered abuse repeatedly over time and space. Describing the sorrow of an elderly black couple taking refuge in Pittsburg, Kansas, after the 1903 lynching and riot in Joplin, Missouri, she finds that it was not the first time their family had been victimized:

> Over the preceding two years, they had escaped the wrath of an angry mob when a race riot erupted in the Oklahoma town they lived in, and blacks were expelled. The couple then moved to Pierce City, Missouri, to live with their son. But in August 1901, a mob lynched three black men and expelled that town's black residents. In the panic that ensued, the couple lost track of their son. They escaped to Joplin, but their son was less fortunate. Wounded, he traveled to the safety of Springfield, only to die of his injuries. The couple, once again penniless and without relatives nearby, settled at Joplin. . . . But when a Joplin mob of over one thousand whites lynched Thomas Gilyard, a young black migrant, . . . the couple had once again to run for their lives.[65]

With these findings this chapter achieves for the study of racist violence what other historians have urged in the study of lynching: the pursuit of new theories and methodologies "for excavating," in the words of Michael J. Pfeifer, "the lived experiences of lynching victims, their families, and their communities."[66]

5 Missouri's Little Dixie, 1899–1921

"They flog a negro up there every week"

"The negroes continue sullen and rebellious and are still using every means to conceal fresh outbreaks of smallpox in their homes," reported the *Paris Mercury* as the disease raged in that small northeast Missouri town in 1899. They were anxious to conceal the malady because they rightly feared that, if it was exposed, whites would impose harsh and indiscriminate sanctions on *all* blacks rather than provide the necessary care for the sick ones, as would be the case if whites acquired the disease. "The negroes of Paris are hiding every case they can," charged the *Monroe City Democrat*. In the midst of this health crisis and the racially charged unrest that it provoked, the *Mercury* reported an episode of violence "that threw the town's population, white and black, into a furor of excitement."[1]

A white doctor went into the black quarter to investigate and allegedly encountered "an older brother of [a] sick negro, who approached him with a huge knife and made a move as if to cut him." The doctor drew a pistol to hold the attacker at bay and alerted white townspeople. "The news spread rapidly and intense excitement ensued," continued the *Mercury*, and the "negro was soon in the hands of a half-dozen [white] citizens, who took him into the alley, where he was flogged with a blacksnake whip, until he screamed for mercy." According to the *Democrat*, the vigilantes "horse whipped him till the ground around him was damp with blood." Authorities then imposed the very sanctions that blacks had hoped to avoid in the first place. "They have been repeatedly threatened," chronicled the *Mercury*. "All the stores of the city have put up placards excluding the negroes."[2]

After the report appeared in the news, visitors shunned the town, injuring its reputation and economy. "Trade left Paris," wrote the *Stoutsville*

Banner. The community was "forced to spend several thousand dollars to keep the disease from spreading among the whites. After the disease was finally corralled and there was nothing doing in the business circles, Miss Paris sat down on the hillside and communed with herself in regard to the 'nigger' and the loss they had caused the town." After she had thus considered the matter, "many niggers were driven from the town, several were horsewhipped, and what few were left in town were ordered to stay in the niggers place." The *Banner* reported approvingly that "Paris received many compliments from visitors to the town for this important move. Women and children were [no longer] forced to walk the streets with some black buck."[3]

The whippings and expulsions in Paris—as well as the smallpox outbreak—were not unusual events in northeastern Missouri at the turn of the twentieth century. Neither was the immediate reaction of the whites to the initial victims of the disease, as Palmyra's *Marion County Herald* observed in 1901.

> Palmyra has now had two visitations from smallpox. In both cases it was brought here by negroes. The city and the county have been put to great expense and in both cases the negroes have done their best to thwart efforts to stamp out the disease. Do our negro citizens know that up in Monroe City the negro school has been closed, that they flog a negro up there every week and that they are gradually driving the negroes out of town? Do they know that Paris has run off half of her negro population in the past year? Do they know that Elsberry is driving out all the negroes and that Perry will not permit a negro to stay in town over night?

In a terrifying threat to blacks there, the *Herald* concluded: "And don't they realize the danger of a thinning out here in Palmyra?"[4]

With its focus on fourteen counties in northeastern Missouri between 1899 and 1921, this chapter examines these two interlocking themes—whippings and expulsions. First it details the whippings, focusing on the actions and motivations of the members of the mobs, the widespread support of these actions by whites, and the assistance rendered to them by law enforcement officials. Then it examines the variety of sundown towns found in the study area during this period and the role of whippings in creating and enforcing sundown practices. Finally, it evaluates the findings and speculates on their significance for the study of antiblack mob violence and sundown towns.

The fourteen counties under investigation are Audrain, Boone, Callaway, Chariton, Howard, Lincoln, Macon, Marion, Monroe, Montgomery,

Pike, Ralls, Randolph, and Shelby. They are located in an area identified historically as "Little Dixie." Though defined in various ways for different purposes by local residents, journalists, and scholars, twelve of these counties were associated with Little Dixie in a majority of the seven definitions of this region reviewed by the historian Douglas Hurt, and two of them are mentioned in a minority of those definitions.[5] Before the Civil War, Little Dixie was associated with southern white slaveowners who settled the area, took advantage of its temperate climate, fertile soil, and riverine location, and established a slavery-based hemp and tobacco economy. As a result it claimed a relatively substantial slave population before the war. Whereas most counties in Missouri claimed just a few hundred enslaved people in 1860, slave populations in Little Dixie ranged from 660 in Macon County to 5,886 in Howard County.[6] The white population across Little Dixie retained a distinct fondness for its southern identity and made frequent gestures toward it, as the *Mexico Missouri Message* did in reporting an antiblack outbreak in a neighboring jurisdiction: "Monroe County," it noted, "is settled largely by Southerners."[7] Before turning to whippings and expulsions in Little Dixie, I must first address the spatial and temporal contexts for both activities: Missouri between the Civil War and the turn of the twentieth century.

From the time when they established their first settlements in the state, most slave masters owned only a relatively small number of slaves.[8] Nonetheless, they employed violence of all kinds to maintain control. Over the course of three days in 1859, for example, whites lynched four slaves in Saline County, burning one alive.[9] Much more commonly, masters or mob members employed whipping. Allowing for exaggeration, an abolitionist painted a vivid portrait of a whipping that took place in Lexington in 1856. Taking the victim from jail, a mob decided to administer "ONE THOUSAND lashes [to] his bare back, two hundred to be administered this evening (if he can bear it), and the remaining eight hundred from time to time, as in the judgment of the Committee his physical nature can bear up under it."[10] As will become evident, whites in Little Dixie would retain this proclivity for whipping.

When the Civil War erupted in 1861, whites in Missouri were already torn by competing loyalties and divergent attitudes toward blacks, slavery, and the economy. As a result, they soon went to war with each other, plunging the state into a guerrilla conflict involving Union soldiers and irregular fighters.[11] In her analysis of the situation at that point, the historian Diane Mutti Burke indicates that "enslaved Missourians understood the potential implications of the sectional conflict" from the outset, "capitalized on the presence of the Union military and the political divisions among the white population and left their owners by the thousands." Slaveholders fretted continuously over the possibility of such losses but could not imagine their eventual scale. By the midpoint of the war, concludes Burke, "the institution of slavery had been seriously compromised."[12]

After the war white Missourians, once bitterly divided, now coalesced behind a white supremacist ideology targeted against blacks.[13] They demonstrated their growing unity in 1869, according to an account in the *St. Louis Democrat*: "A gentleman, as he alighted from the stage at Fulton, heard one man address another in jubilant tones, giving the news: 'We hung a nigger last night,' uttered just as if he had been to a circus, and was delighted to report what a good time he has had."[14] Writing about lynching in Missouri after the Civil War, the historian Michael Fellman notes, "If blacks were to be free, many whites believed they had to leave the region or else be hanged, as they were impermissible in the community as other than utterly subordinated slaves."[15] Whites continued their racist violence across the state throughout the late nineteenth century. After an alleged rape in La Plata in 1889, for example, a posse seized a black suspect. "The men took the prisoner from the guards and throwing a rope around his neck hung him from the timbers of the bridge across the stream known as East Fork."[16]

During that same period whites established an unknown number of all-white sundown towns and counties, places where they never allowed a substantial number of blacks to collect at all or terrorized and expelled the occasional unsuspecting black settler or traveler. In 1905 a former resident chronicled the sentiment in Lancaster, located near the Iowa border as follows: "20 or 25 years ago, there was one family of negroes living near Lancaster." Since then, he declared, there had "been no permanent residents. Lancaster has been particularly hostile to the black man. When a negro enters town he is gently informed that it would be safer for him to move on before night fall." If he failed to honor the warning, he suffered the consequences. "At first they only use ancient eggs and vegetables," he related, "but if they are insufficient to enforce respect you will notice clubs and brick bats flying in the air. As a rule the latter method is not necessary, though it has been resorted to several times." This individual then contextualized Lancaster's aggressiveness towards blacks by stating, "The other towns are not as vigilant as Lancaster in running out the negro, but somehow the colored men do not feel at home any place in the county."[17]

By the end of the nineteenth century, white Missourians enforced their social order primarily through racist *practices* that did not comply with state laws but possessed the power of law in day-to-day life nevertheless. In an exchange between Governor Arthur Mastick Hyde and some of his black constituents in 1916, the former demonstrated that reality. In a letter to the governor, some black residents in Fulton explained that for many years whites there had denied them the use of the restrooms at the county courthouse by means of slurs and threats to keep them out. When a black minister refused to accept his expulsion from the facilities, the whites retaliated by mounting two signs reading "DARKIES—KEEP—OUT," one of which was so large that it "may be read the distance of a block away, from the outside." The blacks argued that whites had no basis for denying blacks the use of these facilities under Missouri law and that, like whites, blacks paid for their use through their taxes. "Negroes feel that the courthouse is common property," they wrote, and were "maintained at public expense." They demanded answers to several reasonable inquiries:

(1) Is there any law upon Missouri's statutes permitting this kind of discrimination?
(2) Are the colored citizens entitled to protection against these insults?
(3) If this discrimination is not statutory, shouldn't the county officials be asked to see that it is discontinued, and have those signs removed?
(4) What suggestions, if any, would you offer?[18]

In his response, Hyde acknowledged that such discrimination was illegal but casually declined to challenge these Jim Crow practices, stating,

> The control of the Court House is entirely in the hands of the county court. There is no law permitting discrimination that I know of on the statute books. Colored citizens are entitled to protection. The county court has absolute control of the Court House and can make such order as they see fit with reference to the toilets. I would suggest that you take the matter up with them.[19]

In this way Hyde surely frustrated his black constituents and reinforced just how these illegal practices continually replicated themselves.

Nonetheless, white Missourians did enforce some racist *laws*. With regard to education, for example, they had mandated school segregation in an effort to reduce the potential for racial mixing. Around the turn of the century, however, their legislators attempted to expand these legislative initiatives. Prominent state and national black newspapers criticized them. "Hanging over the negroes['] heads in the state of Missouri is a 'Jim Crow' bill which was introduced by certain legislators for the purpose of pushing the negro to the wall and making him cringe before the onslaughter [*sic*]

of the white man's prejudice," declared the *Rising Son*, angered by attempts
to circumscribe further access to education, ban interracial marriage, and
impose other indignities.[20] The *Freeman* (Indianapolis) challenged a bill
proposing discrimination in transportation. "Missouri now comes to the
front with a proposition to inaugerate [*sic*] the 'Jim Crow' car system," it
spat. "Will the many Negroes of Missouri stand the proposed insult?"[21]

Notwithstanding the challenges facing them, black Missourians across
the state organized to confront and address these issues. "Missouri negroes
are in nearly every small town organizing clubs and associations and
meeting to discuss in a careful and temperate way problems affecting their
business and social life," declared the *St. Louis Globe-Democrat* in 1906.
"There is a large and well defined movement among Missouri negroes
looking toward self-improvement."[22] Blacks periodically came together
against the unrelenting efforts to suppress them. "Negroes Organize
against Jim Crow," thundered the *St. Louis Palladium* after a conference
of two hundred of "the most prominent negroes of Missouri" took place
there in 1907. "Use of the Ballot Urged in Order to Prevent Discriminating
Laws."[23]

Blacks in Little Dixie were, of course, subject to the legislative initiatives wending their way through the state government in Jefferson City, to
the many Jim Crow practices they faced, and, to the racist violence long
practiced by whites across the state. In 1899, for example, a mob of five
hundred men hanged a certain Frank Embree near Higbee in Randolph
County. According to the *Moberly Weekly Monitor*, "He was neither burned
nor shot, as was predicted." The *Monitor* did not object to the lynching
but drew the line at using it for promotional purposes. "It is very bad
taste, to say the least, to use the ghastly circumstances of the mobbing
of the negro, Embree, as an advertisement for the Moberly fair. This is
especially so, when language is put in his mouth, which he never used."[24]
The *Monitor* did not specify in what manner someone used the lynching,
but probably one of the three known photographs of it was modified in
some mocking way. In 1914 members of another mob hanged a prisoner
in Fayette, Howard County. "So quietly did the mob form and execute
its work that few outside of those actually engaged in the lynching knew
of it," reported the *St. Louis Post-Dispatch*. "Spectators at a theater across
the street were not aware of the lynching until they came out after the
performance."[25]

In a lynching that garnered considerable attention, members of a mob
in Bowling Green hanged and shot one Roy Hammond in 1921 after effort-
lessly seizing the youth from local officers. In a letter to Governor Hyde,

U.S. Senator Selden P. Spencer of Missouri summarized his concerns about the affair, "particularly because the lynching immediately followed a judicial trial, conviction, and sentence." Spencer also lamented the receipt of a letter from a prominent resident of Bowling Green who wrote that "the sympathy of the [white] community was very much in favor of the lynching."[26] The members of the Green Tree Negro Republican Club of St. Louis complained to Hyde that "a Mob, like a storm, . . . wrecked the machines of Justice and cast the honor of Missouri, to the winds, when [it] lynched that poor innocent negro lad."[27] In addition, Walter White, the assistant secretary of the NAACP, wrote a letter of protest to Hyde.[28]

In perhaps the best-known lynching to take place in Little Dixie, townspeople in Columbia, including many students from the University of Missouri, lynched James Scott, a janitor at the university, hanging him from a bridge off campus in front of hundreds of spectators. In his report, Colonel John F. Williams of the Missouri National Guard related what he had seen after the mob took Scott from the jail. "I saw a Columbia policeman in uniform standing beneath the bridge and asked him where that part of the mob was that had the negro," he wrote.

> [The policeman] pointed up above on the bridge. I asked him if anything could be done to stop the mob activity and he said "no." Just then someone yelled: "here he comes" and the body of the negro was thrown from the bridge and [he] swung just above my head. I immediately went up on the bridge to underneath an arc light where the body had been suspended and asked those milling a round [sic] if they knew who had done the actual hanging. All said: "they left right away," and no one seemed to know who they were or where they were from.[29]

Given the location of the hanging and the participation of university students, the Scott lynching generated national coverage and provoked a substantial outcry from blacks in the state. In the *Crisis*, the magazine of the NAACP, the scholar and activist W. E. B. Du Bois remarked bitterly, "We are glad to note that the University of Missouri has opened a course in Applied Lynching."[30] Representatives of the Kansas City Negro Women's Republican League wrote to the governor to "deplore the horrid occurrence at Columbia" and to "request that the promoters of such disgraceful occurrences be brought to justice."[31] Heedless of the negative publicity, however, University of Missouri students attempted another lynching in 1928. "Unchastened by [the earlier] lynching," declared the *Kansas City Call*, a black paper, some "again persuaded [themselves] that the very charge of rape justifies doing away with trial and the processes of the law," and "only the removal of the prisoner kept the mob, among whom university students were conspicuous, from again committing murder." Concluded the *Call*, "education in Missouri is not a guide to better living," because "Columbia lusts to kill."[32]

Much more often, whites in Little Dixie opted for whipping as their preferred method of terrorizing blacks, an affirmation that the habits of slavery did not die in 1865. "There is no whipping-post law in Missouri, but this does not prohibit the citizens [of] Monroe City and Paris from using the lash on worthless culprits just the same," asserted the *Shelby County Herald* in 1901. It added that whipping was "an effective proceeding and should be the law of the land."[33] The *Sedalia Weekly Democrat* echoed its sentiments two years later. "The whipping post law went into effect in Fayette Thursday night without waiting for the bill to pass the legislature," it reported. "A band of 'regulators' escorted several bad negroes to the corporation limits, and, after whipping them, gave them until 10 o'clock Friday morning to leave town."[34]

In some instances vigilantes stormed jails, seized prisoners, administered floggings, and expelled them from the area. In one such case "the jail door was broken open and the negro was taken about one-half mile from town, tied to a telegraph pole and given 150 lashes with a harness tug," reported the *Moberly Evening Democrat* after an episode in Armstrong.[35] In other instances vigilantes seized their victims off the street, from their homes, or at their workplaces. In Elsberry they raided a livery stable, apprehended a porter, "marched him to a rock quarry, one-half mile below the city, beat him severely with switches, and warned him . . . to leave town."[36] In another incident in Armstrong, a mob grabbed William Harvey, a black man, who "was taken out to a pasture and given a severe whipping . . . for using profane language in the presence of a large crowd of women," reported the *Sedalia Evening Democrat*. After his narrow escape from a possible lynching, his tormentors ordered him to leave town.[37]

Amid their whipping sprees, whites sometimes revoked the rights of blacks generally to freedom of assembly and movement. During the aforementioned smallpox outbreak in Paris, the authorities closed black churches, schools, and meeting halls, the very institutions that blacks used for organizational and medical purposes. In a prolonged episode provoked by alleged criminality in Monroe City in 1907, whites imposed a curfew. "Many well known citizens have banded themselves together to keep the negroes from the streets," reported the *Mexico Missouri Message*. They made clear that they would take whatever steps necessary to ensure compliance. "Placards have been posted," declared the *Message*, "warning negroes that if they are not off the streets at 8:30 P.M. each day they must 'suffer the consequences.' A bell is rung at this time each night, and now all Monroe City negroes wend their way homeward when the curfew rings."[38] The whites, added the *Weekly Monitor*, "have openly declared that if the negroes are not in their homes" by bell time, "those on the streets will be caught and lynched."[39]

Instead, "a crowd of white men armed with whips searched the streets," an observer reported. "Only one negro was found and he escaped after a hard chase."[40] A couple of black visitors challenged the curfew and suffered the consequences. "Two negroes of Shelbina heard of Monroe City's curfew and determined to show their friends here that they would not obey it," an unsympathetic observer noted.[41] One of them supposedly removed a curfew notice from a pole and, in the words of the *Monroe City Democrat*, "tore it to bits, and with the remark: 'No sich d——n things could go in Shelbina,' threw them into the gutter." He soon found himself the victim of a severe whipping. "He was then given a hand full of the yellow posters and told: Put those up when you get home. Now git, and he got."[42]

On August 11, 1907, the *St. Louis Post-Dispatch* reported that whites had lifted the restrictions in Monroe City. "After having been compelled for nearly one month to comply with an 8 o'clock curfew, the negroes of this city again have been given the freedom of the streets," it declared. "The curfew was lifted . . . contingently. The citizens who comprised what is known as the Vigilance Committee, however, are still organized, and declare they will take steps to drive every negro from the city, if the situation again becomes menacing."[43] When a few blacks vowed vengeance on a vigilante leader who had "embittered" them with his brutality, whites jailed them. Although they did not whip these prisoners, they did threaten that, "if a white man should be shot as a result of the racial troubles here, many negroes will summarily pay the penalty."[44]

White newspapers took undisguised pleasure in describing the fear and agony experienced by whipping victims. In the account of one such paper, the *Monroe City Democrat*, "midnight came, [and] so did a l[o]t of men with buggy whips and a board. [Bud] Davis was placed astride the one inch board and the whips plied with a vengeance." The newspaper joked about the speed with which Davis fled town, carrying one of the curfew placards thrust into his hands after he had gained his freedom. "When he flashed by the Burlington depot the operator mistook the handful of yellow cards for the headlight of a wild locomotive and wired ahead to close all switches and look out. . . . It is said [that Davis] overtook and passed the freight on the Salt river bridge."[45]

Mobs targeted their victims for alleged offenses ranging from so-called insulting remarks to theft, assault, and rape—threatened or otherwise. In 1901 members of a mob in Monroe City whipped Marvin Washington, a fifteen-year-old who supposedly possessed "a heart blacker than his skin" and attempted an assault on a white girl. The *Monroe City Democrat* reported that Washington was "taken to the pasture and almost flayed alive. (He should have been emasculated to save future trouble.) He was then turned loose with instructions to never return." When Washington's father protested the treatment afforded his son, whites threatened him, too. "The best thing for him to do," warned the *Democrat*, "is to keep quiet and behave himself or some fine morning there will be a shortage of raw hides in the harness shops and a surplus of them on some backs."[46]

Although they most commonly targeted young men, mobs did not spare other members of the black community. When, for example, in early 1901 vigilantes in Elsberry whipped and expelled Frank Bradshaw, his mother was also targeted. Evidently unnerved or exasperated by the objections of Frank's relatives to the whipping, the vigilantes went to the Bradshaw home, dragged his mother Betty and his brother Joe from their beds, and flogged them both, along with another black man. Making distinctions by age and gender, the mob expelled the two men under penalty of death, giving Bradshaw "ten minutes to get out of town" and the second man "five minutes to accomplish the same act. Both negroes were beyond the city limits in half the time," noted the *St. Louis Republic*.[47] The mob did not expel Betty but it may have committed some act of sexual violence against her, a possibility usually not documented but often associated with such situations. With these whippings whites underscored the fact that they often targeted certain black families for repeated and aggravated abuse, suggesting that the Bradshaws may have been a particularly resistant family, not unlike those identified in chapter 4.

The 1900 census data from Elsberry underscore the degree to which mob violence against young black men could have a substantial effect on many others close to them. When the vigilantes attacked Frank, twenty, Joe, twenty-four, and Betty, sixty-five, it surely inflicted terrible psychological wounds on the young men's other siblings, sixteen-year-old Maggie, fourteen-year-old Charley, and twenty-three-year-old Sallie Davis, and on Joe's twenty-five-year-old wife, Oliva Bradshaw. The mob must have terrorized the younger members of the household as well, including

nine-year-old Guy and eleven-year-old Sussay. Although two-year-old
Louis was probably too young to understand these events, the attackers
ensured that he and the other children would experience even deeper
poverty than they might otherwise have known and the loss of the familial
bonds that might have protected them.[48]

By keeping their victims under surveillance, whites from different towns
shared information and coordinated their efforts. In Fayette a mob invaded
the homes of "three notoriously bad negro women, dragged them from
their beds to the court house square, where they were severely whipped,"
reported an observer. "They left town on the first train."[49] Some black men,
treated to the same inhumane violence, fled as well. None of the fugitives
found solace. "Some of the negroes, who were flogged at Fayette not long
since and directed to leave the city, found quarters at the home of a negro
man" in Myers, reported the *Moberly Evening Democrat*. "As soon as this
was learned by the good people of the neighborhood they were ordered
to leave." When the blacks failed to follow the directive or failed to do so
quickly enough to suit the whites, "they were waited upon with the view
to inflicting the same punishment as was administered to them at Fayette.
The men made their escape, but the woman was captured and given a
severe whipping and ordered to leave, which she did the next day. 'The
way of the transgressor is hard.'"[50]

Mobs enjoyed the widespread approval of whites, as evidenced by
their tacit acceptance, explicit endorsement, or participation. The mob
in Fayette expressed the self-righteous indignation of the town's residents
when it ousted some blacks who were deemed criminals. "In response
to a call issued from the pulpits of the several churches," reported the *St.
Louis Post-Dispatch*, "a public meeting was held at the courthouse Monday
night and a committee of five appointed" to deal with the problem. With
a broad coalition arrayed against them, "a number of the worst class of
negroes left [town] without being told."[51] Some whites in Fayette and in
other municipalities probably disapproved of the whippings because of
concerns about lawlessness, but few probably did so because of concerns
about the welfare of blacks. If some did, they expressed it in such a muted
way that it amounted to acceptance.

In the 1907 episode in Monroe City, some whites apparently criticized
the *excesses* of the mob members but not the whippings themselves. "The
boys of Monroe City began the campaign to keep the negroes off the
streets at night, but when they carried their methods to the extreme, older
citizens took the matter in hand," reported the *Mexico Missouri Message*
cryptically.[52] The *St. Louis Post-Dispatch* allowed only that "many citizens

have opposed the drastic measures adopted by the 'vigilantes,' but all admit that they did an effective work." Neither paper, however, elaborated on the nature of these "extreme" methods, an oversight which suggests that white opposition was neither effective nor sustained.[53]

Given such widespread approval, mobs had little to fear from the authorities—and much to gain from collusion with them. In Monroe City it was the marshal who jailed Bud Davis, the black visitor from Shelbina. "The negro was released at midnight . . . but before he could reach the station," according to the *Mexico Missouri Message*, "a crowd of citizens seized him, and, carrying him to the eastern edge of town, gave him forty-nine lashes."[54] The *St. Louis Post-Dispatch* reported a yet more egregious incident in Lincoln County. "Alton and Ella Pearl, negroes, went to Troy last Monday and applied to the county authorities for warrants against the whites who participated in the flogging" of their son. "The news was telephoned to Silex and when the couple returned that afternoon they were met at the train by an angry mob. The negress was dragged to a warehouse and severely lashed. The couple were released upon their promise to make no further effort to prosecute and to leave the village at once."[55]

In 1900 the authorities in Fulton played the role of the mob in violation of their sworn responsibility to their prisoners and the law. "Prosecuting Attorney D. H. Harris asked the [two] negro boys in a jocular way which they would rather do—take twenty-five lashes each on their bare backs or go to jail," reported the *Mexico Missouri Message*. Each allegedly expressed a preference for the whipping. On the following day, the two jailed youths supposedly declared that they were prepared to accept the whipping and to leave town immediately thereafter, prompting the authorities to pursue that option. "Constable Garner, who weighs 218 pounds, was hunted up, and the negroes were brought to the sheriff's office, where the big constable laid the rawhide on their backs in the good old-fashioned way. At every blow from the rawhide the negroes groaned with pain, but they took the punishment they had chosen and were released."[56] It is quite possible that the whites in Fulton simply decided to whip and expel the blacks and then to justify their decision with a story that placed the responsibility for the outcome on their victims.

Whites warned that whipping was a generous alternative to lynching but that lynching was acceptable if floggings proved insufficient. For instance, in reporting that a black man in Chariton County had been "twice whipped out of the county because of indignities to white girls," the *Sunday Morning Democrat* speculated that he must be "trying to get burned at the stake."[57] The *Mexico Missouri Message*, too, advocated harsher measures when alleged criminality continued despite floggings. After reporting that a black man whipped in another town had come to Mexico and turned once again to theft, it warned that he "either did not get the stripes thick enough and heavy enough—or the whipping post won't do."[58]

Two of the recorded lynchings included whipping, a testament to the thin line between these types of racist violence. Before Frank Embree was hanged, "he was stripped of his clothing, and beat with rods," reported the *Moberly Weekly Monitor*.[59] In two of the three extant photographs of the lynching, Embree stands naked before a crowd of white men, his body covered with welts, cuts, and blood; in the third he is dead.[60] In 1902 members of a mob near Higbee flogged Oliver Wright to death. "His back and arms were one mass of scars and bruises, and his clothing, torn to shreds, lay about," reported the *Chillicothe Constitution*, "the ground being strewn with hickory [s]witches used in punishing Wright." He was "a horrible sight," continued the report. "He was covered with blood and on both arms were slashes and cuts as though some one of the vigilantes had wielded a knife."[61]

Because of their numerical superiority and the ferocity of their violence, whites exercised extraordinary control over blacks. Nevertheless, against great odds blacks fought back. In Monroe City, for instance, a few of them opposed the 1907 curfew. "The race trouble seems to be nearing a crisis," observed the *Paris Appeal*. "Negroes, some of them, resent the order to keep off the streets at night." By making their objections known, they provoked reprisals. "The whites who have been enforcing the order are determined that it shall be respected," continued the *Appeal*. Two men "asserted that they had as much right on the streets as the whites and refused to stay at home. The Vigilance Committee attacked them and administered a severe beating."[62] Even though some blacks appealed to justice via the court system, they could not expect a positive response, as the experience of Alton and Ella Pearl confirmed.

One victim who demonstrated extraordinary courage in the wake of a whipping was a bootblack named Bud Davis. After his whipping in Shelbina in April 1914, he sued his attackers for seventy-five hundred dollars in damages.[63] According to the *Chillicothe Constitution*, "The negro in his petition asserts, the eight defendants seized him and took him to a [location] one and one-half miles from Shelbina, in an automobile." There, he claimed, "the men put a rope around his neck and hanged him until he was forced to grab hold of the rope to keep from choking. As he hung from the tree, the negro declares, the men horse-whipped him." After the flogging, the whites drove him to neighboring Monroe County, abandoned him, and warned him never to return. Having sustained serious injuries, Davis claimed that he would "be crippled for life."[64] In all likelihood, this Bud Davis was the same individual targeted by the vigilantes in Monroe City in 1907.

When his suit came to trial in 1915, the legal system dashed Davis's hopes. All of the defendants pled guilty, paid a nominal fine of twenty dollars, and had their guilty pleas read into the legal proceedings. In spite of this, the jury awarded Davis an insulting one cent in damages. The *Chillicothe Constitution* betrayed its satisfaction: "Negro Sues . . . , Gets Lincoln Penny: Bud Davis, Who Sued Six White Men at Shelbina for Attacking Him, Receives 'Souvenir.'"[65] As Davis surely understood, the courts often did little more than ratify the right of whites to humiliate, terrorize, injure, and kill blacks.

Using whippings and other types of violence and intimidation, whites in Little Dixie established their dominance; with sundown towns they reinforced it. By 1899 some towns were in effect all-white. According to the *St. Louis Post-Dispatch*, Stoutsville, for example, had not "permitted a negro within its boundaries after sunset for 25 years."[66] Until recently, added the *Moberly Weekly Democrat* in 1907, a sign was posted near the railroad station that read: "Negroes, don't let the sun set on you in Stoutsville."[67] Amused by the troubles endured by whites in neighboring towns that allowed at least a few blacks to remain, the *Stoutsville Banner* encouraged these towns to impose a similar ban. "Stoutsville has a good plan—do not allow any negro of whatever character, class or sex, to live in town, or even to stay over night. Try it."[68]

Elsewhere, whites drove blacks from town in sudden, wholesale expulsions. With the whipping of the Pearls and their son in Silex, they "brought race feeling, which has been growing strained for months, to a climax," and "little cause [was] needed to fan the smoldering flames to race-war pitch."[69] To avoid such an outcome, whites ordered all blacks to leave town. The *Post-Dispatch* noted that the few "negroes still remaining at Silex are making every effort to comply with the command of the whites that they leave the village by next Saturday night. The disposition of their property is the only cause of delay to several families, while others have already loaded their household effects on wagons and fled."[70] Although there had been no further floggings, any black found in the town after the expiration of the time limit was to be flogged. With this expulsion, whites in Silex—like those elsewhere in the Midwest—demonstrated both their resentment of blacks who dared to accumulate wealth or property and their willingness to assuage that resentment by banishing blacks by threat or violence. Under these circumstances, fleeing blacks could not arrange to take their possessions or to sell their land at a fair price; thus, truculent whites obtained black-owned property at little or no cost.

Whites in Elsberry took longer to drive the blacks out of their town but did so at an accelerating rate. They began as early as 1901 but undertook a more focused effort in 1906. On March 6 they whipped two blacks. On March 19 they whipped three more, expelling two of them.[71] Calling themselves "the Whipping club," they banded together again on April 3, shooting one man, whipping another, and expelling both. "The negroes whipped last month have all left with their families and relatives, about twenty-one in all," summarized the *Sedalia Evening Democrat*. "They sold their property, most of them going to St. Louis. The colored population advises others of their race not to move here."[72] With regard to Fayette, the same paper reported in 1903 that twenty-five black families had fled the town. Although they apparently left of their own volition after the whippings took place, they also did so because they believed that these attacks foretold an escalation in antiblack persecution. "The whites," it noted, "have openly threatened to battle with negroes and drive them from Fayette and vicinity."[73]

In Paris and Monroe City whites whipped and expelled many blacks between 1899 and 1907 but never established conventional sundown towns, nor did they intend to do so. Instead they tolerated a small, ruthlessly subordinated group of blacks that lived under severe constraints. After driving out "more than one-third of its negro population," as the *Moberly Weekly Democrat* recalled in reference to the events detailed at the outset of this chapter, Paris allowed the rest to remain.[74] In Monroe City, where vigilantes ousted an unknown number of blacks in 1907, whites permitted an unknown number of "good" blacks to stay. "Because some niggers are not good citizens does not mean that all colored people are bad," reasoned the *Monroe City Democrat*. "[But] there is no room in Monroe for the would be bad nigger."[75] After a 1916 whipping the *Democrat* elaborated on its distinction between good blacks, who knew "their place," and bad ones, who did not:

> There are other niggers in Monroe who are candidates for the same treatment, unless they mend their ways. Monroe City has several respectable, deserving colored people who know their place and make good citizens. Then the city is cursed with a lot of impudent, loud, profane, indecent niggers both male and female who are a disgrace to any community. It is no use

to haul them up before the courts and fine or give them a jail sentence . . . as they have no shame and do not mind going to jail. For all such a whipping post should be provided by law. Moral suasion in such cases is not as good as the whipping post."[76]

In both of these places new black residents gradually settled, increasing the black population and prompting renewed demands for a thinning out. In 1903 newspapers in neighboring towns condemned Paris for its inaction. Recalling the expulsions that had taken place a few years earlier, the *Marion County Herald* concluded that "those good days are all passed. The niggers are most in evidence."[77] The *Monroe City Democrat* related the recent experience of its editor during a trip to Paris. "Arriving at the depot we found niggers here, niggers there and niggers everywhere," it raged. "This should not be, it need not be and the city authorities owe it to their city, to their county[, and] to their state to stop niggers loafing at the depot."[78] The *Stoutsville Banner*, for its part, floated the idea of a shift in the locus of political power. "If Paris can't respect the gift of Monroe county [then] move the county seat to Stoutsville, where the nigger is not allowed to live."[79]

Whites in Monroe City took stock of another increase in the number of blacks in 1915. "Let's call a halt on the negro population," counseled the *Democrat*. "Monroe City is overrun." Referring to the 1907 whipping campaign, it recalled that "the negro population was not large in Monroe City [then] due to the fact that a vigilant committee took things in their own hands and used a black snake whip when it was necessary." Reporting an alleged recent act of criminality, it added that "with a little encouragement a whipping committee could [again] be organized. Let's do something, for if we do not in a few more weeks it will be unsafe for our mothers, wives and daughters to be on the street after dark. A stitch in time will save a lot of heartaches and trouble later."[80] In the same issue the *Democrat* vented its frustration with the behavior of some black residents: "There will be some dead 'niggers' hereabouts if the bathing stunt in the city reservoir is ever pulled off again."[81] Nearly two months later it declared that whites had suffered enough. In an apparent call for expulsions, it published a banner at the top of the front page one week asking, "WILL IT BE DONE?" The following week it published another asserting that "IT SHOULD BE DONE."[82] Despite its rhetoric, the *Democrat* was not calling for a *complete* expulsion but for a targeted one: "Monroe City has a few energetic and law abiding negro citizens—they should be encouraged, but the trash, or 'niggers' should be told to 'beat it,'" the paper averred.[83] Furthermore, it was relying on the dependability of the mob to differentiate between the two types, as it tacitly acknowledged the following year in an article titled "Nigger Horsewhipped."[84]

The threats uttered routinely by the *Democrat* and the violence unleashed periodically by the mob may have had their intended effect by encouraging the departure of "the would be bad nigger"—often in substantial numbers—and the retention of a few trusted blacks. Yet they also confirm that sundown towns did not always conform to the practice of banning all blacks evident in places like Stoutsville or to the definitions of *sundown town* used by some scholars.

With their violence, whites drove beleaguered blacks from place to place in a vain search for succor. In some instances they targeted the same people repeatedly, and in other instances they targeted the same families for multiple attacks. Banned from Perry, Stoutsville, Silex, and Elsberry, always ill at ease in Paris and Monroe City, and unsafe in Fayette, Fulton, and Mexico, blacks found themselves in perpetual turmoil—on the run, forced to forfeit family and personal relationships (not to mention property), and vulnerable to the whims of their oppressors.

Ultimately, many blacks migrated to the largest or fastest-growing urban centers, where they hoped to find more opportunity and greater security. Others fled to regional cities like Moberly, where, as the *Moberly Weekly Monitor* complained in 1912, they compounded the concerns of urban whites. "If these people in a few counties . . . have a problem they should be compelled to solve it themselves and not burden other communities with it," the paper argued. "The negroes in those counties are compelled to live somewhere. To drive them forth en masse is only to shift the solution of the problem to another community. No community has the right to do this."[85]

Whites in the large urban centers responded to these migrations from the countryside, from the smaller towns and cities, and, increasingly, from the South with a series of racist spectacles. In 1917 mobs in East St. Louis, Illinois, sister city to St. Louis, invaded the black quarter, killing dozens of its residents and burning houses and buildings in one of the worst race riots in twentieth-century America.[86] In 1919 a mob reportedly "composed of Randolph County citizens went to Macon and overpowered the officers," abducted their prisoner, James Anderson, and returned to Moberly, whereupon they lynched him.[87]

Given their persistent antiblack attitudes and their open expression in the *Moberly Weekly Monitor,* whites in Moberly set about creating sundown neighborhoods within their growing city. As early as 1908 the *Moberly Weekly Democrat* reported their efforts. "The residents of Miller's

Park addition, who a few weeks ago organized an association to keep negroes from settling in that addition have started something in Moberly," it cheered. "A few nights ago about 100 of the residents and property owners in Northeast Moberly organized a similar association and expect to make good at their work." Unfortunately, the blacks already living in such places now confronted another difficulty. "This association does not expect to have any trouble with the colored population but in case their wishes are disobeyed they all stand ready to make their word good."[88] With their creation of sundown neighborhoods within a segregated but multiracial city, the residents of Moberly provided another reason for scholars to expand their understanding of sundown towns.

This examination of Little Dixie in the early twentieth century provides insight into the racist practices employed by whites there. It demonstrates, first, that members of white mobs engaged in frequent whippings—a practice that emerged from slavery—to enforce their dominance and in a number of cases to expel part or all of the black population of a town. Underscoring the degree to which whipping was a legacy of slavery, my study of racist violence in the *entire state* of Kansas over the course of seven decades identified only three whippings—substantially less than the number uncovered in these fourteen counties in a little more than two decades.[89]

In employing whipping, mob members enjoyed the widespread and often raucous support of whites and the collusion of public officials. Under these circumstances blacks often were little more than fugitives from the caprices of their oppressors. After fleeing from one town to another, many eventually migrated to the larger cities. As they concentrated there, they attracted the animosity of urban whites, who again sought to subordinate them and force them into segregated districts.

At a time when influential whites were challenging the legitimacy of lynching because politicians and businessmen increasingly feared the implications of such violence for the reputation, stability, and growth of their state, they may have concluded that whipping was preferable because it attracted less scrutiny and reduced the odds of an investigation. Nonetheless, many whites resented this encroachment on their prerogative to use lethal vengeance against blacks. Such a complaint was registered by a Missouri editor as late as 1938 when he used the headline "Can't Even Lynch 'Em Now."[90]

If Missouri whites were reluctant about lynching black women, they were far less so about whipping them. Furthermore, though the sources employed in this study are largely mute on the subject, white mob members probably assaulted female victims sexually at some point before, during, or after the whippings. Contemporary newspaper accounts, for example, indicated, that the vigilantes who whipped Ella Pearl in Silex did so not in public but in the seclusion of a warehouse, a distinction suggesting that they may have sought for unstated reasons some privacy in the whipping of a woman. Indeed, subsequent research is likely to confirm what a 1938 study found with respect to lynching: "Negro women who attract the attention of lynchers are, regardless of age, invariably mob-raped before being executed."[91]

As indicated by the experiences of the Bradshaw family in Elsberry and the Pearl family in Silex, mobs tended to target the same families repeatedly, sometimes within the same town and sometimes in multiple towns. In the process they inflicted profound physical and psychological damage on family members and occasionally tore families apart. The mob members who whipped and expelled fifteen-year-old Marvin Washington in Monroe City, for instance, provoked the anguish of his father, who pled for mercy but elicited only the threat of further whippings. The activities of such mobs underscore the conclusion reached in chapter 4 that some black families were particularly resistant to white oppression and that whites retaliated against these families with merciless acts of violence intended to break and destroy them.

Despite their intentions, whites were not always able to maintain the all-white character of their towns in the aftermath of an expulsion. Once they had rid themselves of the perceived threat—*too many blacks*—they allowed small (and perhaps not so small) numbers to locate once again in their midst until some catalyst provoked another round of expulsions. In some cases they permitted "trusted" blacks to remain, a self-interested acknowledgment of the need for some types of inexpensive labor. In other cases they simply recognized a demographic reality: the large number of blacks in this formerly slaveholding area of the state. The *Moberly Weekly Monitor* identified this difficulty when it simply stated that "the negroes . . . are compelled to live somewhere."

By whipping and expelling blacks, whites demonstrated plainly that they resented blacks who managed to accumulate property and wealth and achieve independence. In his classic study of racist violence in Kentucky, the historian George C. Wright argues that these kinds of attacks show, "far more clearly than does lynching, that most of the violence blacks experienced resulted from economic activities, not from alleged attacks on white women." In sum, "blacks who were prosperous or independent threatened the entire system of white supremacy."[92] Furthermore, with attacks of this kind against blacks occurring all over the Midwest—indeed, all over the country—for more than a century, whites ensured that blacks would have little to pass along to their heirs and that whites would have more than they had legally earned. In this sense, white mobs perpetrated acts of generational theft that virtually ensured poverty for generations of blacks thereafter. The criminal justice scholar Geoff Ward summarizes the results as follows: "The lasting meaning of racial violence from the more and less distant past is attributed to lingering traces in psyches, identities, attitudes, behaviors, structural inequalities, and other dynamics of successive generations. In places where, historically, black life has been trivialized by lethal and often sadistic violence, typically without protection or recourse through law, linked notions of 'white dignitary privilege' and black devaluation may persist or grow more pronounced over time."[93]

In terms of historiography, this chapter offers critical insights into antiblack mob violence and sundown towns. With respect to the first, historians have focused on lynching as the principal indicator of racist violence and have given other indicators short shrift. The historian Crystal Feimster recognized this when she observed that "between 1880 and 1930 lynch mobs murdered at least 130 black women" but "many more were tortured, mutilated, tarred and feathered, shot, burned, stabbed, dragged, whipped, or raped by angry mobs."[94] In *This Is Not Dixie* I theorized this concern with a call for a more capacious model of racist violence. In this study I have addressed another type of racist violence that was widely used in this particular region of Missouri (though not everywhere in the Midwest), and I have demonstrated its utility in the establishment and maintenance of white supremacy. With time historians, sociologists, social scientists, and others will be able to integrate these findings into a more comprehensive model of racist violence and ultimately provide a much broader understanding of those who deployed or suffered under it, and of its consequential impact on American history.

Since the publication of *Sundown Towns* by James W. Loewen in 2005, scholars have sought to compile lists of towns that banned blacks from their limits and analyze their characteristics.[95] They have provided a wealth of new insights; they have also made some problematic assumptions. Just as the study of lynchings obscured the understanding of other types of racist violence, so too does the study of only the towns that would not allow a *single black* obscure the understanding of those that did allow *some* blacks and, in so doing, imposed on them conditions that were no less restrictive. In this sense this chapter affirms the conclusion of the historian Guy Lancaster, who wrote in his study of sundown towns that "racial cleansing should be understood not as an absolute but as existing along a continuum."[96]

6   The Missouri Ozarks and Beyond, 1894–1930

"Whence all negroes have been driven forth"

Eighteen-ninety-four was a bad year for blacks in the Missouri Ozarks. In January posses spread out around Verona and Aurora in search of a man alleged to have raped a white woman. "A tireless search is being carried on for the black demon," reported the *Springfield Democrat*. "The feeling of the people is intense."[1] Announcing an arrest, the *St. Louis Post-Dispatch* predicted that, if linked to the crime, "the brute" would be lynched. The residents of the area were overwrought, and the paper feared it would not be possible for officers to prevent mob violence. For miles around every white man seemed to be "hunting for the fiend. One of the hardware stores has donated all of the cartridges free for those who wanted to hunt the negro."[2] Never welcoming, whites now banned blacks. Aurora was "negroless," the *Post-Dispatch* would later note. "No negro families are permitted to settle in the city of 5000 inhabitants." The entire region was becoming a place "whence all negroes have been driven forth."[3]

In May whites in the ironically named town of Fair Play took vengeance against a black man named Pete Mitchell, who barely survived the ordeal. According to the *Springfield Democrat*, the mob initially intended to hang Mitchell for the attempted rape of two white women but, deferring to a prominent white resident who counseled moderation, the attackers punished him in a different manner. "The negro was stripped of his clothing and tied to a tree. Then with buggy whips each member of the mob took a turn at belaboring the negro," noted the *Democrat*. "How long this was kept up cannot be learned, but it was continued until the wretch fainted away unconscious. Then after administering restoratives the mob gave him twenty-four hours to leave the country. He was unable to obey at first, but finally left or hid himself."[4]

In June a mob in Monett lynched a black man accused of shooting a white man, reported the *Pittsburg Daily Headlight,* adding, "Previous to the lynching they drove every darkey out of Monett."[5] Whites then established a zero-tolerance policy: blacks were unwelcome at any time for any reason. The following year the *Monett Leader* reported that there "were three strange coons in town this morning but they did not tarry long among us. Monett is not particularly stuck on darkies, and their sojourn in this city is of short duration."[6] In 1901 the *St. Louis Post-Dispatch* noted that for seven years "no negro has been permitted to set foot in Monett." The Missouri Ozarks, that paper concluded, were becoming "'colorless.'" In a memorable phrase, it added, "Down here they call it the white man's heaven."[7]

Eighteen-ninety-four may not be the definitive year for the *start* of the sundown movement in the Missouri Ozarks but, it does provide investigators with a convenient moment at which to begin the study of the movement in the three decades that followed. Building on the work of historians and journalists, this chapter examines incidents of racist violence used by whites to control and expel blacks and to establish and maintain sundown municipalities there. It also places this region in a larger geographical context by addressing the contiguous areas of neighboring states and examining the reciprocal impact of these racist practices across state lines. Finally, the chapter considers the implications of its findings.

Whites in the Missouri Ozarks used various types of threatened or actual violence to control blacks, trigger their departure from the region, and discourage their arrival. In late 1901, for example, whites in Monett threatened a few blacks who—notwithstanding the prohibition against them—came to town as employees of the railroad. "Several porters were in a restaurant near the depot at Monett, when a group of whites came in and threatened to lynch them," noted the *Leader-Democrat.*[8] In 1902 a large mob in Springfield attempted to lynch a black prisoner and, when it learned that he had been spirited away by officers to another jail, the mob members clamored for another man incarcerated for an unrelated offense. Although they failed to secure either, they succeeded in smashing a hole in the wall of the jail and, more important, in terrorizing blacks in the area.[9] In 1922 a mob in Carthage failed to lynch two prisoners but it, too, spread fear among blacks for a prolonged period. "The effort to seize the negroes . . . was the climax of several days of rumors on the streets," reported the *Joplin Globe.*[10]

Conditioned by outbreaks elsewhere, blacks in Carthage lived in such a state of fear that in 1903 they fled for their lives on hearing a false rumor

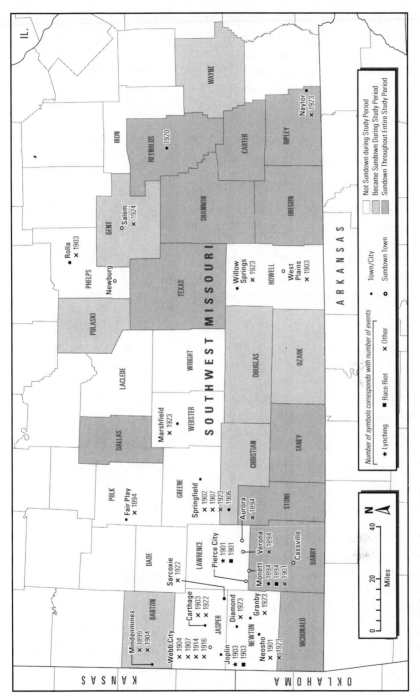

Map 2. Racist Violence in Southwest Missouri

one night that whites had instigated a race riot, had already lynched several blacks, and were now targeting the black quarters. "The frightened people scattered out in all manner of costumes, many running barefooted," reported the *Springfield Republican*. "They tore out for Carter's woods, crawling through the hedge fence with their naked feet, frightened mothers clinging to their crying babies, trying to quiet them, least [*sic*] their screams should betray the direction of the flight." After they learned that the rumor was a hoax, the frightened blacks slowly and cautiously returned to their homes.[11] In that same period a mob in Webb City threatened to lynch a stranger who had not only visited the town—a sufficient offense, perhaps—but had defied conventions and laws against interracial marriage. "A black man and his white wife came into this city, but the citizens would not tolerate them, and after keeping them locked in the city jail all night and frightening the 'darky' almost to death, they were given thirty minutes to leave town, the next morning," observed the *Webb City Daily Register*.[12]

Like those in Fair Play a decade earlier, whites in Rolla seized a victim in 1903, tied him to a tree, and whipped him. The *Missouri Sharp Shooter* portrayed Rolla as a generous locale in an otherwise inhospitable area, explaining that "Rolla is the only town in Phelps county where colored men are permitted to have an abiding place and those who conduct themselves properly and keep their place are treated kindly by our white citizens, but insulting white ladies is an outrage which no civilized community will allow, and this [victim] should be thankful he was let off with nothing worse than a whipping."[13] The following year, whites in Webb City used a whipping to expel a resident. "Great excitement prevailed on the street" and "all sorts of rumors were afloat," noted the *Webb City Daily Register*.

> While nothing definite can be learned by any one, it is generally understood that the nigger was taken quietly from the jail by a crowd of 18 or 20 persons headed by a leader with a black snake whip and driven out of the city with a severe cut from the whip at every step. He was asked in what direction he wished to go, and as a result it is understood that he was thrashed all the way to the old Memphis depot, and down the railroad track into the gravel piles and there left to suffer from the injuries he had received.[14]

In Mindenmines the town marshal killed Andrew Rector in 1904. As police officers and their supporters always claimed when black men died at the business end of a service revolver, the officer insisted that he killed Rector in self-defense when the victim (supposedly clutching a razor and stating, "I am not afraid of your gun") attempted to pull a pistol. "The negro, who still had his knife, changed it from his right hand to his left and reached for his right hip pocket as if he intended to draw a gun," reported the *Webb City Daily Register*. "The marshal did not wait for him to finish the motion but immediately fired. The bullet entered the negro's heart and caused almost instant death." Justifying the killing, the paper described Rector as "a bad negro" and accused him of picking fights with whites and warning them that he could do whatever he wanted. As expected, a coroner's jury "completely exonerated Marshal Barr for his action, claiming that he shot in self-defense."[15]

In 1903 whites in West Plains ousted nearly all blacks from the segregated section of town. Although the *Post-Dispatch Sunday Magazine* claimed that the exodus resulted merely from letters of warning, the blacks left in such numbers and with such haste as to belie its claim. "Where lately was a village of a hundred and fifty families birds and bats are the only occupants of the houses," it noted afterwards. "'Coontown,' that portion of the 'Gem City of the Ozarks' where the negro population of this city have long resided, is now deserted. Birds chirp in the grave-like stillness where formerly laughter and song echoed. But few of the 150 negro families who once resided here remain and these are hourly expecting the visit of an avenging nemesis."[16]

Without sympathy the *Post-Dispatch* chronicled the despair and suffering of fleeing blacks who sacrificed everything, and the greed and hostility of insensitive whites who pocketed a windfall.

> All day long a continual stream of humanity, both black and white, passed to and from 'Coontown' across the Frisco tracks [from] the business portion of the city. It was a busy day for the second-hand dealers and draymen. The former bought goods for a song, while the latter reaped a harvest hauling trunks and furniture to the depots and downtown stores.
>
> Some of the blacks left their furniture in their homes and took the first train, caring little where they went, just so they got far from West Plains. Others who had teams put a few goods on their wagon, gathered up the children and calling the dogs started southward to Arkansas to pick cotton.
>
> Everything was sacrificed. One negro sold three cows and calves for a trifle. Another deserted a growing corn crop of 40 acres. Carter Woodson, who has been a familiar figure on the streets of West Plains for 20 years, where he peddled leaf tobacco, lost no time in nailing up his storage house and leaving on the first train.
>
> The negro school, in charge of Cora Moore, recently of Cairo, Ill., closed on hearing the news. Mammies came and took their picaninnies [*sic*] home and even the teacher sought a place of retreat to await the first train going in the direction of Cairo.[17]

The *St. Louis Post-Dispatch Sunday Magazine* published this image, "How They Depopulated 'Coontown,'" after the white residents expelled the entire black population of West Plains, Missouri, in 1903. With its mocking tone, its stereotypical representation of black residents, and its defamatory caricature of a black victim fleeing the scene, this image epitomizes the vicious racism that defined Missouri and the Midwest generally at the turn of the twentieth century.

Between 1901 and 1920 lynch mobs killed at least eight black men in four incidents in the Missouri Ozarks. In the first of these incidents—the one addressed in chapter Four in conjunction with the Godley family—a mob in Pierce City first hanged a black prisoner, then invaded the black quarters and killed two more, burned five of their houses, and expelled at least two hundred residents. "In the order issued by the mob there were no exceptions," declared the *St. Louis Post-Dispatch.* "All persons of negro blood . . . were compelled to flee for their lives."[18]

In towns across the region, hostile whites flushed out fugitives in the ensuing days. According to the journalist Elliot Jaspin, "The newspaper in Neosho, about fifteen miles from Pierce City, reported that whites 'requested' its blacks to leave and that twenty-two had. Neighboring Barry County became all white when its last remaining black resident sold his farm and left. The *Cassville Republican* said that, in the days following the Pierce City riot, blacks were boarding trains at every depot along the Frisco line to escape to either Joplin or Springfield."[19] At intervals blacks, racing on foot across the backroads toward safety—somewhere—encountered "armed men patrolling the roads and were told to move on. Each negro was warned never to return, on peril of his life."[20]

In known sundown towns in surrounding areas, whites used the lynching and riot at Pierce City to reinforce the rules. The *Aurora Argus* declared: "Better [to] hang a dozen innocent black brutes than let one guilty one escape."[21] Armed men picketed Monett to ensure that no fugitive would mistakenly enter their town. "While the cleaning out process was going on in Pierce City," noted the *Pittsburg Daily Headlight,* "guards were out around Monett with [W]inchesters ready to shoot the first negro who dared to light in the town, but the past reputation of Monett and the antipithy [*sic*] its citizens hold against the colored race caused the Pierce City negroes to go around the town."[22] Further south "one negro was permitted to dwell in Cassville until a few years ago, when he died."[23] Another sundown town, "Webb City, west of Peirce City, and about midway between Joplin and Carthage, denie[d] to negroes the right of settlement," according to the *Post-Dispatch.*[24]

In 1903 members of a lynch mob in Joplin hanged a prisoner accused of killing a police officer and then turned their fury on the black population generally, frightening "every negro . . . off the street, stated the *St. Louis Post-Dispatch.* "All fled to the north part of the city, where the black population resides." The attackers began to stone black people and to set fire to their houses, many of which were destroyed despite the arrival of the firemen. After the mob members vented their "wrath in the north end of the city, they rushed to the southern, where lived a number of negroes. Their houses were vacant and not a negro could be found. Three more houses were fired." Although numerous blacks were injured, the newspaper did not record any fatalities.[25]

Afterward, an observer noted that "all day long there has been a migratory movement on the part of the colored population. The report that there is to be a general cleaning out tonight has caused almost every negro in the city to pack up or sell out and leave." About six hundred boarded trains bound for Carthage, Springfield, and Kansas City. Many declared that "under no circumstances would they remain another night in Joplin," and "scores of them could be seen wending their way along alleys and side streets, carrying bundles of every conceivable description."[26]

In Springfield members of a mob hanged three prisoners in 1906, then doused their bodies with coal oil and set them aflame. "The slow contortions of the muscles contracted by the heat were ghastly," noted the *St. Louis Post-Dispatch*. "A leg would contract, while its mate would straighten out toward the flames. Men would take torturing brands and hold them against remaining parts of the body, uttering unprintable things and reveling in the stench of burnish flesh." Some well-dressed white women stood about gawking "at the dangling, naked forms of those negroes and smile[d]."[27]

Blacks in Springfield reacted immediately: "Nearly all negroes had fled from the streets at the first shouts of the mob." An unknown number escaped from the city during or after the burnings, and with good reason, because "there [were] threats to attack the Jail again and lynch every negro prisoner remaining. There [were] threats to burn every negro house in the city."[28] A quarter of a century later, the *Springfield Leader* recalled the consequences of this event: "Since the riots of 1906 negro influence has been rather low in this city. Negroes never are appointed to public office and many of the most prominent left when excitement was high and never returned."[29] In 1907 whites in Springfield again sent blacks packing. "There may be another race riot," reported the *Parsons Daily Sun*. "Many of the negroes, fearing trouble, have left Springfield."[30]

As the lynchings in Joplin and Springfield demonstrated, white residents there were more than willing to reinforce their supremacy over blacks. Yet they faced different issues than did their counterparts in the small towns and rural municipalities. First, living in large urban centers, they were often confronted by the in-migrations of blacks expelled elsewhere and now seeking shelter and safety among the substantial concentrations of blacks already living there. Seventy-five of those who fled Pierce

City headed to Springfield. When they arrived, the fugitives met more hostility. Asked to comment, the mayor of Springfield told the *St. Louis Post-Dispatch* that there were already tensions and that, since the riot at Pierce City, whites had surreptitiously posted a sign in "a Springfield negro neighborhood, warning all negroes to leave the city." Nonetheless, he claimed, no one took it seriously.[31] If that was the case, it was probably because the whites feared the consequences for themselves if they engaged a reasonably large number of blacks determined to defend themselves.

Second, because the white residents of the larger urban centers relied to a much greater extent on black labor in various low-paid sectors of the local economy, they recognized the practical need for some minimal number of black workers. When Springfield's mayor asserted that there appeared to be, "south and west of here, an overwhelming public sentiment against permitting negroes to become citizens of the towns,"[32] he was probably ignoring a similar majority sentiment among whites in his own community but acknowledging the economic necessity of black labor there.

Given the need for cheap labor, whites in these urban centers permitted the return of some blacks after expulsions. Following the Joplin riot, the *St. Louis Post-Dispatch* correctly predicted that some "negroes will be allowed to return."[33] In her account the historian Kimberly Harper found that some of them returned to their homes the day after the riot, although they endured an even more stifling brand of racism than had existed before it: "Joplin was no longer home. The *Joplin Daily Globe* gave a 'conservative estimate' of blacks who planned to leave and never return at around 200 individuals out of an estimated population of 700." However, she added, Joplin's expulsion, unlike those that occurred in Monett and Pierce City, "would not be permanent. By 1910, 801 African Americans lived in Joplin, up from 773 in 1900."[34]

Scholars generally assume that the residents of sundown towns barred *all* blacks at *all* times, an assumption predicated on some persuasive evidence. The *Post-Dispatch* provided some of this evidence for the Ozarks. "Newburg . . . is a small place," it noted, "but sufficiently powerful to exclude the colored race."[35] The *Kansas City Star* reported further evidence from Reynolds County. In 1920 residents of the county objected to the importation of fifteen black convict-laborers to work on a road by lynching one of them. During the manhunt, the *Star* added, "the prison officer in charge of the company, removed the fourteen remaining negroes back to the penitentiary as fast as the trip could be made. It was feared the prison camp would be attacked by the mob, in which event it would have been a question if a single one of the convicts escaped with his life."[36] Reporting the lynching, the *Current Local* indicated that "feeling was intense all over [Reynolds] county, which like others in this section of the state, contains no resident negroes."[37]

Even in the strictest sundown jurisdictions, however, whites occasionally allowed a limited number of blacks for very particular reasons. In Ozark County, for instance, there were two, both old, infirm, and isolated. According to the *Post-Dispatch*, "they [were] 'Aunt' Ann and 'Uncle' Andy. Before the war they were brought to Ozark County" as slaves. "Old Andy has become totally blind and his sister Ann plows the field, cultivates the corn and cotton crop and cares for her sightless brother. They reside on North Fork, in the wildest portion of the Ozark mountains."[38] In other places whites repeatedly allowed small numbers of blacks to accumulate before thinning them out. In 1907 the *Webb City Register* warned of an ousting:

> For the past month, it has been quite noticeable that a large number of negroes were coming here to live and during the past few days, they have increased in number to such an extent that they are becoming quite insolent. The Webb City people will leave the negroes alone as long as they keep their place, but will tolerate no insolence from the blacks, and unless such actions are stopped, it will likely result in trouble, for Webb City has never had the reputation of being a "nigger" town.[39]

The *Register* reaffirmed this pattern in 1914. "When too many negroes begin to congregate in this city, then trouble begins to brew and when they get too numerous and the whites will no longer stand for such depredations," it declared, "there has been an aggregation who eliminates this city o[f] all its colored population by a system that they call 'Hot Footing Niggers.'"[40]

As they aggressively expelled blacks from the region, whites always blamed the blacks for *being* expelled. In a tale published in 1903 about Christian County, Missouri, the author addressed the exclusion practiced there but explained that it was the result of blacks' efforts to escape the consequences of their many crimes: "There were not many negroes in Christian County, for the simple reason that they had to stand for about everything that happened in the criminal line, and consequently got considerably thinned out."[41]

Once the white residents of the Missouri Ozarks had established sundown municipalities in the more rural areas of the region and devised an acceptable modus vivendi in the larger cities, they used the threat of

violence or actual violence well into the 1920s to refresh their reputations and discourage the settlement of unwelcome migrants. In 1916, for
example, the *Webb City Register* called for another of the city's periodic
expulsions of those who had "drifted in from Joplin, Oklahoma and cities
and towns to the north and east." It reasoned that "the negro tribe is getting a bit numerous in Webb City" and, with about forty blacks present,
it was time "to break up their business in Webb City. We are just as well
off without them."[42]

Over the course of several decades whites in the Missouri Ozarks created a white man's heaven, a sundown belt from which blacks were largely
excluded. They tolerated some blacks in the larger cities but controlled
them by means of geographic segregation, economic exploitation, and
personal insecurity. The local newspapers periodically reported on their
success. In 1917, for example, the *Cassville Republican* observed that "there
is said not to be a single colored family living in [Barry] county."[43] The
Aurora Advertiser mused about the results of these sundown practices in
1930, concluding that "there are not many negroes in the Ozarks except in
Springfield and Joplin. This is not a new condition but one that has long
prevailed. There are rural communities within a few miles of Springfield
where a negro is a great curiosity to children."[44]

The collected correspondence of Governor Arthur Mastick Hyde demonstrates that whites across southwestern Missouri formed chapters of
the Ku Klux Klan in the early 1920s to drive out blacks or keep them
at bay. In 1922, P. W. Burden of Sarcoxie wrote to the secretary of state's
office to advise officials that representatives were "now engaged in organizing a klan at this place, and scattering litature [*sic*]."[45] In a 1923 Western
Union telegram, members of the Willow Springs Ku Klux Klan proudly
announced their existence to the governor. In a notation at the bottom of
the telegram, a member of the governor's staff wrote that thirteen other
Klan chapters had sent "identical telegrams," including chapters from such
southwestern Missouri towns as Naylor, Springfield, and Marshfield.[46] In
a telegram sent two days later, Klan chapters from Neosho, Granby, and
Diamond likewise promoted their existence.[47]

It is not surprising that these Klan chapters often sprang up in the all-
white towns or counties that comprised most of the region. On January
23, 1924, a woman in Dent County wrote to Governor Hyde to advise
him that there "has been organized in Salem lately, a Ku Klux Klan." She
noted that there were in the county very few of the "outsiders" customarily
targeted by the Klan. "As you know they are against Catholics[,] Jews &
Negroes. There is but one Jew here, no Negroes, and but 6 or 7 families

of Catholics." Nevertheless, by starting an active chapter, the Klan helped ensure that Dent County *remained* all-white. After all, as the writer recognized, nobody wanted "to be terrorized with such an unlawful and wicked thing as the Ku Klux."[48] In a breezy reply, the secretary to the governor told this constituent that "there is no state law prohibiting such an organization, and there is nothing that could be done about it as long as such an organization commits no violations of the law."[49] His response may help explain why so many chapters across the state were eager to go on record with the governor as "decrying mob violence and unconstitutional methods."[50]

Klan chapters also formed in black population centers. In 1921, a resident of Springfield wrote to the governor to advise him of the emergence of a chapter there.[51] He provided a clipping from that day's *Springfield Republican* which explained that the "announcement was made yesterday that an organization of the Ku Klux Klan will be formed in Springfield. The kleagle of the order has been in Springfield several days and is reported to have accepted nearly 50 persons for membership." According to the kleagle, the *Republican* added uncritically, "the Ku Klux Klan is an organization to bring about law enforcement through legal means and to cooperate with officials in time of emergency" but its "membership is by selection, and only native Americans of the white race are eligible."[52]

The federal censuses enumerated between 1900 and 1930 corroborated the anecdotal evidence found in the local newspapers. They also documented the change in the "condition" that supposedly had "long prevailed." Over the course of these thirty years the black population of the Missouri Ozarks decreased from 8,194 to 4,463, falling from an already meager 1.4 percent of the total population to just 0.8 percent. The blacks who remained fled to the large cities from the rural counties. In Joplin and Springfield they concentrated to such an extent that they accounted for 37.1 percent of all blacks in the entire region in 1900 and 56.8 percent in 1930. However, blacks accounted for less than 1 percent of the total population in twenty-one of the thirty counties in the region in 1900 and twenty-four in 1930. Viewed differently, the number of counties with fifteen or fewer blacks—an arbitrary but modest number equal perhaps to only two or three families—increased from twelve to eighteen, and the number with no blacks whatsoever increased from one to nine, almost one-third of the total. If the eleven counties with fewer than fifteen blacks in all four censuses are plotted geographically (see map 3), it is striking because they cluster along the southern border with Arkansas and in the east central part of the region. If the seven counties that claimed fewer than fifteen blacks at some point after 1900 are also plotted on this map, they are almost entirely contiguous with the previous cluster. Clearly, all- or nearly all-white sundown counties were the norm in the region.[53]

The violence and expulsions experienced by blacks in the Missouri Ozarks influenced and, in turn, were influenced by events in contiguous areas of the surrounding states. In one such instance, whites and blacks clashed repeatedly over the course of several days in 1899 on the Kansas-Missouri border. In the most spectacular incident, members of a white mob in Weir City, Kansas, raided the jail, dragged out a prisoner, and lynched him. Armed blacks and whites then took to the streets of Weir and neighboring coal-mining towns in Crawford County such as Yale, threatening to ignite race riots. By nine o'clock on the morning after the lynching, "the streets of Weir City were thronged with an excited crowd of both whites and negroes and a few hasty words would soon have resulted in a bloody battle," reported the *Pittsburg Headlight*.[54] Some of this violence spilled back across the border when a white man, Walter Uer, died in Mindenmines, Missouri, as a result of a shooting by a black man from adjacent Yale.

The *Pittsburg Daily Tribune*, a white paper located just over the state border in Kansas, claimed that the shooting of Uer was "unprovoked, the result of a fool nigger being allowed to carry a gun." According to its account, a black man and woman from Yale pulled up in a wagon in front of Uer's saloon in Mindenmines and the woman asked for the restroom. In response, Uer advised her to relieve herself in the grass. The woman then supposedly revealed herself to be a prostitute by asking Uer "if he was going to spend any money with her. He declined." During the conversation, the *Tribune* added, "the colored man seemed to be getting mad and when Uer told this bold prostitute to go to a vacant lot," drew his gun and fired.[55] The *Pittsburg Plain Dealer*, a black paper, told a more likely story. "The white man had committed an assault up on [sic] a pretty Colored girl [and] when her assailant heard some one approaching he attempted to run but was shot by the colored man."[56]

White men in Yale exacted revenge for the Mindenmines violence. When a black named Isaac Owens walked into a saloon, "some one in the crowd of white people stirred up over the unprovoked shooting of a white boy in Mindenmines by a Yale negro, resented the intrusion of the colored man and a shot was fired in the direction of Owens," wrote the *Pittsburg Daily Tribune*. Suffering from a bullet wound in the arm and finding himself in a hostile environment, Owens produced a knife with which to defend himself. When police officers arrived, they arrested

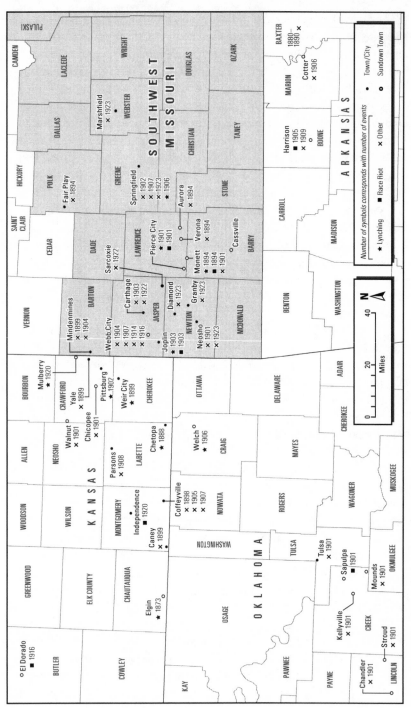

Map 3. Racist Violence in Southwest Missouri and Its Borderlands

Owens for drawing his knife but made no effort to identify his assailant. They soon spirited Owens to nearby Girard to protect him from a potential lynching.[57]

Two years later, the riot in Pierce City provoked antiblack incidents in several Kansas towns. A couple of weeks after that event, whites in Chicopee posted warnings advising all blacks to leave. When the members of one family resisted the order, whites whipped them, tarred and feathered them, and expelled them.[58] The *Walnut Advance* declared that Walnut would from that moment forth enforce sundown practices, noting,

> Public sentiment at Pierce City, Mo., is at fever heat. . . . The citizens organized themselves into posses and searched the town and country for the brute. Violent mobs were also organized and as a result three negros [*sic*] were lynched, a few killed in their houses and the remainder of the negro population was driven out of town. They have decided never to allow another negro to live in Pierce City, which has been the decision of many another town, and Walnut is one of them.[59]

In some instances black refugees fleeing expulsions in Missouri sought sanctuary in Kansas. Following the lynching in Joplin some fled to Galena, Kansas, which "took on 'somewhat of an emancipation day appearance'"; others "'went far west' in the direction of Columbus and Baxter Springs," writes Harper.[60] Within days of the Pierce City lynchings and riot, whites in Pittsburg learned that some of the refugees were headed in their direction. Based on intelligence from an unnamed railroad man, the *Pittsburg Daily Headlight* reported that a number of the "vicious class of negroes" from Pierce City were in the Pittsburg area and were planning to settle there. In a later dispatch it confirmed that some of the Missouri refugees had relocated to that city and that among them were the Godleys, one of the oft-targeted families discussed in chapter 4.[61]

Predictably, whites in Pittsburg kept the newcomers under surveillance. After closely monitoring the Godley family for more than a year, the white residents acted on Christmas Eve and Christmas Day 1902. They lynched Mumpford, jailed Jess, beat Gus, and shot Joe, who fled the state seriously wounded. Thereafter, they harassed the family repeatedly, making their lives more difficult than they already were, as detailed in chapter 4.

Immediately after the Pierce City event, whites in Oklahoma used it to justify their own antiblack movements. In Stroud whites formed mobs for "the purpose of ridding the town of its colored population. The mob visited the various tents and houses occupied by the negroes and drove the twenty terror stricken blacks from the town," according to a local

newspaper. It justified these actions as "the outgrowth of considerable
recent insolence on the part of certain negroes toward the whites, and a
heavy immigration of negroes within the past few days, believed to come
from Peirce City."[62] In Sapulpa rioters expelled the black population within
a few days of the incident in Missouri. The *Muskogee Daily Phoenix* also
linked that incident to the one in Missouri, writing that "this movement
is the direct outcome of the lynching of Will Godley at Pierce City, Mo.,
last Tuesday night."[63] In all likelihood, the whites in the growing towns
of Stroud and Sapulpa were eager to exclude blacks at a moment of rapid
growth and prosperity resulting from new railroad connections and repair
shops, and they saw in the Pierce City incident an opportunity to advance
that objective.

As they had in the Missouri Ozarks, the expulsions in Oklahoma drove
blacks into larger or growing cities where their numbers improved their
chances for protection and employment; they also precipitated further
unrest in these urban centers. Reporting from Tulsa, a correspondent told
the *Muskogee Daily Phoenix* that "the negro question is getting to be a
serious one at this place, and attention is being directed to it by the recent
outrage at Pierce City, Mo. Negroes are being driven out of Sapulpa and
other towns, and many of them are coming to Tulsa." In order to promote
growth, the residents of Tulsa had "voted for a wide-open town at the
last city election, and the result has been the accumulation of a large and
worthless negro population. Some of them were active agencies in carrying the election, and it has made them feel their importance, and much
insolence on the part of some of them has been the result."[64] As suggested
by this news report, whites in Tulsa interpreted the participation of blacks
in the recent election as an act of gross impertinence.

In northern Arkansas, an area dominated topographically by a south-
ward extension of the Missouri Ozarks, whites maintained practices
indistinguishable from those used across the border. In fact, in a report
titled "Negroes Driven from Southwest Missouri Towns," the *St. Louis
Post-Dispatch* regarded towns over the state border as a logical and seam-
less extension of southwestern Missouri. South of Cassville, it wrote, "is
Rogers, just over the state line, in Arkansas." Rogers, too, "has no negroes
and will permit none to live within its limits."[65] Writing about the Ozarks
in 1914, the *Arkansas Gazette* noted that "there are counties in Arkansas
where there are so few negroes that a negro attracts attention."[66] When it
addressed the issue eight years later, the *Gazette* focused on a small black
colony in Bentonville, calling its residents "the only negroes in Benton
county."[67]

When they deemed it necessary, white Arkansans had enforced sundown practices well before the end of the century and continued to do so thereafter. According to the historian Guy Lancaster, those in Baxter County, sixty miles southwest of West Plains, Missouri, had driven out the black population during the 1880s.[68] In Harrison and across Boone County, whites expelled blacks in 1905, prompting an observer to speculate that "a movement has begun [there] which it is believed will result in the driving out of most of the negroes."[69] They drove out the remaining blacks in 1909. "If all the negroes in Boone County should join in the reputed exodus, their absence would scarcely be noticed," joked the *Arkansas Democrat*. "An exodus of white men from Liberia would make a greater hole in the population."[70] In 1906 whites in Cotter expelled some blacks. "Negroes have never been welcome in Cotter, and a few weeks ago a gang of seven were run out," declared the *Arkansas Gazette*. "Since that time, no new negroes have been allowed to live here, and in [the] future none will be allowed to live in Cotter."[71]

Within Missouri and between and among its sister states, whites encouraged one another to create or maintain sundown practices and assisted one another in enforcing them. Those from neighboring towns converged on Pierce City to assist during the conflict there, for example. "Monett came down to Peirce City, represented by several hundred of her male citizens, in extra coaches attached to the Monday evening train," noted the *St. Louis Post-Dispatch*. "Monett and Peirce City and the farming community joined hands. During Monday armed men came in from other points, swelling the mob to nearly a thousand men."[72] In his account of the Pierce City episode, Jaspin concluded that "if there was any doubt about what would happen, the arrival of the Monett contingent dispelled it."[73]

On several other occasions newspapers suggested that whites from one place or another were working together to terrorize blacks and create new sundown towns. Although the authorities denied it, the *Post-Dispatch* reported a rumor that, as blacks took shelter in Springfield after the Pierce City riot, whites from the scene of the lynching and riot were preparing to pursue them. According to the story, "a train load of men from Peirce City and Monett was bound to Springfield, to drive the Peirce City refugees away."[74] After the Joplin lynching, the *Evening Star* informed readers that "'Negro Chasers' from Pierce City are coming this evening to assist in the extermination of the negro."[75] Similarly, the *Sedalia Evening Democrat* stated that "several hundred strangers are in the city, and the report is circulated that many of them are from Peirce City, where a race war occurred over a year ago, and where negroes are not allowed to reside."[76]

With ongoing riots in Stroud and Sapulpa, Oklahoma newspapers reported that whites in nearby towns, eager to banish blacks, were providing assistance. A reporter from Sapulpa indicated that "cowboys from Kellyville, and horsemen from Mounds, will arrive this afternoon to take part in driving out the blacks."[77] In Stroud whites posted a sign declaring: "Nigger, don't let the sun go down on U."[78] Furthermore, the *Guthrie Daily Leader* related that the residents of both "Stroud and Chandler . . . have also taken up the fight on negroes and citizens at Tulsa have warned [them] not to stop off there."[79]

As these accounts demonstrate, the *same whites* often expelled blacks from multiple towns and cities; in some cases they targeted precisely the *same blacks*, people who had already fled a succession of towns. The Godley family, of course, suffered mightily on both sides of the Kansas-Missouri border. The blacks who fled Springfield after the lynching there included those who had lived through previous expulsions. "An unknown number of men, women, and children headed for the train depot and bought tickets to Joplin, Carthage, Kansas City, and St. Louis," writes Harper. "It is probable that among those that left Springfield were survivors of the race riots in Monett and Pierce City."[80] Viewed in this way, the expulsions may be understood not as individual events but as a series of skirmishes in an asymmetrical race war designed to establish the so-called white man's heaven.

Periodically, whites in sundown towns on one side of a state line killed blacks from the other, spreading terror across the border area. In 1906 whites in Welch, Oklahoma, purportedly killed three youths who passed through from nearby Chetopa, Kansas. According to investigators, they attacked the visitors and accidentally killed one or more of them. In order to conceal their crime, they killed the other (or others) and placed their bodies on the railroad track, where they were mutilated by a passing train. "Many of the negroes think the boys had a mixup with young white boys at Welch, as no negroes are allowed there, and that in the melee they were killed and their bodies afterward removed to the place where they were run over."[81] Regardless of the uncertainty surrounding the particulars of the incident, the white perpetrators succeeded in reinforcing the reputation of their town for intolerance and spreading fear among blacks in both states.

As a consequence of their success in establishing control over black residents, the white residents of the Missouri Ozarks enjoyed largely unchallenged dominance through World War II. Those in Monett, for example, were so proud of their whiteness that "until the 1930s the letterhead on the town's official stationery bragged that Monett had '6,000 good citizens—all white.'"[82] After World War II, however, whites encountered rapid and, for them, bewildering shifts in racial policy as national leaders moved to wipe away the Jim Crow system that during the Cold War undermined America's international leadership role, its claim to represent freedom and democracy, and its capacity to attract allies in Asia, Africa, and Latin America. As a consequence, they complied very reluctantly. After the Supreme Court vote in *Brown v. Board of Education, Topeka*, for example, the local school board in Neosho buckled to the demand and integrated the city high school in 1954. When the *Neosho Daily News* reported the change in policy, it reflected the continuing whiteness of the region when it noted that "six Negroes, four boys and two girls, are now enrolled at Neosho high school."[83] Whites elsewhere were generally reluctant to end the racist practices that they had enforced for decades. In an article titled the "Plight of the Negro" in Missouri in 1963, the *St. Louis Post-Dispatch* underscored the continuation of sundown practices. Citing a report by the Missouri Commission on Human Rights, it painted a bleak portrait of places outside areas of the state with larger black populations including St. Louis and Kansas City. "'In a number of counties, a Negro can be served food in the kitchen, a back room or in a screened-off area. Negroes traveling through Missouri, are at a great disadvantage in obtaining eating accommodations or overnight lodging.... A Negro can actually travel the width and breadth of the state and not [find] one cafe, restaurant, hotel, motel or resort that will accommodate him.'" Although the *Post-Dispatch* focused on the whole state, it did cite a revelatory example of the prejudice found in the Ozarks: "A Greene county (Springfield) motel owner told the commission: 'We have been tempted to take Negroes. Usually those who travel are of a very high type—if only they would stay in their rooms!'"[84]

In recent decades scholars have told and retold the story of the lynchings and expulsions that occurred in the Missouri Ozarks. The historians Michael J. Pfeifer, Dominic Capeci Jr., and Kimberly Harper, the sociologist James W. Loewen, and the journalist Elliot Jaspin have all grappled with either the Pierce City events specifically or with the series of events in Monett, Pierce City, Joplin, and Springfield.[85] Loewen provided a précis of these events that constitutes a blueprint of sorts for the other studies: "A series of at least six race riots in the Ozarks, along with smaller undocumented expulsions, led to the almost total whiteness of most Ozark counties," he wrote. "In 1894, Monett, Missouri, started the chain of racial violence.... After the lynching [there], whites forced all African Americans to leave Monett. Pierce City, just six miles west, followed suit in 1901." After the lynching in Pierce City, "the mob then turned on the black community." Some blacks "fled to Joplin, the nearest city, but in 1903 whites rioted there." In 1906 whites in Springfield "staged a triple lynching they called an 'Easter Offering.'"[86]

Some investigators have expanded the story of the Missouri Ozarks by including a handful of the Arkansas border towns—particularly in Harrison and surrounding Boone County, which experienced violence and expulsion in 1905 and 1909. Loewen and Harper tied their analyses of Monett, Pierce City, Joplin, and Springfield to those of towns across the border. Loewen indicated that in 1905 "whites in Harrison, Arkansas, expelled most of their African Americans, and in 1909, they finished the job."[87] At the end of her Missouri-focused study Harper devoted a chapter to Boone County.[88] Jaspin linked the Pierce City event to the riot and racial cleansing that took place in Stroud, Oklahoma, a few days later.[89] More recently, the historian Guy Lancaster dealt holistically with the history and formation of sundown towns in Arkansas, including those in the Ozarks.[90]

This chapter expands the story of the creation and maintenance of the white man's heaven in three significant and interrelated ways. First, it expands the standard notion of antiblack violence—defined implicitly but narrowly as lynchings and race riots in most works—to include a broader range of attacks including whippings, killings by police, and threatened lynchings. In so doing, it enables the identification and analysis of a larger sample of incidents than would result from the examination of only two types of violence. Without these incidents this study would not have been able to chronicle the pervasive racism that governed Webb City and expressed itself in multiple violent expulsions. In detailing the major incidents, Loewen rightly noted that a series of lynchings and race riots "in the Ozarks, along with smaller undocumented expulsions, led to the almost total whiteness of most Ozark counties, which continues to this day."[91] With its expanded definition of antiblack violence, this study identifies some of those smaller expulsions.

Second, this work expands the temporal framework for this well-known story, focusing not only on the period from 1894 to 1909—the years when whites relied on the most sensational and well-known lynchings and riots to create their sundown towns—but also on the period from 1910 to 1930—the years when they utilized these and other practices to preserve those towns. In addition, it summarizes the legacy of these sundown towns for decades to come. In this context, it also suggests that historians interested in antiblack violence in the Missouri Ozarks might profitably turn to the years prior to 1894. The anecdotal evidence suggests that whites routinely resorted to mob violence to keep blacks under control, initially as slaves and then as nominally free citizens. In 1854, for example, whites converged on Carthage to burn two blacks. A century later the *Joplin Globe* republished a contemporary account. "The whole community was wrought up to a state of the most intense excitement and the expiation of their crimes by their fearful death at the stake was witnessed by thousands," it recounted. "The people from adjoining counties had come . . . a distance of 50 miles to witness the sight."[92] In addition, the residents of Springfield lynched blacks in 1859 and 1871. In the first incident, members of a mob seized Mart Danforth, an enslaved man, and hanged him for the alleged rape of a white woman. In the second "another negro, Bud Isbell, was hanged by a mob, almost on the same spot, and for the same [alleged] crime. In neither of these cases were any arrests or indictments had for any of the mob."[93] Surely other acts of racist inhumanity litter the history of the Missouri Ozarks, awaiting investigation.

Third, this study expands significantly the geographical area involved in the study of racist violence in the Missouri Ozarks. Within Missouri it encompasses not only the extreme southwest corner of the state, which has been the focus of previous studies, but the south central part as well. In so doing, it demonstrates that whites in Newburg, West Plains, Rolla, and Reynolds County were as aggressive as those in Monett, Pierce City, Joplin, and Springfield in imposing and enforcing sundown practices, if their selection in some instances of less sensational violence earned them less attention from the press. As a consequence, this chapter demonstrates that the southeastern part of the Missouri Ozarks was *more* fully white than the southwestern part. The study also expands the geographical area by placing the events in the Missouri Ozarks in dialogue with similar—often related—outbreaks of violence and expulsion in the adjoining areas of Kansas, Oklahoma, and Arkansas.

By expanding the analysis across state lines, this study provides new insights into the historiography, demonstrating that the customary acceptance of state lines or the arbitrary imposition of other constraints for academic purposes can impede the ability to reckon with the *lived experiences* of those located contemporaneously on both sides of these political boundaries. In my study of antiblack violence in Kansas, for example, I found that whites in southeast Kansas drove blacks out of smaller places that were often sundown towns, such as Caney, Elgin, and Mulberry, and into larger cities, such as Chetopa, Coffeyville, El Dorado, Independence, and Parsons, where whites used violent methods to control swelling black populations. Although I investigated these acts *within* Kansas, I did not account for those in neighboring towns across state lines that played equally important roles in shaping *local* experiences. I included an 1888 double lynching in Chetopa, for instance, but did not include the 1906 lynching of several blacks *from* Chetopa in sundown Welch, Oklahoma, ten miles away, simply because it occurred outside of my defined study area.

A hundred and fifty miles north of Joplin, the *Kansas City Star* posed several interesting questions after a Kansas City policeman gunned down a resident in 1907. "In which state was Harrison Anderson, a negro, killed? Missouri or Kansas?" The *Star* also wondered: "Who's to Hold the Inquest?" In asking these questions, the *Star* was trying to address an issue of legal jurisdiction because the "shooting occurred in Missouri, but the negro fell dead in Kansas." A coroner's jury in Missouri "decided it had no jurisdiction—that the negro's body belongs to Kansas." Officials across the border, it said, had to hold the inquest.[94] These questions intersect directly with the scholarly questions posed in this study concerning the problem of state lines and antiblack violence. The answer, as blacks in the Missouri Ozarks and beyond could have attested, was that the legal jurisdiction where the killing took place was irrelevant to their experience; no matter where he was shot or fell dead, Anderson's death at the hands of an officer terrorized Kansas City blacks on both sides of border.

In a well-known 1901 essay "The United States of Lyncherdom," Mark Twain penned his response to one of the series of horrors that gripped his home state of Missouri at the turn of the century. "The tragedy occurred near Pierce City, down in the southwestern corner of the state," he wrote. "Although it was a region of churches and schools the people rose, lynched three negroes," torched "five negro households, and drove thirty negro families into the woods." Awash in a culture that increasingly believed that antiblack lynching was a recent phenomenon, one that in the main had emerged in the 1880s and 1890s and increased fearfully since, Twain wrote of the event as if it were a new phase in race relations rather than merely another event in a long history of racist violence. He also wrote of lynching as something that was essentially rooted in the South but which only began reaching its tentacles north into the Midwest at the turn of the century, amid the so-called nadir of race relations: "Lynching has reached Colorado, it has reached California, it has reached Indiana—and now Missouri!"[95]

"And so Missouri has fallen, that great state! Certain of her children have joined the lynchers, and the smirch is upon the rest of us," Twain mourned. Had the author been more familiar with the history of Missouri, he might have been more circumspect in denouncing the injustice of character assassination that he saw being perpetrated against white Missourians by a national media that painted with a broad brush, unfairly portraying the murderous lynch mob as representative of the entire white population. Instead, he believed, the press ignored the overwhelming majority of white Missourians, the fine, law-abiding people who denounced mob violence. The "handful" of whites who led the assault on blacks in Pierce City had "labeled [Missourians] with a name" as lynchers, he wrote,

> and to the dwellers in the four quarters of the earth we are "lynchers," now, and ever shall be. For the world will not stop and think—it never does, it is not its way, its way is to generalize from a single sample. It will not say, "Those Missourians have been busy eighty years in building an honorable good name for themselves; these hundred lynchers down in the corner of the state are not real Missourians, they are renegades." No, that truth will not enter its mind; it will generalize from the one or two misleading samples and say, "The Missourians are lynchers". . . . It would say, "There are a hundred lynchers there, therefore the Missourians are lynchers"; the considerable fact that there are two and a half million Missourians who are *not* lynchers would not affect their verdict.[96]

This chapter demonstrates the fallacy in Twain's claims. With lynchings in Carthage and Springfield in the antebellum period, with a lynching in Springfield during Reconstruction, and with the lynchings, whippings, and expulsions in towns like Monett and Fair Play in the 1890s, whites in southwestern Missouri (and elsewhere in the state) had been committing atrocities against blacks for decades. In the context of these findings, it is clear that the Pierce City event in 1901 was not, as Twain believed, a moment when Missouri had fallen. In addition, with whippings, lynchings, riots, killings by police officers, expulsions, and other acts of racist malice, many thousands of whites in the Missouri Ozarks participated in these acts of racist violence over the course of decades, not simply a "hundred lynchers." Whites who did not actively participate in this violence endorsed it, refused to investigate it or punish the perpetrators, and maintained the white supremacist ideologies and practices in whose service the violence was perpetrated.

7 The Old Northwest, 1890s–1930s

*"If we do our duty no mob can ever
get into this jail"*

In 1903 thousands of whites in Danville, Illinois, demanded that the mayor, John Beard, surrender to them John D. Metcalf, a black prisoner accused of murder. Intimidated, he did so immediately. The whites dragged Metcalf through the streets, hanged and shot him, and then threw him—possibly still alive—onto a makeshift pyre that they set ablaze. The mayor justified his timid response by claiming that he was powerless in the face of a mob determined to wreak fury, a claim that did not pass muster with some. "'If [the mayor] had been . . . brave in opposing the mob at the city building . . . the lynching would have been averted," charged a local clergyman. "The fact is the mayor did not do his duty."[1]

"Not satisfied with their fiendish work," reported the *Decatur Herald*, Danville whites clamored for John Wilson, another black prisoner. "It required nothing more than a suggestion to incite the attack on the jail."[2] As the mob encircled the lockup, however, Sheriff Hardy Whitlock refused to repeat the mayor's act of deference. Instead, he vowed to repel the mob at all costs. "If we do our duty no mob can ever get into this jail, and we are here to do our duty," he told his deputies. Because of his resolute stand, the sheriff ensured that Wilson remained physically—though surely not psychologically—unscathed. "There was only one way to get into that jail, [and] that was to dynamite the building from the outside," an admirer of Whitlock marveled. "There was a report that this was to be done, that men had gone after dynamite. That did not frighten the sheriff; he said the mob was too cowardly to do anything of that kind."[3]

This chapter investigates the development of official white resistance to mob violence against blacks in the Old Northwest—Illinois, Indiana, and

Ohio—from the 1890s to the 1930s. First, it details the methods deployed by local authorities to protect prisoners threatened with mob violence and the conditions required to trigger their appeal to state authorities for support. It then explores the responses of "ordinary" whites to these efforts. Next, it traces the transition made by the authorities—and specifically the police—as they offset their success in mitigating mob violence by appropriating mob tactics to control blacks themselves. Finally, it assesses the implications of its findings for the scholarship. Before proceeding, however, the chapter provides a brief overview of the sometimes very thin line between police officers and lynch mobs in the Old Northwest during the study period.

In the quarter of a century after the Civil War, the authorities took proactive steps on occasion to protect blacks from white mobs in the region. All too often, however, they concluded that the defense of black lives—to say nothing of the law—was not worth their loss of standing in the community. Instead, they handed victims over to mobs or stepped aside as they invaded jails. Officials in Coshocton, Ohio, for example, made no effort to stay the mob that seized Henry Howard from his cell in 1885. Marching in columns to the jail, reported the *Coshocton Age*, the vigilantes surged unopposed into the building, secured Howard, and, "half dragging and half pushing, rushed with him to the Court yard square, where a rope was placed about his neck, and in a few seconds he was dangling from the limb of an elm, where he was left suspended until near ten o'clock of the next day."[4]

In other cases, officers took active roles in the lynchings. In 1882 they did so during their search for Bill Allen, a black man accused of killing an officer in Chicago. The lawmen set out in pursuit with "the understanding that he must be taken dead or alive, dead preferred."[5] In order to capture him, they threw a dragnet around the black community. "Trains were searched at the depots, and even after they had been started on their journey," reported the *Daily Inter Ocean*. "Colored houses of ill-repute and resorts of all kinds were frequently visited by officers. Allen's known friends and acquaintances were shadowed night and day."[6] In addition to about 150 officers, thousands of Chicagoans, many carrying their own weapons, participated in the hunt for the accused, it explained. "Others procured ropes to hang him, if he should happen to be taken alive."[7] Eventually, some of them discovered that he had hidden in a mill. As they surrounded him, Allen attempted to surrender. "He had a revolver in his hand, but before he could use it Officer Beck fired and he dropped [it,] crying, 'I give up.'" Unfortunately, the newspaper concluded, the officer's "first shot was a signal for a regular fusillade, [and] everybody having a pistol" opened fire.[8] A correspondent for the *Bloomington Daily Pantagraph* corroborated that account, writing that Allen "threw up his hands, and offered to surrender; but the police . . . refused to listen to his pleas, and he fell, completely riddled with bullets."[9] Although Allen died before the officers could convey his body to the patrol wagon, whites on the scene, believing that he was merely wounded, clamored to lynch him.

When the patrol wagon approached the station bearing Allen's corpse, it "was surrounded by a struggling mass of humanity, perfectly wild with rage," reported the *Chicago Daily Tribune*. "The body of the negro lay in the bottom of the wagon. The crowd pressed eagerly forward, shouting, 'Lynch him,' 'String him up,' 'Bring a rope.' The rope was soon ready, and the crowd made a determined rush for the wagon." After the officers passed the body through a window into the building, the mob threatened to invade it. Because a major riot looked inevitable, the police chief mounted the wagon and assured his listeners that Allen was dead. The members of the mob grew more and more disorderly nonetheless. "To quiet them down, Chief Doyle had the naked body laid on a mattress, supported by ladders, and placed in front of a grated window, from which it could be seen from the alley," the *Tribune* related. Those outside let loose "a shout of triumph," it observed, "and then a strange scene was enacted." Whites formed a queue, then filed by the corpse and gawked. "All afternoon that line moved steadily along, and the officers were busily occupied in keeping it in order. The crowd increased rather than diminished." Into the wee hours, "the crowd was just as large and just as eager, and the remains of the late Bill Allen, deceased, continued to furnish a show for thousands."[10] The dry goods box in which Allen was hiding when surrounded and shot, reported the *Daily Inter Ocean*, was "sold to some speculative young men, who [broke] it into pieces and [were] selling bits as souvenirs of the hunt."[11]

Most commonly, white authorities simply failed to act, lacking the nerve to stand up against mobs made up of friends, neighbors, or constituents. In his classic 1908 study *Following the Color Line*, Ray Stannard Baker demonstrated this phenomenon in his analysis of a 1904 lynching in Springfield, Ohio. "No official in direct authority in Springfield that evening, apparently, had so much as an ounce of grit," he observed. "The sheriff came out and made a weak speech in which he said he '[didn't] want to hurt anybody.' They threw stones at him and broke his windows." The chief of police then dispatched some men to the scene but did not go himself. "All of these policemen undoubtedly sympathised with the mob," he wrote; "at least, they did nothing effective to prevent the lynching." Abdicating his responsibility, the mayor refused to send out the fire companies to douse the mob with water because he feared that the mob members might cut the hoses. "The local militia company was called to its barracks, but the officer in charge hesitated, vacillated, doubted his authority, and objected finally because he had no ammunition *except* Krag-Jorgenson cartridges, which, if fired into a mob, would kill too many people!"[12]

As the incidents in Coshocton, Chicago, and Springfield demonstrate, those responsible for enforcement of the law were often indistinguishable from those who broke it. Beginning in the 1880s, however, police officers became increasingly professionalized and committed to the defense of law and order as a measure of their manhood and honor. As a consequence, they began, unevenly but certainly, to confront mobs, though they had the same negative attitudes toward blacks as did whites generally. In many instances of sensational crimes attributed to blacks from the 1890s to the 1930s, the authorities minimized the possibility of mob violence by transferring the accused from local jails to safer, more distant ones. In 1903 they did so in Hillsboro, Ohio, when a mob raided the lockup but found nothing more than an empty cell. "The negro could not be found, as he had been taken away a short time before [by the] Sheriff," reported the *Piqua Daily Call*.[13]

In some instances officers did not have the time required to undertake an orderly transfer, especially when they confronted mobs that formed quickly and moved rapidly. In those situations they muddled through. In 1906 officers and a prisoner in Franklin, Ohio, had a harrowing escape. As a mob smashed into the jail, the sheriff and two deputies took the inmate "out the front way, placed him in an automobile and made a speedy run for Lebanon, the county seat," noted a report. "The departing automobile was fired at."[14] In 1924 the sheriff in Pulaski County, Illinois, had a similar experience. "Pursued by roaring automobiles filled with angry citizens, many of them reported to be klansmen [*sic*], intent on taking the law into their own hands, Sheriff Hudson today started on a spectacular run in his automobile to Metropolis, Ill., with [several] negroes," reported the *Daily Independent*. "More than 400 automobiles were declared to be in the pursuit."[15]

In circumstances when they could neither transfer prisoners nor risk an attempt without a confrontation with a mob, the authorities occasionally faced down mobs with calming or threatening words backed with a display of arms. The sheriff in Danville did that in 1903, despite the heckling and abuse of the townspeople. "The performance of Sheriff Whitlock was full of merit," noted the *Daily Review*. "He is a cool man and one of nerve. For almost five hours he held that mob at bay and twice he drove it away after it had partly beaten in two doors of the jail. Almost all of this time he was on the outside of the jail, in plain view of the mob. Twice he was struck by a stone, and yet he did not lose his temper for a moment." Although he had to retreat periodically when the mob charged the doors, he resumed his argument when tempers cooled. "As soon as he had beaten the mob each time he immediately went out in front and talked to the excited men. Twice he got them to take the railroad iron away."[16] In addition, Whitlock accepted the assistance of a minister who mixed admonition with spiritual counsel as he "spent ten minutes beside the sheriff on the jail steps imploring the rioters to disperse. He was hit several times with stones and narrowly escaped a bullet."[17]

In the days-long incident in Pulaski County in 1924, Sheriff I. J. Hudson deputized an ardent white supremacist who possessed the influence to quell the mob, at least temporarily. As the officer surely hoped, "H. F. Moreland, a Ku Klux Klan organizer . . . pleaded with the crowd and offered a brief prayer," buying the sheriff enough time to escape with his prisoners but failing to dissuade his listeners of their intentions altogether, as the four hundred automobiles in hot pursuit of the officer made clear. "With the crowd temporarily quieted, the . . . negroes were brought here followed by many of the persons that had at first threatened violence. Fearing a new outburst of mob spirit, the sheriff deputized sixteen men and placed them on guard at the jail [in Mound City]."[18]

After a victim fell into the clutches of a mob, the authorities could intervene, sometimes by calming tempers sufficiently and, when they could not, by placing themselves at personal risk. In 1903 officers intervened in Chicago when whites pummeled a black man. Into the fray raced four officers who wrested the victim from his attackers and pulled him into their wagon under a shower of bricks. "During recent years there have been many inconsequential cases of 'threatened lynchings' in Chicago," reported the *Tribune*, "but this is the first case where a crime stirred such indignation and race hatred that the police were barely able to save the prisoner from death at the mob's hands."[19] Four years later, a mob in Terre Haute, Indiana, seized a man and dragged him toward the spot of a lynching that had occurred six years earlier. Instead of allowing a repeat of that incident, an official intercepted the crowd "and started to reason with the angered men." He notified the police, who dispatched an officer, who "arrived before the crowd had decided what to do," reported the *Indianapolis Star*. "Superintendent Jones and several patrolmen arrived in the wagon a few minutes later" and whisked the man away. "It was only by rapid work that violence was averted."[20]

On less laudable occasions the authorities claimed prisoners from the clutches of mobs because of the efforts of the would-be victim rather than their own. In 1902, for instance, a mob took one Ardee Wilson from the jail in Sparta, Illinois, and prepared to hang him. When Wilson threw off the noose and ran, the mob unloaded a volley of shots that struck but did not fell him. The sheriff and a posse then hunted him, neutralized him with another round of buckshot, and took him, more dead than alive, to a different jail. Although Wilson was in critical condition, the officers thereafter protected him from mob violence, and he evidently survived.[21]

In other instances the authorities neutralized mobs because of their well-founded fears that, if they did not, armed blacks would do so, with potentially volatile consequences: "Mounted on fast horses and having in their midst a manacled, frightened negro, for whose life a mob was clamoring, officers from Mounds reached Mound City late the other night, thus preventing a lynching and probably a bloody battle between the blacks and whites," reported the *Cook County Herald* after an episode in Illinois in 1906. As the whites began to gather in Mounds, "two hundred negroes seized whatever arms they could lay their hands on and assembled to prevent the lynching, and it looked as if a battle could not be avoided. The officers, however, averted the clash by removing the prisoner to Mound City."[22] Once they learned that the blacks were ready to meet them, whites customarily lost interest in mob violence. The *Alton Evening Telegraph* hinted at this when it stated, "There is some talk in Mounds of going to Mound City and lynching the negro, but it is not believed this will be done."[23]

In 1924 local blacks in Alexander County, Illinois, threatened whites who had attempted to oust newly arrived southern laborers. "One hundreds [*sic*] shots were exchanged in a battle last night between whites and imported negro cotton workers from the south," reported the *Daily Independent*. "Northern negroes . . . have been enraged by the attack on their newly arrived brethren from the south, and . . . have threatened to retaliate in kind against the whites," it explained. "Cairo negroes have expressed sympathy for the 'pickers' from Dixie and are said to be arming and defying any clique or clan of whites to further harass the new arrivals." The newspaper recognized the gravity of the situation, which soon took "on all the aspects of a real race riot, with local peace officers doing their uttermost to quell the trouble."[24]

Where the local authorities questioned their capacity to maintain order when confronted by mobs clamoring for jailed suspects or by armed blacks preparing for a showdown with such mobs, they took more aggressive action. On one such occasion in 1931, officials in Bucyrus, Ohio, made patently unjust efforts to ensure that blacks could not confront the mob that had collected for days at the jail. "Homes of 750 Negroes were searched for firearms tonight after trouble was feared in the threatened violence to two Negroes held in the county jail at Bucyrus, a few miles away," reported the *Cincinnati Enquirer* after the raid in Crestline, a small town near Bucyrus and the hometown of the prisoners. "The search was ordered by Mayor Leonard F. Waldboudar and resulted in the finding of a number of firearms, officers said." By disarming blacks but not whites, the authorities ensured that the minority would be less likely to engage the mob in an armed confrontation at the jail and less able to defend against an armed invasion of their quarters by the mob.[25]

More often, local officials requested that the governor muster the state militia and keep it in readiness near the scene of the disorder or dispatch it to the spot. In 1906 a local sheriff in Indiana telephoned the governor to express his concern about the possibility of mob violence and request his assistance in that eventuality. In response, "Adjutant-Gen. Oran Perry went to Bloomfield, last night, at the direction of Governor Hanly, to investigate the report that there was danger of mob violence at the trial of Robert Williams," who was accused of killing a white railroad worker. Should the troops become necessary, explained the *Indianapolis News*, "Company B. of Terre Haute, will be sent, as it is the nearest company to Bloomfield."[26]

In 1910 a sheriff in Vienna, Illinois, opted for a more urgent response. One Sheriff Mathis took action after mobs from Eldorado and Harrisburg threatened to invade his jail in search of three blacks. "The mob had cut the telephone wires between [Vienna] and Eldorado and Harrisburg, but Sheriff Mathis got his appeal to the Governor for aid away before the wires went down," noted the *Inter Ocean*. In response, Governor Charles Deneen sent four companies. Underscoring his commitment to prevent mob violence—a commitment elevated by the hanging and burning in Cairo a few weeks earlier that had brought the state terrible notoriety—the governor coordinated additional measures. First, he stopped all freight trains from entering Vienna, dashing the plans of whites who planned to reach the lynching in that way. Second, he advised Mathis to swear in as many men as needed to ensure order until the troops arrived. Accordingly, the sheriff garnered "300 deputies, or nearly every available man in the village."[27]

By their presence alone, soldiers often dampened the resolve of mob members. Furthermore, as outsiders, they usually did not know, and were unknown to, local residents, thereby eroding one of the central concerns that caused local policemen to waffle when confronted by mobs. Quite simply, soldiers did not have the same personal ties to mob members as did local officers, did not have to live with them later, and did not rely on their support for their livelihood. When the soldiers arrived in Danville in 1903, they brought the unrest to an end, despite resentful grumblings. "With the city patrolled by the militia quiet has been restored," reported the *Chicago Daily Tribune*. "Bayonets are in evidence on all sides, and it is hoped that further rioting can be prevented." Although some whites vowed to continue their racist campaign, they faced overwhelming odds because the soldiers were armed and prepared to resist them. In this situation the vigilantes chose to express their disdain in subtler ways. "Much feeling has been shown against the soldiers, and difficulty was experienced today in procuring food for them."[28]

Despite their overwhelming firepower, the commanding officers of activated militia units preferred to exhaust nonviolent options before considering violent ones—surely a calculation that reflected the political concerns and reelection hopes of the governors who dispatched them. In 1915 Illinois guardsmen coordinated with the local authorities to avert violence: "A mob of several hundred who surrounded the Harrisburg, Ill., jail, intent on lynching Joe Deberry, a negro . . . was outwitted by a sheriff's party last night," explained the *Tribune*. "Deberry was smuggled out of the Harrisburg jail and under the protection of three companies of Illinois state militia was brought here and placed in the local jail at 1 o'clock this morning." In a bait and switch the local officers created a diversion for the militia. "While the crowd was in front of the Harrisburg jail the doors were thrown open suddenly and an automobile filled with deputy sheriffs dashed out," continued the *Tribune*. "The crowd rushed for this machine, believing that Deberry was in it. Almost at the same moment the negro prisoner was taken out of the jail from the rear and between three companies of soldiers was hurried to the train."[29]

The militia, however, could not necessarily guarantee the safety of blacks. After the sheriff of Logan County, Ohio, hastened to Rushsylvania to secure a prisoner, he confronted a mob that refused to surrender him. He tried to deputize some citizens and compel their assistance in resolving the matter. When that effort yielded no success, he requested the militia from Bellefontaine. "When the militia arrived at Rushsylvania they were met by a large body of citizens who declared that the prisoner must not be removed," noted a reporter. "Sheriff Sullivan, who was in command of the soldiers, was informed that there were six dynamite cartridges under the calaboose" and that they would be detonated if an effort was made to remove the prisoner.[30] Under the pressure of the moment, Sullivan capitulated, dispersed the militia, and granted custody of the prisoner to local citizens. Within an hour the mob seized the prisoner and hanged him. The sheriff, an editor lamented, "virtually allowed the mob to work its will rather than bring on a conflict between the angry citizens and the military and posse he had summoned."[31]

When mobs refused to disperse, the authorities occasionally resorted to force. The stalwart but patient sheriff who repeatedly appealed to reason ultimately turned to a method guaranteed to gain the attention of the mob members attacking his jail in Danville. After they resumed the battering of the door with a railroad tie, Sheriff Whitlock warned them to desist. They ignored him. "The door was bent in the lower part, where the rail was striking it," noted the *Daily Review*. "Through the small opening the sheriff fired a couple of shots to scare the men away, not aiming to hit any one. They would not quit." Finally, the sheriff lost patience and grabbed his shotgun. "In this were shells that were loaded with No. 4, 5 and 6 shot. He pointed the gun down the rail, where the men's hands had hold of it, and fired." Not surprisingly, the men then dropped the rail, many of them nursing wounds to their hands. Without causing any fatalities, the sheriff achieved his objective.[32]

In a handful of highly publicized incidents, local officers resorted to lethal force. In 1910, three months after the burning of Will James in Cairo, Illinois, a mob there attempted to lynch two more black men. Unwilling to allow another such spectacle, the newly installed Alexander County sheriff and a dozen deputies, some of them black, defended the jail. As the mob advanced, he warned its members: "'Stand back, or my men will fire on you.'"[33] To prove the point, they fired a volley over the mob, prompting the crowd to return fire. At that point the sheriff and his men unloaded a second volley that tore through the mob, killing Alexander Halliday and wounding several others. "Halliday, son of a former mayor of Cairo, lay for three hours dying, beside the courthouse steps, with the temperature near zero. During that entire time Sheriff Nellis, acting on the order received by telephone from Governor Deneen, refused to permit anyone to remove the wounded man, or allow a physician to enter the enclosure."[34]

Later that night and over the course of several days, the militia descended on Cairo and confronted a volatile situation. "The civic issue in Cairo has been reduced to one sharp phrase—the right of certain of her citizens to fare forth to 'lynch a nigger' when the call of savagery stirs them," observed the *Weekly Sentinel*. "The situation in the Illinois city is tense and ominous of danger," it added. "Troops parade the streets with loaded rifles and are prepared to meet an outbreak. Because the sheriff met a mob bent on lynching a negro charged with a minor offense and repelled the hoodlums with firearms Cairo is bent on more disorder and the outlook is full of promise for complete gratification of the desire."[35]

In Cairo the soldiers kept matters under control. In other instances, they eventually had to use force. In 1894 state troops from Columbus descended on Washington Court House, Ohio, to protect a black prisoner. Colonel A. B. Colt, in command of the troops, ordered the mob at the jail to disperse. The mob members ignored his order and rushed the jail. When its door collapsed, the soldiers let loose a volley of shots, scattering the townspeople. They regrouped, however, and threatened to kill the soldiers and dynamite the courthouse, prompting the state to dispatch more troops. With their arrival, Colt reported that he would have enough soldiers "'to control all the people in Fayette County.'" By the time the smoke cleared, however, five mob members were dead and about twice as many wounded.[36]

In the bloodiest incident, the militia in the Hoosier State responded aggressively to racist violence in Evansville in 1903. After two days of antiblack rioting and several attacks on the jail, the militia—which had tried to curb the chaos for days—increased its numbers. Resentful of the increase, a mob pushed its way into the militia line, driving the soldiers back. Its members snatched at the guns of the soldiers, slapped their faces, lit matches under their noses, and subjected them to verbal abuse. When the soldiers finally opened fire, the crowd fled as the dead and wounded dropped all around, some of them with bullets in their backs. When the gunfire ceased, twelve people had died or were dying and many others had sustained injuries.[37] The *Evansville Courier* reported the aftermath two days later: "Evansville was quiet last night. There was nothing to indicate that for the last few days scenes of violence had been enacted or that an angry mob had but the night before attacked and been repulsed with awful loss of life by the militia guarding the county jail."[38]

After rebuffing the mob in Danville, Sheriff Whitlock claimed that he had felt little fear. "I was not afraid that any one in the mob would shoot me. It takes some courage to fire a gun in such a place, especially at an officer. The man would have to raise his gun to fire and in doing this many would have seen him."[39] His pluck notwithstanding, he underestimated the danger that could result to himself, his officers, his prisoners, or the

residents from such a decision. A mob in Urbana, Ohio, exemplified the
risk in 1897. Though Charles Mitchell had already been sentenced for his
alleged crime, the mob made a late-night attack on the county jail with
the intent of lynching him. The militia responded with gunfire, killing
three, wounding ten, and enraging white Urbana. Fearful that his small
force could not cope with the larger mob that had formed by dawn, the
militia leader withdrew his guard. Coincidentally, the mayor dismissed
a newly arrived company from Springfield because, in his judgment, it
would not be required. At that point and in broad daylight, thousands of
people, including many women, gathered at the jail and, with the military
offering no resistance, hanged the prisoner from a tree limb.[40]

While they paid lip service to the pursuit of color-blind justice, the
authorities at all levels rarely demanded the punishment of the whites
who threatened or perpetrated antiblack violence, no matter how egregious their actions or certain their guilt. The mayor of Danville, who had
handed Metcalf over to the mob that lynched him in 1903, epitomized the
typical response. "Mayor Beard, who has made no move to investigate
the lynching, is coming in for severe criticism for his plea that he was
unable to recognize the men in the mob who faced him on the city building steps," explained the *Chicago Daily Tribune*. "If nothing comes of the
plan to prosecute the lynchers, political considerations will be to blame."
A local minister excoriated the official, noting that Beard was publicly
"'urging punishment of the mob leaders'" while "'asserting that he could
not identify one of them.'"[41]

Eventually, the authorities began to prosecute some of the perpetrators
more aggressively, particularly toward the end of the study period. In 1930
policemen arrested four whites near Makanda, Illinois, who had stoned a
home and committed considerable property damage in an effort to drive
out the blacks, whom they blamed for recently "coming to the vicinity
and taking work away from white men." Although their efforts in this case
to prosecute the vigilantes were laudable, the authorities probably acted
more from concern for the property owner who employed the blacks at
low wages than for the blacks themselves, a supposition predicated on the
sundown history of the area. "Makanda . . . is a fruit and vegetable center
and negro families have been few and ofttimes [*sic*] none," explained the
Carbondale Free Press. "In Union county to the south, hardly a negro lives
in the county. Several years ago they were terrorized out of Anna and
Cobden, the principal towns in the county."[42]

Whites responded in sometimes volatile ways to the efforts of the
authorities to quell mob violence. At times the vigilantes turned their

anger toward the blacks, assaulting them, expelling them, or both. In one case an officer in Shawneetown, Illinois, brooked no threats from the mob that demanded his prisoner in 1903 and warned that "any effort to force the jail would be at their peril," reported the *Indianapolis Star*.[43] As a result, the mob vented its anger elsewhere. "There has been an ill feeling among a class of white men here against the negroes for several months," reported the *Inter Ocean*, and the unrest "has served to intensify the feeling. Negro resorts and dives were stoned last night and many of the colored people took refuge among their friends in the country. At least fifty have left the town within two days."[44] Similarly, in 1906 a mob in Casey, Illinois, redirected its anger after it learned that the authorities had prevented the lynching of a prisoner by hustling him away from town. The *Alton Evening Telegraph* reported that the mob members "became furious, and immediately started to free the city of the negro," giving their victims just minutes to leave. According to the report, Casey was now "without a negro. In the future none will be permitted to stay more than a few hours."[45]

In Urbana, Ohio, whites responded forcefully to the aforementioned lethal acts of the militia in 1897. The members of the militia company that fired on the first mob to storm the jail soon sensed the public outrage. As a consequence, they did not resist when faced with the second mob. With their first action they enflamed public anger; with their second they faced potential charges of dereliction of duty. "While the Urbana company is overwhelmed with local sentiment against their action, they are also liable for abandoning their post of duty," noted the *Democratic Standard*. For his part, the sheriff feared for his safety. "Some citizens of Urbana asked for protection by troops for Sheriff McLain, against whose life threats had been made." The sheriff did not wait; he fled to Dayton. "He escaped by the back door of the jail, and claims that dynamite was being prepared to blow him up. In the excitement that prevails it is almost impossible to get at the facts as to the responsibility for the loss of life, but it is generally claimed that Sheriff McLain ordered the troops to fire."[46] In turn, the sheriff shifted the blame, claiming that he had requested more militiamen but the governor had denied that request. "'The Governor's reply was that I must first exhaust the resources [already] at my command,'" he explained. "'My idea was that with a superior display of soldiers I could thus overawe the mob and prevent fatalities.'"[47]

The authorities in Urbana fared well by comparison with those in Akron, Ohio, in 1900. In that case the members of a mob did not believe the authorities who told them that their prisoner had been moved to

Cleveland. Showering officers with rocks and ignoring a volley of gunshots fired over their heads, whites began to batter the jailhouse door. At that point "the police began shooting in earnest," wrote the *Akron Daily Democrat*. "The lights were turned off and darkness prevailed." As mob members and bystanders fell, several mortally wounded, the others retreated, peppering the building with rocks and shattering windows. Once they learned that the militia was being mobilized, the mob members invaded a hardware store for firearms. Then they opened fire on the officers, who returned the barrage. As the riot grew, the mob set fire to Columbia Hall, which adjoined City Hall, in the hope of flushing out everyone inside. "Columbia hall burned and with the assistance of dynamite the City building was soon destroyed," the *Daily Democrat* lamented. When the firemen arrived, the mob warned them not to use their hoses and, when one disregarded the warning, the attackers shot him and three other firefighters.[48]

Although the use of force to repel a crowd was the act most likely to precipitate such fury against the authorities, it was not the only one, as demonstrated by a mob in Lima, Ohio, in 1916. Unaware that the sheriff had transferred his prisoner out of town in anticipation of violence, the mob stormed the jail and the sheriff's adjoining home, doing substantial damage. "The residence portion of the county jail [was] tracked with mud and stained with tobacco juice, the furniture battered and scratched and the family rooms littered with the wearing apparel and other things tossed about the home by the ransackers intent apparently on pilfering as well as on finding the sheriff, who was obeying his oath and protecting his prisoner in accordance with [his] duty," reported the *Lima Times-Democrat*. Unsatisfied, the mob turned its ire against the sheriff himself to "'make him tell where the coon [was].'"[49]

Seizing Sheriff Eley, the mob members, numbering in the thousands, beat and tortured him, cracking two ribs in an effort to extract information. "Eley firmly refused to tell where Daniels could be found" and remained steadfast even after the attackers procured a noose and slipped it around his neck. When the fire department arrived to disperse the crowd with water from high-pressure hoses, the mob slashed a tire on the fire truck, disabling it. "By this time Eley was well nigh exhausted by the rough treatment of the crowd, and was about ready to collapse," noted the *Times-Democrat*. The city prosecutor pushed his way through the mob and persuaded the sheriff to divulge the location of the prisoner in Ottawa. At that point thirty mob members commandeered another truck, piled inside—taking Eley with them—and set off for Ottawa. If they could not gain custody of the prisoner, they clearly intended to take revenge on the sheriff. Fortunately, other officials regained custody of the sheriff and alerted the officials in Ottawa to move the prisoner to a more distant jail.[50]

In 1908 a mob took vengeance against Harry T. Loper, a white business-man who assisted police officers in removing from Springfield, Illinois, two black prisoners facing possible mob violence. Enraged by his complicity, mob members destroyed his restaurant. "'There isn't much left besides the four walls, and even they are dented,'" he told the *Inter Ocean*. "'There isn't a chair or a table left in the place, or a dish, that isn't broken. It was wiped out.'" The attackers also destroyed the automobile that he had used to hurry the prisoners out of town. Despite his losses, Loper refused to repent for his act of citizenship. "'Would I help get the negroes out of town again? I certainly would,'" he declared.[51] In addition to the retribution against Loper, the vigilantes attacked blacks, lynching two men, burning entire neighborhoods, and temporarily expelling many black residents.

Certainly, some whites recognized the injustice exhibited by whites who targeted blacks more aggressively and more frequently with mob violence for lesser crimes and on less evidence than they did whites. "There are bad negroes and bad white men," counseled Indiana's *Columbus Republican*. "The bad negroes ought to be dealt with just the same as the bad white men are dealt with. The same law is for both and not one law for one race and another law for another race." Nonetheless, in moving against rac-ist violence, whites were rarely motivated by lofty commitments to the defense of blacks. Despite its nominally egalitarian position, the editorship of the *Republican*, like most whites, held blacks to a communal standard— treating them as a monolithic group whose individual members were responsible for the actions of *all of the other members*—to which it did not hold whites. "Many negroes are insolent and lawless and they need to be promptly suppressed by the law, but not lynched and burned," the paper averred.[52] Similarly, the *Bremen Enquirer* was relieved that policemen had intervened to prevent a lynching in Valparaiso, Indiana, but it left little doubt about its harshly racist attitudes toward blacks, attitudes that surely reflected the views of most of its white readership. "Northern Indiana was threatened with a 'nigger barbecue,'" it wrote, but, after capturing the suspect, "the sheriff with a large number of deputies prevented him from being mobbed."[53] In short, influential whites—editors and authori-ties alike—in the Old Northwest subscribed to the same negative attitudes generally held by ordinary whites toward blacks.

Around the turn of the century, however, the authorities at all levels became increasingly concerned about the impact of these incidents of mob violence on their own interests and on the interests of those whom they served. They worried about the reputations of their municipalities, counties, and states, and about the infusions of financial and human capital that depended on those reputations. They also responded to the pressure exerted by like-minded business, spiritual, and editorial leaders in the community. Harry T. Loper shared that view, saying: "'I did not help the sheriff take the men away from the jail because I had any sympathy for them.'" Instead, he sought to advance what he perceived to be his own interests, explaining that he was principally interested in defusing a crowd that (he was correct in believing) might do damage to the city and its name. "'I have been in disturbances like this before and I felt that the crowd was in an ugly mood.'"[54] Reflecting these concerns as well as their particular anxieties about spiritual depravity, ministers in Danville deplored the burning there. The *Tribune* reported that "sermons on the disgrace to the city were preached this morning and tonight in nearly all the churches."[55] The Carbondale *Daily Free Press* was more forceful in its demands. "For the second time within a period of less than two months the State of Illinois has been disgraced by the lynching of a negro," it worried in 1903. To overcome the "anarchy" and "save the good name of the state," mob members "must be brought to justice."[56]

Local civic leaders revealed in unmistakable terms their concern about the reputation of Wilmette, a "fashionable suburb" of Chicago. After they formed the Wilmette Civic Association to discourage the growth of the black population, they quickly achieved that purpose. "Every negro in the suburb received a short polite note saying that the white residents of Wilmette desired the entire town to themselves and that hereafter there will be no employment for negroes," noted the *Rockford Republic*. "Today they were confident of having an all white population within a short time."[57] The attention from the press caused them embarrassment—but did not derail their plans. "In an effort to stem the unwelcome publicity which has attended the efforts of the Wilmette Civic [A]ssociation to drive the colored race from its village, Vice President W. C. Reinhold last night urged the members of that organization to bar all representatives of the press from future meetings," reported the *Inter Ocean*. Although Reinhold insisted that the association's purpose was not to expel the blacks, its actions belied its statement: "Only white property owners are eligible for membership."[58]

At all levels the authorities attended to the interests of those whom they served. At the local level they opposed racist violence in order to enhance the economic success of business owners, who could now hire black workers at low wages and thereby suppress the pay of working whites. They did so in Decatur, Indiana, in 1902. "Until a few months ago Decatur had not for years had any negro inhabitants," reported the *Indianapolis News*. At that point employers cracked the prohibition: "Several [blacks] were brought in for hotel and domestic work." In response, working-class whites made anonymous threats against the businessmen, advising them to fire the newcomers and send them packing. When they were unsuccessful, a mob chased most of the blacks from town.[59] Indignant over this assault, the businessmen and the officers who supported them opposed another attempt a few weeks later to drive out the remaining black. "The one colored man who is now in the city is being protected by white friends and the officers," reported the *Fort Wayne Daily News*. "An attempt was made last evening to form another mob to drive him from the city, but about seventy-five excited friends of the colored man, well armed, gathered and the mob dispersed."[60]

On occasion, police officers acted surreptitiously in their efforts to balance the competing demands of local whites. In 1913, for instance, the *Dixon Evening Telegraph* revealed that the police in Freeport, Illinois, had quietly conducted a campaign supported by many of the white residents in the town and targeted at a reduction in the number of its black ones. When confronted by the report, the police chief refused to comment on it because he feared that "some of the corporations here will raise an objection because they want the colored men to work for them."[61]

In 1904 the authorities in Vanderburgh County, Indiana, demonstrated their indifference to the protection of black lives with their blasé response to an event near Armstrong in which a fugitive committed suicide by drowning rather than take his chances with the mob pursuing him. Although this suicide near the county seat of Evansville was circumstantial, officials did not view it as the result of mob violence. "As soon as it was learned that the negro had drowned himself," reported the *Evansville Courier and Press*, "there was a feeling of relief among the officers at headquarters. Chief Heuke was determined not to take any chances on a repetition of the scenes of last July when an attempt was made to mob the slayer of Patrolman Massey" and the state militia had shot down members of the mob during a confrontation at the jail.[62]

At the state level the authorities also became increasingly concerned about the threats posed by mob violence to the legal system and to their control over the social order. On August 2, a few weeks after the shooting of mob members by soldiers in Evansville in 1903, Governor Winfield T. Durbin detailed these concerns in an address to the members of Company

E, First Regiment of the Indiana National Guard, the soldiers involved in that event. "Behind you in that moment" of bloodshed, he told them, "stood every loyal citizen of Indiana; behind you and behind all those who wear the uniform of the Indiana National Guard, in all that you do in defense of the state's integrity, the law's majesty and the honor of the flag, they stand today and will stand forever." To those who championed mob law, he declared, "There is only one name for talk like this, and that is treason. There is only one name for the man who utters it, or the man who applauds it, and that is traitor."[63] The *Columbus (IN) Republican* reinforced this view. "The mob . . . kept up its riotous conduct until it came into collision with the militia," it reminded its readers. "For three days disorder had reigned in Evansville, owing to a mob of rioters that was intimidating the city and it had grown so powerful and law defiant that it even provoked the militia." The governor, too, expressed little sympathy for the mob. The only appropriate response to such violence was to quell it: "It is no use to temporize with a mob."[64]

In this instance the governor and other influential Indianans had grown exasperated after a series of lynchings that state authorities had done relatively little to prevent. In 1899, after a mob lynched five white men in Ripley County, Indiana, Governor James A. Mount, in his biennial message, expressed his frustration that the "good name of Indiana has been dishonored by a lawless mob." Every person "charged with crime has the right, under the Constitution and laws of the State, to a fair and impartial trial. For a better guarantee of this right and to awaken a more lively interest in the counties against lynchings . . . I recommend the enactment of a law making the county responsible for such conditions and liable in a civil suit."[65]

Following this series of lynchings, leaders seemed determined to assert the authority of the state. Governor Durbin expressed his views in his 1905 address to the Indiana House of Representatives when he recollected the Evansville militia shooting eighteen months earlier. "Deplorable as was this tragedy, its effect as an object lesson has been most salutary," he declared, noting a substantial decline in the number of threatened lynchings in the intervening period. "It will perhaps be some time before a company of the Indiana National Guard, in the discharge of its sworn duty, will again be attacked by a mob."[66]

In the case of Evansville, even the president of the United States was eager to state his support for the Indiana governor's use of force to disperse the mob. On August 6, 1903, Theodore Roosevelt wrote a letter from his home in Oyster Bay, New York, to Durbin commending him. "Permit me to thank you as an American citizen for the admirable way in which you have vindicated the majesty of the law by your recent action in reference to lynching," he wrote. "I feel, my dear sir, that you have made all men your debtors who believe, as all far-seeing men must, that the wellbeing, indeed the very existence, of the Republic depends upon that spirit of orderly liberty under the law which is as incompatible with mob violence as with any form of despotism."[67] In turn, Durbin told Roosevelt that his letter "struck the keynote of a national necessity" by advocating the "doctrine that 'We must show that the law is adequate to deal with crime.'"[68]

In response to the growing sentiment against mob violence, state leaders, usually prompted by some embarrassing event, did begin to enact laws against mob violence. On April 10, 1896, the Ohio legislature passed a law making the county in which the violence occurred liable for it and subject to fines. The *Cincinnati Enquirer* reported that its passage "took place [after] Roscoe Parker, colored, was taken from the Sheriff of Adams County in November, 1895, and lynched. It was introduced by Harry C. Smith at the succeeding session of the Legislature." The *Enquirer* explained: "The act provides that not only the heirs of the person mobbed, but all other persons killed are entitled to $5,000 damages, and those injured from $500 to $5,000." Although the success of laws like these depended heavily on their enforcement, those responsible for enacting them placed a brake on unrestrained mob violence, particularly among the authorities and influential citizens concerned with or responsible for the management of financial affairs in each county. After the 1897 lynching of Mitchell in Urbana, the *Enquirer* noted that the "law [had] never been applied, and the Urbana case [would] probably be the first trial of it." Although doubts were expressed about the law's constitutionality, the paper summarized the conventional wisdom after the death of several mob members at the hands of the officers and the subsequent lynching of the prisoner: "Champaign County is liable [for] anywhere from $15,000 to $30,000 damages."[69]

After prolonged wrangling in court, Harrison Wilson, an Ohio circuit court judge, found that the Ohio mob law was constitutional. The county itself, he noted, could not be trusted to determine what penalties should follow mob violence because it was the site of the unrest and would be predisposed towards leniency. "It is not very likely that a community which will tolerate . . . mob violence would furnish a jury that would give much damages for the death of the party and it would defeat the law," he wrote. "I think that fact has been made plain to the people of the county in that no one has been prosecuted for the death of the party."[70] Nonetheless, those responsible for carrying out the law undermined its effectiveness.

"The jury in the suit brought against Champagne [*sic*] county to recover $5,000 damages for the lynching . . . returned a verdict against the plaintiff," reported the *Daily Herald*. The father of the victim, therefore, received nothing.[71] In addition, the Supreme Court dismissed the charges against the Urbana sheriff and mayor for dereliction of duty. "It is thought that this will be the last echo of the case," opined the Massillon, Ohio, *City Item*.[72]

In 1905 Governor Charles S. Deneen of Illinois signed a bill proposed by the state's only black legislator, Edward Green, and characterized by a combination of fines against the county where mob violence occurred and sanctions on officers who allowed it. "Green's anti-mob violence measure," reported the *Inter Ocean*, "provides two sets of penalties. It authorizes the heirs of a mob victim to collect from the county $5,000 for the loss of life and $5,000 for damages to property, and requires the Governor to issue a proclamation vacating the office of any sheriff who permits a prisoner to be taken from him by a mob and lynched."[73] Philip Dray adds that the extralegal execution of a person in police custody "was 'conclusive evidence of the failure on the part of such sheriff to do his duty.'" Four years later, Sheriff Frank Davis of Cairo, Illinois, lost his prisoner, Will James, to a mob, despite his efforts to outrun it. Davis lost his job to the law. "It was ironic that Davis would wind up the target of this effort, as he had . . . hardly been complicit with the mob," notes Dray. Nonetheless, antilynching activist Ida B. Wells-Barnett, who lived in Chicago, campaigned to ensure that Davis would be subject to the penalty. She argued that, if the officer was not punished, "the state would miss an opportunity to show convincingly that mob violence would not be tolerated." Three months later, Sheriff Nellis (or Nelis), the successor to Davis, gunned down the Cairo mob that attempted to lynch two more blacks. "Wells-Barnett had convincingly shown that antilynching laws had the potential to reform officers' behavior," Dray writes, "for the fate of his predecessor had clearly been on Sheriff Nelis's mind."[74]

In addition to these concerns, many of the police officers who opposed mob violence did so because of their evolving sense of professional responsibility, sworn duty, and personal honor. Before he faced down the mob in Danville, Sheriff Whitlock of Vermillion County, Illinois, "had never been looked upon as an especially remarkable man—except, as I was told everywhere, he had a record as *a strict sheriff*, as a man who did his best to enforce the law in times of peace," writes Baker in *Following the Color Line*. Raised by strict Presbyterian parents who possessed "stern . . . conceptions of right and wrong" and who made their son "obey the law with peach-tree switches," Whitlock brought the same mentality to his work as sheriff. "When the crisis came that night with the mob howling around his jail, Hardy Whitlock had become so accustomed to doing his duty that he didn't know how to do anything else. Here was the jail to be protected; he intended to protect it."[75]

While they suppressed mob violence, the authorities—civil and uniformed, local and state—increasingly assumed the role of the mob by repressing blacks. In 1904, a year after the militia opened fire on the mob in Evansville, signaling a growing intolerance for lynching on the part of influential Indianans, an officer in Carlisle, Indiana, took vengeance against Jasper Hammond, a so-called troublemaker. "Hammond live[d] on a farm a short distance out of town. He [was] married to a white woman and [had] been the source of much trouble," according to the *Indianapolis Morning Star and Journal*. During an attempted arrest, the officer shot at him five times as he attempted to flee, wounding him. In this instance the other officers then protected Hammond. "When he was taken through here on the way to Sullivan a large crowd gathered and numerous threats of lynching were heard. The officers hurried him on to the county seat in order to prevent trouble." Though the officers prevented a lynching, they could not or would not prevent the subsequent expulsion of nearly every black resident from town.[76] Increasingly, however, officers intentionally killed black suspects in a variety of ways, much as mobs would have done earlier.

Law enforcement officials incurred the wrath of whites in Illinois when, as described above, they resisted the efforts of mobs to execute Joe Deberry in 1915. After the prisoner was convicted of murder and sentenced to hang, however, the sheriff of Jackson County evidently decided to allow the would-be vigilantes to view the spectacle and devised a novel means for doing so. "Joe Deberry, negro, was hanged at 9:30 o'clock this morning . . . , 2,000 spectators within the stockade witnessing the execution," the *Dixon Evening Telegraph* observed. Three thousand more "crowded on the streets around the jail. The law provides that hangings shall be private, and to legalize the presence of so many in the stockade the sheriff commissioned them special deputies."[77] Given the terrifying circumstances under which the officers extracted the confession—a confession likely made in return for protection—and under which the sheriff reached his decision in support of a public execution, the hanging of Deberry resembles what the historian George Wright called a legal lynching.

In 1916 Chicago policemen murdered Henry and Hattie McIntyre. Accusing Henry of several violent crimes, a squad of officers approached his apartment to make an arrest and took incoming fire from the suspect, leaving several officers wounded or dead. At that point the officers declared their intent to kill McIntyre; as one of them vowed, "I'm going to get that guy." After cordoning off the area, they slipped into an adjacent apartment and set off dynamite that "exploded directly over where the Negro and his wife were hiding in a corner of the bedroom." A policeman then entered the apartment and finished off Henry, who was badly injured, with a point-blank gunshot to the head. Officers found Hattie "on the floor dead, her body mangled by the dynamite." Hattie was, of course, accused of no crime and was a hostage. Prior to the bombing, officers at the scene had sought and received the support of the police chief for the drastic step that they were preparing. Afterwards, the chief openly applauded the work of Captain Wesley Westbrook, who set off the charge, calling it "fine work, bully work." With an eye for melodrama, the *Chicago Daily Tribune* provided the exchange: "Capt. Westbrook's face lighted. . . . 'Did he say that, now, really? Come on. Did he say that?' he asked. . . . 'Yes—he gave out a statement saying you had done excellent work.'. . . 'Capt. Westbrook surveyed the scene. . . . 'I'm glad,' he said.'"[78]

In 1922 posses fanned out around Lafayette, Indiana, in search of Henry Poole, who was accused of assault. "The assault had aroused such intense excitement and feeling in Lafayette that, had Poole been taken alive, it was feared a lynching would follow, and arrangements had been made by the police to take the negro out of the city," observed the *Indianapolis News*.[79] According to the questionable story told by those present, Poole emerged from his hiding place, failed to recognize either the officer or the handful of posse members with him, and, although covered in blood, breezily asked for directions to Lafayette. Confronted by all of these armed men, Poole then attacked the officer, William Condra, with a club. In response, the members of the posse tackled Poole, who somehow in the resulting commotion suffered a bullet wound to the heart. Nonetheless, the local authorities and white residents were in no mood to ask questions: "The negro fell over dead. Condra will get a medal."[80]

In 1931 officers in Bucyrus resisted mob violence before and after they killed one of three prisoners—all brothers—in their care. Following the brothers' arrest, whites milled about, muttering threats and constantly increasing in numbers. "With the rising tide of indignation," officers made preparations to remove the prisoners if necessary; as a deterrent to possible mob violence, they also added a number of guards. At the same time, however, they killed one of the youths themselves. According to their story, they were interrogating Elijah Ralls when he "leaped from his chair, eluded the grasp of his questioners and jumped through the window." An officer ordered Ralls to halt and, when he failed to do so, shot him. Immediately thereafter, the officers renewed their efforts to prevent mob violence. "Attracted by the shooting, the small group of spectators was joined by others and quickly the crowd grew to more than 200," noted the *Cincinnati Enquirer*. The officers drove the crowd back and hurried Elijah inside, where he died. "Rumblings of violence against the other two brothers were [again] heard" but, rather than capitulate, the officers "recruited additional guards in the hope they would be able to placate the crowd."[81] Ultimately, the officers protected the other two prisoners but, as mentioned above, preemptively disarmed the black population of nearby Crestline.

This chapter demonstrates that local and state authorities in the Old Northwest used a range of tactics to protect blacks from impending or ongoing violence at the hands of whites. In most instances they used preemptive tactics, spiriting prisoners from local to more distant or better-protected jails, fighting off mob members and claiming custody of bloodied but still-living victims, or delivering impassioned speeches to crowds, demanding their withdrawal or dispersal. When mobs refused to be cowed by threats of force, local officers used force—nonlethal if possible, lethal if necessary—to curb assaults on jails. When necessary, local authorities called on the state to assist them in maintaining or restoring order by requesting the militia. If this show of force was insufficient, they sometimes used violence to suppress mob action. To encourage the authorities to stand against mobs, lawmakers eventually passed legislation making such violence costlier to the perpetrators, the officials who permitted it, and the jurisdictions in which they occurred.

In taking these actions, the authorities could place themselves in grave danger from uncontrolled white mobs, sometimes suffering threats and beatings, and at other times incurring damage to public and private property alike. In undertaking these acts, officials usually reflected their concerns—or the concerns of those they served—about issues such as the reputation of the community, the impact on its economic growth, and the protection of the legal system, rather than concerns about racial justice. Not infrequently, they incurred the wrath of the white community, placing themselves in uncomfortable positions, buffeted by the demands and threats of the more numerous but less influential white advocates of mob violence, on the one hand, and the desires and mandates of the fewer but more influential advocates of law and order on the other.

The authorities were not the only ones who resisted mob violence. Blacks did as well. In Mounds they took up arms and converged on the jailhouse to defend a prisoner who was under threat of lynching and, in addition to stimulating resistance by the local police officers, they succeeded in dispersing the mob itself. Near Elco both black residents of long standing and black newcomers imported from the South to pick cotton allied to challenge the racist vigilantes who menaced them, burned and dynamited their houses, and opened fire on residences under cover of darkness. The authorities who preemptively raided the black community in Crestline during the threatened lynching in nearby Bucyrus obviously signaled their deep concern that the black population was armed and preparing to defend itself from a potential lynching or armed invasion of their quarters.

These findings challenge some of the most deeply ingrained tenets of the historiography of racist violence. Although many scholars have concluded that the authorities almost invariably colluded with mobs, this study shows that for a variety of reasons they strenuously and successfully prevented mob violence long before the 1920s and 1930s, when by many accounts they finally began to reject mobs. Furthermore, while many have assumed that blacks responded to violence with either meek submission or with acts of dissemblance, this study demonstrates instead that they routinely inserted themselves into the action, deterring mobs and influencing the behaviors of police officers who may not have defended their prisoner otherwise.

As they curbed mob violence, however, the authorities, and particularly the police, co-opted the role of the mob in controlling and intimidating blacks and in dispensing pain, torture, and sometimes death. In so doing, they achieved the same sort of compromise between liberal reformers and advocates of "rough justice" described in Michael J. Pfeifer's work on the relationship between the decline of lynching and the expansion of capital punishment.[82] The officers in Carlisle and Bucyrus displayed a firm determination to suppress mob violence and at the same time to gun down the black targets of would-be mob violence in very public ways. The sheriff who hanged Joe Deberry in Jackson County offered a similar compromise when he deputized a vast crowd of whites—many of them members of a mob that had been stymied in an effort to lynch Deberry—in order to skirt state laws against public executions. In Lafayette an officer gunned down a fugitive after capture by himself and a posse, and earned vigorous applause from whites. In Chicago in 1882 and 1916, police officers flagrantly executed—indeed, *lynched*—Bill Allen and Henry and Hattie

McIntyre in hails of bullets supplemented in the latter case by a charge of dynamite.

In many respects black authors have demonstrated a firmer grasp of the pervasive nature of racist violence committed by the police and their abettors in the Midwest than have scholars. In his 1940 novel *Native Son*, Richard Wright tells the story of Bigger Thomas, a black youth accused of raping and killing a white woman in Chicago. Fighting bitter cold and gnawing hunger, and on the run from impoverished tenement to impoverished tenement, he slips out to buy a copy of an extra edition in which he learns—without surprise but with deepening fear—what he is up against. According to the fictional reporter:

> Immediately a cordon of five thousand police, augmented by more than three thousand volunteers, was thrown about the Black Belt. . . . Indignation rose to white heat last night as the news of the Negro's rape and murder . . . spread through the city. . . . Police reported that many windows in the Negro sections were smashed. . . . Every street car, bus, el train and auto leaving the South Side is being stopped and searched. Police and vigilantes, armed with rifles, tear gas, flashlights, and photos of the killer, began at 18th Street this morning and are searching every Negro home under a blanket warrant from the mayor. They are making a careful search of all abandoned buildings, which are said to be hideouts for Negro criminals. . . . Reports were current that several Negro men were beaten in various North and West Side neighborhoods.[83]

Ultimately, the searchers trap Thomas on a rooftop, bringing his flight to an end with a high-velocity water hose that in the bitter cold transforms him into a shivering, icy, and defeated man.

If Wright captured the nature of racist violence in large cities like Chicago, Gordon Parks captured similar violence in a fictionalized version of Fort Scott, Kansas, in the 1920s. In *The Learning Tree* he addresses police violence and the justice system: "Here, for the black man, freedom loosed one hand while custom restrained the other. The law books stood for equal rights, but the law (a two-pistol-toting, tobacco-chewing, khaki-putteed, leather-legginged cop called Kirky) never bothered to enforce such laws in such books."[84] Later, the authorities arrest a black man, and whites threaten lynching; fearful, the accused wrests a gun from a guard in court and commits suicide rather than potentially face a mob. The aforementioned officer—Kirky—soon claims another black life when he opens fire on a youth who is climbing a ledge to escape. "Kirky fired again, and the bullet chipped the stone above Marcus' head," the narrator explains. "Marcus

... slipped and was falling down toward the stone apron, screaming as he plummeted through space."[85] As Parks well understood, lynch mobs still threatened in the Midwest in this period but had largely been replaced by badge-bearing men with a license to kill.

In a passage written in 1993 about *Native Son*, and equally applicable, perhaps, to *The Learning Tree*, the literary critic Keneth Kinnamon wrote that "today's reader of *Native Son* might well regard the racism of the newspaper article" in the scene quoted above "as highly exaggerated." Yet, as he showed, the white Chicago dailies of the 1930s paralleled closely those created by the novelist. "As Wright was nearing the midway point of his first draft, two young black men, Robert Nixon and Earl Hicks, were arrested in Chicago and charged with the murder of a white woman," explained Kinnamon. "Nixon became the central figure in the case, which received sensationalized coverage in the Chicago press, especially the openly racist *Tribune*. Without adducing any evidence of rape, this newspaper began its extensive coverage by calling Nixon 'a colored sex criminal' and continued to use such epithets as 'sex moron,' 'rapist slayer,' 'brick moron,' 'jungle beast,' etc."[86] In short, Kinnamon concluded, there was nothing highly exaggerated about the inflammatory reports created by Wright. In fact, this study corroborates Kinnamon's conclusion, and it posits, too, that police violence in the Midwest may well have exceeded that on display in the literary portrayals by Wright and Parks.

8 The Midwest in the Late Lynching Period

"A queer precipitate of the old and the new"

"The body of an unidentified negro was found floating in the Ohio river opposite South Point ... this afternoon," reported the *Ironton Evening Tribune* on June 10, 1932, in its first reference to what would be the last known lynching in Ohio history and would result in "the biggest and most sensational [court] case in the history of Lawrence County."[1] After fishermen pulled the decomposing body from the water, many residents of South Point, a village of about five hundred, believed that it belonged to Luke Murray, a young black man from Atlanta, Georgia, who had disappeared the previous Tuesday evening. According to the *Tribune*, Murray had fought with two white men on that evening and threatened them. Following his arrest shortly thereafter, "a gathering of South Point residents visited the jail. They broke open the door and after flogging the negro ordered him from town. He has not been seen since."[2]

This chapter utilizes the 1932 lynching as a prototype of the changing nature of this antiblack practice during its twilight years in the Midwest, a time identified here as the "late lynching period." First, the chapter sketches the basic contours of the Murray lynching, details the motivations for it, examines the initial black campaign for justice, analyzes the trial, and explores the black political and legal struggles for justice thereafter. It then focuses on the characteristics associated with mob violence in this period, as identified in the Murray lynching and corroborated by similar lynchings elsewhere in the Midwest. Finally, the chapter considers the implications of its findings for mob violence, the black freedom struggle, and the Midwest. Before proceeding, however, it provides a brief overview of the history of white supremacist activities and black resistance in Ohio generally and in Lawrence County specifically.

Long before 1932, whites in Ohio had employed violence to subordinate blacks, as the preceding chapters show, and had established an unknown number of all-white sundown towns. In the early twentieth century they reduced their reliance on antiblack mob violence but increased their use of the Jim Crow discrimination foreshadowed in the Black Laws of the early-to-mid nineteenth century and introduced via custom and legislation late in the century. "The Ohio color line became more unyielding and restrictive in the 1920s," writes the historian William W. Giffin, and it affected almost all areas of life. Giffin elaborates that the residential segregation of blacks "reached ghetto proportions for the first time in some Ohio cities by 1930. Racial discrimination and segregation were increasingly common in residential housing, schools, and public accommodations, while color bias was still seen in law enforcement and the print media. White employers and various private organizations continued to bar or discriminate against African Americans."[3]

Blacks challenged their oppressors at every step, not infrequently with armed self-defense. During a race riot in Springfield in 1921, for example, a black resident noted that "every section of the city, in which there were any number of our people, was organized for determined resistance to any mob that might molest them."[4] In the early twentieth century blacks launched a systematic assault against Jim Crow with boycotts, court tests, and editorial activism, much of it initiated, organized, or publicized by recently established branches of civil rights groups like the NAACP.[5]

Situated along the Ohio River in south-central Ohio, Lawrence County relied largely on agriculture, mining, and manufacturing in 1930 to support its 44,541 residents, a mere 1,669, or 3.8 percent, of whom were black. Despite these modest numbers, it did, like Ohio generally, have a long history of racist violence and oppression. So, too, did the county seat of Ironton, a city of 16,621 residents in 1930 and the home to 928 blacks (5.6 percent of its total population but 55.6 percent of all blacks in the county).[6]

Local whites handled race relations in Lawrence County in much the same way as white Ohioans did across the state, causing a variety of ugly episodes from the mid-nineteenth to the early twentieth century and including a threatened lynching in Ironton in 1901.[7] In South Point, a village located approximately ten miles southeast of Ironton, whites stringently enforced sundown practices. Although a resident insisted that there was "no feeling on the part of South Point residents against negroes," observers repeatedly mentioned the all-white character of the place.[8] One remarked, "No Negroes live there," while another indicated that "the nearest colored residents . . . are at Ironton."[9] Given the town's whiteness—and its notoriety for *being* all-white—residents of South Point almost certainly practiced far less racist violence than did those in Ironton, although they likely refreshed its sundown reputation periodically with animosity or violence against black strangers.

Blacks in Lawrence County resisted this oppression fiercely. In 1850, for example, six fugitive slaves fought against eight white residents who attempted to capture them and return them to Kentucky. "The negroes were well armed and they fired upon the whites, instantly wounding several," claimed a local antiblack account. "They then fell upon the remainder [of the whites] with cudgels and beat several until they supposed them dead." The fugitives then escaped with a posse of white men in hot pursuit.[10] Recalling the 1901 threatened lynching, the *Ironton News* attributed its failure to a "lack of leadership" among the whites.[11] The *Plain Dealer* suggested a different story. "If the attack had been made a bloody battle undoubtedly would have occurred, as fifty armed colored men were doing guard duty around the jail where their friends were imprisoned," it reported. "Negroes were congregating and openly displaying arms."[12]

Luke Murray, a high school graduate in his early twenties, was a "member of a respectable family of Macon, Ga., [and] was chauffeur and butler for Howard Davidson of Atlanta." He had worked for the Davidsons, a wealthy white Georgia family, for six years and, when they "came to South Point, O., to look after certain farming interests, [they] brought Murray with them."[13] Howard Davidson was the executor of the estate of a recently deceased family member and had brought his family to Lawrence County from Georgia just two months earlier.[14]

On June 7, 1932, Murray purportedly brandished a knife during a quarrel with a young white man named Ben Hall, according to allegations made by Hall and his supporters. A short time later, Hall and others converged on the Davidson farm and renewed their hostilities with Murray, who allegedly drew his blade again. Although Murray was almost surely acting in self-defense, whites claimed that he grabbed James Hall, brother of Ben, and "said he had a notion to cut James' throat."[15] They also claimed that Murray was drunk, although the wife of his employer, identified only as Mrs. Howard Davidson, insisted that he was not and that she had never seen him drunk. Someone summoned the South Point town marshal, "Rip" Winters, who arrested and jailed both Murray and Ben Hall. In an ominous hint of what was to come, one of the whites vowed, "We will get the [s.o.b.] yet."[16]

With a wink and a nod Marshal Winters gave the members of the nascent mob the green light to begin their operation. He moved Murray "from a cell to an open vestibule, and went home to dinner, leaving the jail unguarded, and announced that he would be gone about two hours," noted an observer.[17] Excited by the free reign that he afforded them, the whites hooted: "Get ready in there, here we come[!]"[18] Storming the jail, they hustled out Murray, who supposedly failed to appreciate the murderous designs of the mob. "The negro," one of his slayers recalled, "remarked that he didn't mind taking a beating but he didn't want to be cut."[19] Although the autopsy failed to determine the cause of Murray's death, it did indicate that the whites rendered far more than a beating. "The physicians found evidence of Murray having sustained a blow at the base of the brain, on the right side of the skull, and a dislocation of the second vertebrae [sic] in the neck," stated the Ironton Evening Tribune. "There was no skull fracture and the blow on the head did not cause a concussion inside the skull. It is possible, however, that the blow caused the vertebrae dislocation and the latter injury was sufficient to cause death."[20] When asked if hanging could have caused the dislocation, the coroner said yes. He also found "[e]vidence of a rope having been around the negro's neck." After killing him, the lynchers dumped Murray into the Ohio River.[21]

Blacks regarded this killing as a clear case of collusion because "the 'strong door of the South Point jail' where Luke Murray was confined on a charge of fighting prior to his death, was left unlocked, and . . . it was an easy matter for some 14 or more men and boys . . . to gain entrance to the compartment occupied by Murray."[22] Furthermore, Winters later claimed that on his return he failed to notice that his prisoner was missing or that a door had been battered. "Altho[ugh] the affair occurred last Tuesday night," noted the Ironton Sunday Tribune, "no report was made of the matter and county authorities were not aware of any disturbance at South Point until advised of the finding of the body Friday afternoon."[23]

"Had Murray been mobbed for rape upon one of the fair young women of the village it would have not been so astounding," ruminated a Lawrence County attorney shortly thereafter, but Murray "was lynched for little or nothing." In fact, some whites did try to tar the deceased as a sexual predator, although they found little traction. One was Mrs. Lou Hall, a relative of Ben and James, who claimed that "Murray had threatened to tear her clothes from her," supposedly causing the woman to break into tears.[24] Although it was indisputably true that Murray's lynching was not attributable to an alleged felony, the attorney who made that point failed to appreciate that Murray *had* committed serious transgressions of local racial etiquette, albeit inadvertently.

Fundamentally, whites lynched Murray because they hated and feared blacks. In pragmatic terms, however, they understood that, by refreshing their town's sundown reputation, they might discourage other blacks who might dare settle among them. The basest racism drove them, conceded a resident: "Luke Murray was crucified because he was a negro." More specifically, however, whites were responding to the victim's willingness to defy them and act in self-defense. Like those across the country, whites in Lawrence County expected blacks to submit meekly to abuse; they reacted with fury to the exercise of self-protection on the part of blacks. As a resident asserted, "The negro with his belligerent attitude started it all."[25]

The lynchers also targeted Murray because "he was too popular with his employers for some of the whites in that section."[26] They bitterly resented the wealthy Davidsons as well, of course, but they recognized that they could not mete out their retribution against them as readily as they could against the chauffeur. Since local whites were primarily poor, many of them hired hands, they found it galling to see a black man touring the town in a handsome automobile and decked out in fine apparel, signifiers of status and prosperity that they did not enjoy. In addition, whites watched with smoldering anger as the Davidsons afforded their employee courtesies and responsibilities that they viewed as inappropriate. "Murray lived in the main house on the Davidson farm" rather than in servants' quarters, according to the *Pittsburgh (PA) Courier*, and, "in Mr. Davidson's absence [he] was placed in charge of the house and grounds."[27] As black observers in Lawrence County put it, "Luke Murray's position of trust and confidence in the household of H. G. Davidson incited jealousy on the part of some of the illiterate white people of South Point."[28]

Finally, the lynchers targeted Murray because of their anger about what they viewed as his inappropriate—if not amorous—relationship with "pretty Nancy Adams, niece of Howard Davidson."[29] "He would often take his employer, wife and [niece], auto riding, and most times the [niece] would go without her [aunt]," noted an observer. "And this, I learned, he was warned by some of the whites to discontinue."[30] In addition, young white men were furious about Murray's role as the gatekeeper because he rebuffed their own efforts to court Nancy. "Murray . . . was trying to act as guardian Angel or watch-dog over the girl," grumbled an editor. "His attitude was not pleasant to many of the villagers."[31]

Summarizing these concerns, a black investigator wrote that "Murray's presence in the vicinity [of this sundown town], his position in the Davidson household and the manner and seeming familiar conduct with the family, especially the niece, aroused the enmity of the village men."[32] In a report produced in September about the case at the annual meeting of the Ohio branches of the NAACP in Cincinnati, the authors concluded that "the ruffians accused of causing the premature death of this Colored youth, were hostile to the deceased because he stood too high in the good graces of the feminine members of his employers['] family, and after several attempts to 'frame' him had proven futile, decided to effect his complete removal as a source of annoyance."[33]

As they had always done, blacks in Lawrence County resisted vigorously. In this instance, they responded not with armed self-defense, as they did during still-unfolding acts of violence, but with a formal protest befitting a fait accompli. A local group took the lead. "The Lincoln club, an organization of negroes, has called a meeting of all negroes in Lawrence county to be held . . . for the purpose of organizing in order to investigate the alleged lynching," reported the *Ironton Evening Tribune* three days after Murray's body was found.[34] With hundreds in attendance, the club took action. "Mob violence was condemned and a committee of nine negroes appointed to assist in the investigation of the South Point lynching," explained the *Tribune*. A leading black resident, Dr. L. M. Weaver, led this committee.[35]

The following day Weaver's committee presented to the presiding judge a petition signed by three hundred blacks that demanded an autopsy to determine the cause of death, a request that was subsequently granted; as noted earlier, one had not been performed prior to the victim's burial. The petition also demanded the appointment of an assistant to aid the chief prosecutor, Lee Andrews, whom blacks regarded as unsympathetic to them. When Andrews did not object, the judge "appointed Attorney E. L. Riley [white], who the committee-men explained was their choice." In addition, the petition asserted the widespread opinion among blacks that, "in view of certain credible reports in our possession, we firmly believe that certain valuable information relative to the case is being withheld."[36]

Building on these initiatives, blacks actively recruited support from outside civil rights groups. "It was reported about town today that the Lincoln club, negro organization, planned another meeting . . . at which out of town speakers would be introduced," observed the *Tribune* on June 21.[37] Although it did not elaborate on the identity of the speakers, they almost certainly included members of the NAACP, which would play an important role in the case, and likely included Theodore M. Berry, an attorney and the president of the Cincinnati Branch, who spent July in Ironton in an investigative capacity.

In mid-July the Weaver committee charged that mob members and law enforcement officials had cooperated in the lynching and that the authorities and witnesses were now participating in a cover-up. It also asserted that "all persons responsible for this crime have not been placed under arrest," likely a reference to Marshal Winters, among others, who in effect had handed the prisoner to the mob.[38] Furthermore, blacks called on Governor George White to help bring the attackers to justice, writing, "We firmly believe that the governor of Ohio, with evidence now in his hands, in the interest of justice, should exercise the prerogative of his high office" and demand that the state attorney general "take charge of this investigation and prosecution."[39]

Finally, Weaver himself evidently threatened (or at least intimated a willingness) to sue the county under the state anti–mob violence statute, which enabled a legal representative of the deceased to "file suit against the said county for a sum not to exceed $5,000."[40] Many whites shared the bitterness of one observer who grumbled that the prosecution "should not be done for commercial gain although he pointed out that . . . a local negro organization seemed to have a very personal interest in the case although it was hard to believe they even bore an acquaintance with the deceased southern negro." Reporting this, the *Tribune* "gathered that the reference . . . concerned [the] possible suing of the county for damages in case it was proved that Murray had been lynched. Weaver, besides being chairman of the negro committee, is administrator of the deceased's estate."[41] Evidently, it never occurred to the *Tribune* staff or other whites that such a suit would have been impossible and unnecessary had they adhered to the law. Nor is there any evidence to suggest, as whites did, that Weaver had any personal designs on the money.

On June 21 Andrews, the prosecutor, questioned six young white men regarding their role in the mob violence that had taken place two weeks earlier. Based on those interviews, in which four men allegedly confessed to raiding the jail, the prosecutor filed charges of first-degree murder. On June 30, Judge Jones convened the grand jury for a two-day session to consider the evidence against Taylor Napier (twenty-four), Theodore Johnson (twenty-nine), Garland Massie (twenty-four), Milford Massie (twenty), Lawrence Massie (nineteen), and Clyde Elkins (twenty).[42] Meanwhile, another judge committed Louis McKee (sixteen) to a juvenile detention center for an indeterminate period for his alleged role in Murray's death.[43]

A month later, the attorneys for the prosecution and the defense selected a jury in a process that took several days and attracted a crowd of people of both races, many of whom "stood in the corridors watching and listening through the two large doorways, the four swinging doors having been fastened back to allow a breeze to blow through the overheated room."[44] The attorneys ultimately produced a jury that was anything but inclusive: it consisted of twelve white men. It included at least one juror who "had said on being examined, that he had previously formed an opinion as to the innocence or guilt of the six boys," observed the *Tribune*. "However, he had said that he could cast that opinion aside and consider the evidence fair[ly] and impartially. The matter caused some speculation among bystanders" after the jury had been empaneled.[45]

With the jury selected and the charges reduced to second-degree murder, the judge began the trial in the closing days of July. "Believe it or not, there were persons waiting about the courthouse at 6 A.M. . . . in order to be sure of a seat at the hearing," observed the *Tribune*. "Some of those in attendance brought lunches. If others who occupied seats during the forenoon didn't bring their noon-day meal they must have done without since 90 per cent of them did not leave their seats during the hour and a half noon-recess."[46] Despite the tensions within the county, a black observer reported that attendees on both sides of the color line avoided provocations. "Throughout the tria[l] interest was keen and attendance heavy, but racial feeling was apparently dormant," he wrote. "White and colored spectators mingled in the courtroom and corridors without friction."[47]

To defend the white youths, attorneys painted an endearing portrait for the sympathetic jury. One of lawyers, James Collier, insisted that they were "not representing hoodlums or gangsters" but "six ordinary country boys who were never in any trouble before and with clean records." He added that the boys, "collected at the store in South Point, on the evening Murray was arrested and committed to jail, had no more idea of getting into trouble that night than any member of the jury." He also belittled the prosecutors and civil rights activists who had, he intimated, engaged in theatrics at the expense of justice. "He reminded the jury that he would not, like some others had, yell and carry on but would simply discuss the evidence," reported the *Tribune*. He urged that the trial be conducted in a dignified manner and argued as "a prosecution and not a persecution."[48]

Reflecting and reinforcing local white resentment toward the Davidsons, the defense attorneys harangued the white Georgians, dropping not-so-subtle intimations that they had a peculiar, if not perverted, relationship with their employee, "a low-life southern negro." Turning to the jury, Collier slyly suggested that "he was unable to determine for what reason all the Davidsons seemed to be shielding [Murray]." When Mrs. Davidson took the stand and asserted that her employee did not have a head wound prior to his arrest, Collier implied that she must have enjoyed surprising intimacy with him. "Collier asked her if she had had her hand on Murray's head before he was put in jail." Mrs. Davidson replied coldly, "No, I did not: I'm a Southerner."[49]

Although they were rough on Mr. and Mrs. Davidson, the defense attorneys were particularly aggressive with Nancy Adams, flatly accusing her of intimate relations with Murray. "She denied that she had ever walked hand in hand with Luke Murray," noted the *Tribune*. "The young lady was very much broken up" and fled the courtroom upon leaving the stand.[50] The prosecutor observed that these questions were designed merely to inflame public opinion and sway the jury: "All they wanted was to form an opinion . . . that there was something between this innocent little girl and Luke Murray." Furthermore, he added, it was based on mere rumor. "The cruelest, most unfair tactics I have ever seen employed in this court room came about when the defense cross-examined . . . Nancy," he asserted. "They asked her if she ever held hands with Luke Murray. As if it wouldn't have been common talk if she had. And if she had would not they have produced witness after witness to prove it?"[51]

Research shows that white midwesterners articulated their identity as racially progressive by juxtaposing their own supposed tolerance against the image of "bad" southern racists who routinely used terror to subordinate blacks.[52] The Lawrence County prosecutor placed himself firmly in the former tradition in his remarks during the trial. "Had it been South Point, Miss., or South Point, Ga., it would not have been so astounding," he marveled. "But South Point, O., much more educated than either of the Southern states was indeed surprising."[53] Without a hint of irony he identified the virtue of his own state by comparison with a southern foil identified with racism, ignorance, and violence. Notwithstanding his assumptions, however, the only sympathetic whites to emerge from the Lawrence County drama were the Davidsons—who were not midwesterners but much-maligned southerners. They showered their employee, Luke Murray, with apparent generosity in life and, after his death, testified against the lynchers and plainly desired to see a conviction.

Although several of the mob members admitted to their involvement in the kidnapping of Murray before the trial and elaborated on that testimony during the trial, the defense attorneys nevertheless sought to sanitize the role of these "ordinary country boys." First, they claimed that the boys had no plans to harm Murray; they simply wanted him to leave. "We discussed taking Murray from the jail and telling him to get out of the state," one mob member claimed. "He also said it was decided that [Murray] would not be injured. It was figured Murray wouldn't mind since he was already in jail."[54] Exasperated by this strategy, the prosecutor exclaimed that the defendants "would have you believe that they were doing Murray a favor by getting him out of jail."[55]

After taking charge of Murray, the defendants claimed, they had engaged him in a remarkably civil discussion about the most expeditious way to leave town. "It was suggested he take a freight out of town but Murray said it was dark and he was afraid to attempt to catch one," a mob member told the court. Another supposedly volunteered the money needed for the ferry to Kentucky before realizing that it had quit running for the day. Allegedly Murray "suggested that they get a boat and row across the river since he wanted to get to [Kentucky]." Amenable to this plan, the whites secured one and escorted the visitor across the Ohio. Once the party had rowed a good distance from the shore, however, Murray leapt out of the boat and drowned. Asked why the victim would jump into the water when he was being treated with such kindness, the defendants had no explanation.[56] Furthermore, when asked if Murray knew how to swim, Mrs. Davidson responded definitively: "No."[57]

The report produced in September by the Ohio NAACP raised additional questions about the evidence regarding Murray's supposed drowning, further undermining the story furnished by the mob members and their supporters. "Testimony revealed that the point where Murray was supposed to have sank, (the defendants stating that he jumped from a boat while they were rowing him across the Ohio River), is only wading depth, and it would be impossible for a man to meet his death by drowning without encouragement from his companions or as an after-death act." In addition, "the body was found close to the place where the over-board leap was supposed to have been made even though it had been in the water for some nine or ten days, and it would be natural for the current of the River to carry it somewhat farther."[58]

At trial, however, the defense attorneys presented other arguments that, though equally implausible, appealed to members of the jury and to whites generally. First, they claimed that there had not actually been a crime, that there was no evidence to "prove that the men harmed Murray after removing him from the jail." Second, they suggested that the lynching, if one *had* occurred, was in Kentucky's jurisdiction rather than

Ohio's because there was "insufficient evidence to show that the crime was committed in Lawrence County." Third, they denied that the deceased was the chauffeur. "Failure of the state to absolutely identify the body as that of Luke Murray, without a doubt, lends some support to the contention of belief by the defense that the floater found in the Ohio . . . was not that of the Negro."[59] Despite these claims, however, the Davidsons insisted that the floater was Murray. "A second cousin to Howard Davidson, testified that he had been talking to Murray some few hours before his arrest," observed the *Tribune*. "He . . . testified that the man taken from the river was dressed similarly. Murray, he said, had a small mustache which he described as of the Chas. Chaplin style. The negro taken from the river also bore the same kind of mustache."[60]

Several witnesses provided questionable testimony favorable to the white defendants. Frank Legg, a witness to the jail raid, claimed that he could not identify anyone who participated. "It was 'more dark than light,' he said, and while . . . he was not more than 25 feet from the crowd he was unable to recognize any of the alleged 'lynchers.'" Legg also claimed that he knew the victim because he was the only black in the area and that, after seeing the body of the floater, he could affirm that it was not the same man. Unconvinced, the prosecutor pointed out that Legg was the father-in-law of one of the defendants, a relationship which Legg admitted but the judge ruled inadmissible. Another witness who denied that the deceased was Murray admitted under oath that several defendants had appealed to him in person for testimony supporting their version of events.[61]

After the four-day trial ended on July 29, the jury returned a verdict of not guilty for all six defendants. Following the acquittal, the *Ironton Sunday Tribune*—though not altogether pleased with the outcome—demanded the release of Louis McKee, the only mob member who had been punished by virtue of his incarceration in the juvenile detention center. "Since a jury after a hearing has said that there was no offence of any kind in breaking into a jail and taking therefrom a live man, who is later found dead with a broken neck, we must contend that the youth, who is in a reformatory for participation in the same affair . . . should be brought home, and restored to liberty," it mused. "How can it be otherwise [?]"[62] Shortly thereafter, the *Ironton Evening Tribune* observed that McKee had been released.[63]

A black observer ruminated on additional reasons for the acquittals. Andrews "appeared to be weak in his preparation of the case, shallow and uncertain in the examination of witnesses, and lacking in zeal to obtain a conviction," he wrote. "One gathered that he was performing an unwanted task, and his expression before the opening of the trial, 'I wish this thing was all over,' indicated his attitude." With respect to this last point he identified a local political rift as one possible cause for the prosecutor's lack of 'zeal.' Lawrence County was "split into two major Republican factions, one of which is headed by ... the prosecuting attorney. South Point has consistently provided strong support for his faction, and it is highly probable that he did not wish to disaffect this vote by convicting six native sons." Furthermore, this same observer complained that "it was quite possible for jurors to have been influenced, since they were allowed to go home each night (without any objection from the prosecution)." Finally, he speculated that the jury may have been influenced by the report that, if the defendants were convicted, "Dr. Weaver, administrator for Murray's estate, proposed to sue Lawrence county for $5,000 under the 'death by mob' statute of Ohio."[64] Coming as it did near the nadir of the Great Depression, the possibility of an outlay of tax dollars of this magnitude, especially as punishment for the murder of a black person, was unacceptable to most whites.

During the trial the leaders of the Lincoln Club were visible in the courtroom, to the annoyance of some in the press corps. "The Lincoln club committee, which took quite an active part in the investigation of the alleged lynching, has occupied seats at the press table through the trial," snarled the *Ironton Evening Tribune*. "There has been little room at the table for working newspapermen."[65] In addition, shortly after the acquittal the club pressed new, if lesser, charges. "As the aftermath of the recent trial in which six white men were found not guilty," observed the *Tribune*, "charges have been filed in the court ... charging the same defendants and six other South Point white men with breaking into the South Point jail and kidnapping the negro." Although the magistrate dismissed the charges against five of them on the grounds of insufficient evidence, leaders of the club successfully pressed them against the remaining seven.[66]

Energized by its struggle, the civil rights group reorganized after the trial and set ambitious objectives. "The Lincoln Progressive Club incorporated under the laws of the State of Ohio, for the moral, social and economic uplift of the negro in Lawrence county and elsewhere, in a very interesting meeting held last night," a group leader wrote on August 16. "The membership committee ... has set its goal at 1000 members, by October first." Amid the Great Depression the club made economic opportunity its chief priority. "The organization is seeking employment for members of its group," he added, and "will get information to anyone interested in the movement and a list of capable men and women, desiring employment."[67]

In addition, Walter White, the national secretary of the NAACP, urged Governor White to direct his attorney general to prosecute the case. He charged that the first trial "was . . . little more than a farce and 'gravely reflects upon the integrity of the State of Ohio.'" He predicted that the forthcoming trial would "be 'equally meaningless due to weak and spineless prosecution'" conducted by a lawyer who would not "pursue his duties as vigorously as law and decency demand." Finally, he reminded the governor that the state had not conducted the first trial, as previously requested, that local officials had handled it instead, and that justice had not been served as a result.[68] Since the "opportunity for the convictions for lynching has thus passed . . . we now urge upon you that this second opportunity, less potent for good than the original one, but nevertheless of some considerable value, be taken advantage of." Failure to do so, warned the NAACP official, would "bring still further opprobrium to Ohio."[69]

Once again, Governor White refused to intervene, a reflection not only of his own attitudes but of his well-honed political calculation as well. "Governor White is a candidate for reelection," grumbled the *Negro Star*. If he were to intervene on behalf of a black lynching victim, he would almost certainly create for himself negative and "wide-spread political repercussions in November."[70] With his refusal to act, he assured his reelection but earned the scorn of blacks in the state. At their annual meeting in Cincinnati in September, members of the Ohio NAACP passed a resolution in which they "unreservedly condemn[ed] Governor George White for his refusal to request the Attorney General to send a representative to prosecute vigorously the accused in the Ironton lynching case after having been urgently requested to do so." They added their collective opinion that White was indifferent to the fate of the victim.[71] With the tacit support of the governor, the grand jury in Lawrence County ignored the admissions by the defendants and declined the indictments. "One thing which the grand jury did do was to write 'finis' on the South Point lynching case as a result of dismissing charges of breaking into the South Point jail and kidnapping Luke Murray," summarized the *Ironton Evening Tribune*. Despite the energetic efforts of blacks, the mob members walked free.[72]

In a disturbing indication of just how banal an event it was for a waterlogged black corpse to wash onto shore in Lawrence County, the *Tribune* reported on August 8, just a few weeks after the lynching, that "the body of a negro believed to be between 24 and 40 years of age was found at noon today in the Ohio river." Noting that the coroner believed that it had been there about a week, the *Tribune* was probably relieved to report that the body bore no evidence of violence.[73]

The lynching of Luke Murray provides a prism for understanding the nature of antiblack racism in the Midwest and the ascent of an increasingly cohesive black freedom struggle during the Great Depression and World War II. Situated in its larger temporal and spatial contexts, however, this lynching also assumes historiographical significance because it provides insight into the changing nature of antiblack lynching and antiblack violence more broadly, and of the black civil rights struggle in the Midwest in the late lynching period.

As this book demonstrates, white midwesterners lynched many blacks between the 1830s and the turn of the twentieth century. While they continued the practice at the start of the new century, they did so at a generally declining rate for reasons that are easily explained. Beginning in the early 1900s, white politicians, influenced increasingly by businessmen, newspaper editors, and middle-class voters, and supported by the ever more professionalized police forces that served them, took aggressive steps against such violence by spiriting would-be black victims from mob-encircled jails, deploying the state militia, and passing anti-mob statutes. For the most part they did so not because of their concern for black lives or abstract principles of racial justice but because of their concern for the economic and legal systems from which they benefited and over which they exercised control. In these efforts they received the support of blacks who had long fought against lynching by taking up arms against mobs, establishing black newspapers, founding civil rights groups, and challenging discrimination in court.

At the same time, however, the policemen who actively challenged, dispersed, or outwitted mobs increasingly assumed the role of the mob in protecting white supremacy. Reflecting the informal compromise that they had been forging for decades, they no longer permitted mobs to attack blacks with impunity. Instead, they targeted blacks themselves. After an unknown black man allegedly shot an officer in Chicago in 1926, for instance, the *Broad Ax* reflected on the role of law enforcement in racial control. "The Chicago police force . . . inaugurated a reign of terror in the South Side Negro section," it declared. "More than 350 arrests were made in the 'dragnet' in their 'efficient' search for one alleged criminal." The newspaper quoted an observer who declared that "the action of the Chicago police force . . . was nothing less than the action of a . . . mob, save that they did not string up anybody." During this episode they invaded the homes of many blacks, in some cases smashing in doors that were not opened right away. The *Broad Ax* concluded that the "policemen in American cities are most industrious in hunting down a Negro."[74]

Following a lynching in Chicago in 1924, in which a mob led by a man wielding a baseball bat beat a victim to death in the streets, white midwesterners did not perpetrate another antiblack lynching—or, at least, not another antiblack incident that contemporaries *called* a lynching—until August 1930, when a mob hanged two men in Marion, Indiana, and a photographer captured the event in a haunting and notorious image. For more than three decades before this event such mobs had occasionally aroused condemnation, as residents of cities such as Evansville, Indiana, and Cairo, Illinois, learned at the turn of the century. Coming so long after the last recorded midwestern lynching and after a consequential change in national opinion toward mob violence as a form of racial control, the mob in Marion provoked particularly bitter denunciation, as the sectional and national presses portrayed the city as an embarrassing backwater out of step with the Midwest and the broader North.[75] "Indiana has a black spot," declared the *Repository* of Canton, Ohio. "It should do everything possible to discourage a recurrence of such a disgrace by keeping its people awakened to the responsibilities of civilization."[76] In Massachusetts the *Springfield Republican* called the lynching "lawlessness and mob lust," a "disquieting commentary on the progress, or retrogression, of democratic government."[77]

The Marion lynching proved to be the last time a mob in the Midwest (excluding the outlier of Missouri) executed blacks in a so-called spectacle lynching, a public killing witnessed by a large crowd of supportive spectators who stood about unself-consciously examining their handiwork with no fear of legal or social sanctions. Given the already growing unacceptability of the practice among Midwesterners and then the flurry of negative publicity directed at Marion, the opponents of mob violence successfully prevented would-be lynch mobs from conducting spectacle lynchings thereafter. They did not prevent all lynchings, however. Instead, as the lynching of Luke Murray illustrates, mobs continued to operate successfully but did so by adopting what commentators at the time described as "underground" lynchings.

Underground lynchings were essentially rural affairs. Fearful of the sting of negative publicity, authorities in midwestern cities of any size had by this time effectively crushed the possibility that racist mobs could gain possession of a prisoner in their custody. Simultaneously, police forces in such cities had developed their own methods of racial control, exercised under the auspices of the law by killing or otherwise abusing the blacks whom they had sworn to protect. Accordingly, only those living in rural areas and small towns like South Point, where older forms of communal vengeance still persisted and sundown practices often resonated, could successfully exercise their animosity towards blacks through lynching.

Furthermore, most whites, rural or urban, now understood that lynching had largely lost its legitimacy. Consequently, those inclined to carry it out participated only in small numbers and disposed of the victims' bodies surreptitiously in order to minimize the possibility of capture and avoid the likelihood of publicity. For similar reasons they tended to target black strangers who had few, if any, personal ties to the area. Certainly, had they disposed effectively of Murray's body, the limited number of South Point lynchers would have ensured the silence that they desired—and avoided the historical scrutiny that this work exemplifies.

When underground lynchings were exposed, white communities responded by floating the charge that had long been central to the pro-mob argument: the victim committed or threatened sexual assault against a white woman. Whites in South Point, of course, implied that Murray had established an inappropriate relationship with Nancy Davidson and subsequently threatened to assault a woman, "to tear her clothes from her." Yet because lynching had largely lost its legitimacy in the region's cities and because urban midwesterners increasingly regarded their rural counterparts as rubes, the lynchers and their supporters could no longer count on the urban press to support their charges of rape or to justify mob violence. Indeed, while many white northerners continued to despise blacks, they now realized that accusations of rape were often overstated or invented and, as in the South Point incident, the state, sectional, and national presses largely ignored local claims that Murray was a predator.[78]

Given the reticence of the urban press to support lynchings or accusations of sexual assault, black newspapers and activists, whose influence had grown immeasurably since World War I, stepped into the gap, launching investigations of underground lynchings that identified white racism, not black wrongdoing, as the cause. The members of the Lincoln Club, the NAACP, and the black press exemplified this in the South Point case when they forced local officials to conduct an autopsy and then a trial, threatened to punish Lawrence County by invoking the Ohio mob law, organized public meetings to protest the killing, and, albeit unsuccessfully, lobbied the governor to take an active role in ferreting out and punishing the guilty.

Although lynching may have lost its legitimacy in the Midwest, white supremacy had not. When the perpetrators of underground lynchings saw their violence exposed, they could still be confident of escaping harsh consequences, as the South Pointers understood. Despite the admissions of involvement by several of the lynchers, the testimony of the Davidson family, questionable testimony for the defense, and substantial physical evidence, the young white men in Lawrence County escaped punishment in their first trial because of the refusal of white residents to convict "ordinary country boys" of any crime against a black outsider. In the second trial, on lesser charges, they also escaped prosecution, this time because of the reluctance of the local prosecutor and others in the legal hierarchy to uphold justice.

The characteristics associated with the Murray lynching are evident in other underground lynchings in the Midwest in the late lynching period. The mob that lynched James E. Person in 1942 was certainly rural. Originating in Vigo County, Indiana, it pursued Person across the Illinois border, killing him near Paris, and drawing little attention. In fact, had a farmer not discovered the corpse "in a corn field west of the Illinois-Indiana line, riddled with about 60 shotgun slugs and one bullet," the mob would have received little to no publicity. As it was, the victim lay dead for a month before being found.[79] The small Paris mob also revealed the practices enforced across the sundown belt that straddled that area of the Illinois-Indiana border. "There are no Negroes . . . in the rural community where Person was shot, and in this fact, may lie the key to the killing," maintained Marjorie McKenzie, a reporter for the *Pittsburgh Courier*, a premier black newspaper. "This is the old story of the fate of the stranger in the midst of a homogenous culture. A primitive society will not tolerate a newcomer who looks and acts and smells different from its members because he represents a potential threat to their security."[80]

The Paris lynch mob targeted a stranger who had no personal ties to the area. James E. Person was an outsider—in this case, a veteran traveling through the Midwest in search of work. Like Luke Murray, he was a *southerner* raised under a different system of racism, an outsider from Tennessee who failed to understand the nuances associated with midwestern racial mores and traditions. Apparently, he offended whites unwittingly with behavior that would have attracted little concern among whites in his native South. "His only offense," argued McKenzie, "seems to have been to beg for food from door to door (back doors, of course, as any proper Southern Negro of his class would do). In the South, his appearance would have startled and disturbed no one and he would have been fed, given a coin and sent on his way."[81] Had Person or Murray been native to the Midwest and raised with an understanding of its unique racial etiquette, he would surely have recognized the behaviors that would offend whites there and would just as surely have avoided them.

After the underground lynching in Paris was exposed, local whites claimed that Person had been frightening women. White newspapers failed to support their claims, and McKenzie uncovered and publicized a very different story. "Person had committed no offense," she found. "There was no probable cause to believe that he had committed a felony; neither the sheriff nor his deputies had seen Person commit a misdemeanor, and they had no warrant for his arrest." Instead,

> a woman telephone operator at Libertyville [Indiana], who said that a Negro had "bothered" her several months previously, initiated an active rumor campaign concerning Person's presence and activity in the community. In her strategic position she became a perfect clearing house for gossipy house-wives, and it is further alleged that, finally, the sheriff of Vigo county aided and abetted her by circulating around the county, spreading the rumors, enlisting deputies and beginning the hunt for Person, which he subsequently carried over the State line beyond his jurisdiction.[82]

After the Paris lynchers saw their actions exposed, they could still count on a commitment to white supremacy among local officials and citizens sufficient to ensure that they would escape harsh consequences. In fact, they received a light penalty for the killing of Person. "Nine farmers . . . were fined $200 each . . . on charges which developed from the fatal shoot-ing of a Negro," reported the *Decatur (IL) Daily Review* in 1946. "The nine also were assessed the cost of prosecution, which was reported to have been minor." The other alleged perpetrators, including the Indiana sheriff who led them, saw the charges against them dropped altogether.[83]

The characteristics associated with the underground lynchings in South Point and Paris were affirmed with the lynching of Hollie Willis near the small town of Lewiston, Illinois, in 1943. A posse of just four farmers fatally shot Willis, a black soldier posted at a nearby military facility. Although the details of the case remain murky, the farmers, angry about the alleged rape of a white woman by a black soldier days earlier, killed Willis, who, for reasons that are not entirely clear, stood guard at the vacated house where the rape had occurred and allegedly made a series of "insulting telephone calls" to white women in the area. "The first telephone call aroused several farmers because all phones on the party line ring when a call is placed over it," noted the *Chicago Daily Tribune*. "A woman who answered heard a voice ask for a date and fol-low the request with indecent proposals." With some of the unexplained details in its story, the *Tribune* hinted that whites may have provoked whatever incident occurred and that the killers knew precisely who their victim was and where to find him: "The farmers," it related, "instructed their wives to keep the man talking as long as possible while they located him."[84]

Not surprisingly, Lewiston, like South Point and Paris before it, was an "all-white" sundown town until World War II, when whites temporarily allowed black soldiers from nearby Camp Ellis to enter restaurants, taverns, and stores (or, perhaps, submitted to the insistence of black soldiers themselves to be served). According to the sociologist James W. Loewen, whites in Lewiston relaxed their sundown practices during the war because "everyone in Lewiston knew that the soldiers were never going to stay there permanently." Nevertheless, as the Willis lynching demonstrates, whites in the vicinity were never really hospitable—even when they briefly amended their sundown practices in exchange for the economic opportunities presented by Camp Ellis.[85] As in the other instances examined, the lynchers near Lewiston had little to fear. "A Negro soldier . . . was shot and killed," summarized the *Chicago Daily Tribune*. "No charges have been placed against members of the posse."[86]

In the Willis case the federal government, the military, and the press may have had their own reasons for limiting the publicity surrounding an event involving a soldier on active duty during a world war. First, they may have feared that the lynching of a black serviceman could inflame enmity among whites and blacks in the country generally and in the military particularly, undermining the unity of purpose required to fight Germany, Italy, and Japan. Second—but related to the first—they may have feared that this lynching might provide these same adversaries with an opportunity to discredit America's claim to represent freedom and liberty for all, thereby deflecting "international attention from their own totalitarian abuses and imperial designs, [and] positioning themselves as enlightened."[87]

Because underground lynchings were by definition surreptitious, they became newsworthy only when they were exposed in places like South Point, Paris, and to a more limited degree Lewiston. Some, perhaps many, never became newsworthy because their perpetrators successfully disguised their handiwork. These have not, therefore, been documented and may be irretrievably lost. Others may have received some limited coverage in local papers but, for whatever reason, no coverage outside that area. As a consequence, historians almost certainly underestimate the numbers of underground lynchings. Nonetheless, some of those lynchings that did receive news coverage, however limited, may be posited by a careful reading of these accounts and by an enhanced understanding of the common characteristics associated with such killings in the late lynching period. The following incidents are suggestive.

In 1929 a posse surrounded the home of an accused felon named Louis Seeman in the small city of North Platte, Nebraska. Before long, policemen announced that "Seeman committed suicide after barricading himself against combined forces of police and firemen for two hours."[88] A critical reader may, however, find it difficult to accept the verdict of suicide when the posse burned the home in which he was trapped. Certainly, blacks "expressed doubt that the negro who murdered the North Platte policeman later committed suicide." If Seeman *did* kill himself to avoid certain death from the fire or from the posse that started it, did he really commit suicide, or did he simply end his life more quickly when his death already seemed inevitable?[89] Furthermore, the white residents and the authorities in North Platte cast further doubt on the cause of his death by their actions immediately thereafter. First, a mob expelled all of the other blacks from North Platte and looted their homes. Second, the authorities showed little interest in investigating either Seeman's death or the riot. "County Attorney A. J. Salisbury and Chief of Police James Dorrain of North Platte," reported the *Daily Journal-Gazette and Commercial-Star*, frankly conceded that what white townspeople wanted was for the blacks to leave the county, and "then they would 'not be bothered,' they said."[90]

In 1930 a black stranger named Clarence Hayes died at the hands of members of a posse in rural and overwhelmingly white Burlington, Kansas. According to a nationally circulated wire report, he was "shot to death as he offered to surrender."[91] Local whites, however, vigorously protested this narrative, asserting that Hayes "returned the fire until he was killed," reported the *Emporia Weekly Gazette*. "It is not known who fired the shots that killed Hayes."[92] At the request of prominent whites, the coroner then held an inquest "in order to get a record and as a protection to members of the posse should relatives of the negro ever try to make trouble."[93] It is, of course, impossible to determine at this point whether the posse members gave Hayes an opportunity to surrender. What *is* clear is that local whites understood that the distinction was crucial in determining their liability. Accordingly, they tailored the official documents in a way that would avoid a demand for an inquiry or a settlement by the Hayes family, thereby denying justice to the family and removing their own legal accountability.

The act of mob violence that claimed the life of Luke Murray reinforced the white supremacy that had prevailed in Lawrence County and across Ohio since the early nineteenth century and had hardened into Jim Crow practices in the twentieth. Specifically, it defined once again "appropriate" social roles for black men as brutally subordinated laborers rather than trusted employees, proscribed friendship or intimacy between white women and black men, and refreshed the reputation of South Point as a sundown town. The lynching and its aftermath also warned whites who violated these social norms that they would be ostracized and marginalized, a lesson that the prominent Davidson family and Nancy Adams learned when they suffered social alienation and psychological abuse of different sorts at the hands of the townspeople and the defense attorneys.

The lynching terrorized blacks in Lawrence County and across Ohio, but it also provided them with an opportunity to expand their civil rights activism and to forge linkages with activists elsewhere. Although the South Point mob escaped the consequences of its actions, the Lincoln Club and the Ohio NAACP won important victories: they forced the initially reticent local authorities to conduct an autopsy, to press charges against local boys, and to conduct a trial that brought unflattering publicity on their county. Although the blacks lost in court, they emerged from the South Point affair with a new sense of their power. Certainly, the Lincoln Club emerged with an enlarged and energized membership, and the NAACP used the incident as a rallying cry against an unresponsive governor and as a recruiting tool for a membership drive.

Although racist violence and discrimination were organizing principles across the Midwest, the violence in South Point shows that whites there projected an identity as racially progressive by comparing themselves favorably to white southerners, who were synonymous nationally with racist injustice and were useful therefore in negating symbolically the antiblack sins of white northerners. Had he recognized his own embrace of midwestern mythologies and the history of racist violence in Ohio, the Lawrence County prosecutor would have been more circumspect in claiming that a lynching in South Point, Ohio, was astounding but one in South Point, Georgia, would be unremarkable. Ironically, nearly every white midwesterner identified in the story aided or abetted the lynchers and only the white southerners (the Davidsons) pressed for justice for the murdered man.

Observers have speculated that black midwesterners could find themselves confronted by lynch mobs when venturing into the South because they did not understand the unique racial etiquette of that place. Reflecting on the lynching of Emmett Till in Mississippi in 1955, the journalist William Bradford Huie succinctly summarized this wisdom. His murderers shot Till "because he boasted of having a white girl and showed them the picture of a white girl in Chicago," he declared. "Young Till—he never realized the danger he was in. He never knew. I'm quite sure that he never thought these two men would kill him. And[,] um, or maybe he's just in such a strange environment, he doesn't—he really just doesn't know what he's up against."[94] The historian Stephen J. Whitfield shares this perspective. "Till did not act like his Southern cousins," he wrote. To white Mississippians "he said 'yeah' and 'naw' instead of the customary 'yassah' and 'nawsah.' Even more striking was the photograph he carried in his wallet of a white girl who he claimed was his girlfriend up in Chicago."[95]

This chapter accepts the claims of Huie and Whitfield but argues that the phenomenon that they described as *unidirectional* was in fact *bidirectional*: black southerners who ventured into the Midwest unaware of its unique racial etiquette could likewise find themselves in danger, as Murray, the Georgian, and Person, the Tennessean, learned the hard way. After her assumptions about racism and geography were refuted in the Person case, McKenzie mused that it was "bizarre that a man should have to go north to get lynched."[96] By taking seriously the Midwest as a place with its own unique and uncompromising white supremacist etiquette, this study may erode the assumption that there was something bizarre about such an event.

With its focus on rural and predominantly white areas of the Midwest, this study challenges the heavily *southern* focus of the scholarship on anti-black racism generally and the overwhelmingly *urban* focus of the research concerning the Midwest. Instead, the chapter builds on recent scholarship in documenting the distinctive brand of white supremacy in the largely white and substantially sundown Midwest—a brand that differed from the one prevailing in the rural southern states such as Mississippi *and* in sprawling midwestern metropolises like Chicago. Consequently, it affirms the findings of the historian Clarence Lang, who argues strongly "in favor of the continued necessity of regional specificity in Black Freedom Movement histories" and, quoting Orville Vernon Burton, insists that "historians need to show how race works differently in different regions."[97]

With its focus on sundown towns, this study illustrates the commitment of white midwesterners to the preservation of sundown practices into the 1930s and 1940s. In addition to those in South Point, Paris, Lewiston, North Platte, and Burlington, lynch mobs elsewhere in the Midwest almost certainly murdered other blacks in these years but more effectively disguised their efforts. Although the numbers of lynchings would surely have been smaller in the Midwest than in the South owing to demography alone, the unnamed investigator of a 1940 national study focused on such killings in Dixie and titled "Lynching Goes Underground" might have come to similar conclusions had he studied the Heartland. The declining number of lynchings, he claimed, was misleading. "'Countless Negroes are lynched yearly,' the report stated, 'but their disappearance is shrouded in mystery, for they are dispatched quietly and without general knowledge. In some lonely swamp a small body of men do the job formerly done by a vast, howling bloodthirsty mob composed of men, women, and children."[98]

Whites in sundown towns continued to enforce their practices for decades thereafter, as the *Alton Evening Telegraph* admitted in a 1955 reflection on southeastern Illinois. "We have a number of cities and villages which have somehow kept Negroes out," it noted. "Residents of those communities won't even allow Negroes to reside in them."[99] As late as 1970 the *Southern Illinoisan* reported that "there are no blacks in Thebes," an Illinois town whence whites had expelled temporary black workers with a lynching and riot in 1903. In 1970 locals were tight-lipped about the reasons for this situation. "When visitors ask questions about the absence of blacks," the paper stated, "residents reply in hushed tones or change the subject. Those who do comment insist on remaining anonymous." Claiming that the hanging tree "still [stood] at the edge of town," an elderly resident recalled that "Thebes gained a reputation for being against blacks. To this day, some people stop and stare when one comes through."[100]

With its focus on mob violence in the Midwest in the late lynching period, this study demonstrates that lynchings reveal clear continuities with and distinct discontinuities from earlier lynchings, namely, an ongoing commitment to mob violence and white supremacy but a transition from an emphasis on spectacle to an emphasis on secrecy. Reflecting on these trends after the Paris lynching, McKenzie captured them perfectly, writing that the case did "not fit into the conventional pattern of quaint old lynching customs." Instead, she concluded in a memorable turn of phrase, it was "a queer precipitate of the old and the new in racial interaction."[101] In reaching her conclusion, McKenzie echoed the aforementioned 1940 study, arguing that this type of violence "was not disappearing but rather 'entering a new and altogether dangerous phase.'"[102]

The Midwest, therefore, underwent at this time a phenomenon that would be replicated in the South a few years later. The historian Charles M. Payne recognized the pattern in his study of the Mississippi Delta in the 1950s and 1960s. "By the end of the thirties, NAACP officials . . . thought howling mobs were becoming passe," he wrote. "Small groups of men were doing quietly what large crowds used to do publicly. Kangaroo courts and charges of 'killed while resisting arrest' were giving racial murder a quasi-legal air. Even when large groups were involved, there were more attempts to suppress news of murders—this in a state where lynchings had previously been announced in the newspapers a couple of days in advance in order to give the country people time to get to town."[103] Tameka Bradley Hobbs charted a similar shift. "Secrecy is evidence of fear, especially when considered in contrast to the bold and public lynching bees that dotted Florida's past," she wrote. "The deliberate clandestineness surrounding these events signals that, by the 1940s, lynchers somehow felt less confident that they could participate in extralegal activities and evade detection and prosecution." As this study has, she found another significant indicator of the transformations in the practice, that is, its location: "Whereas lynchings in the 1930s took place all over the state, with nearly half occurring in urban areas, the lynchings of the next decade were confined to rural north Florida."[104]

In addition, this chapter recognizes the significance of continuously evolving communications technologies to lynching. In both Paris and Lewiston, for example, white women used the telephone to aid and abet their menfolk in the hunt, becoming de facto mob members though they were miles from the scene of the killings. In Paris they coordinated by telephone to track Person's flight and to feed that information to the sheriff and his posse. In Lewiston they kept Willis occupied on the phone so that their husbands could find and kill him. Similarly, black activists relied increasingly on the new technologies, particularly newspapers and organizations, both of which, with their increasingly nationwide reach, now had the potential to arouse outrage and organize resistance across a much broader area than they had been able to do when lynchings were more common. In the South Point case, for instance, blacks organized at the local and state levels and secured the support of a national civil rights leader, Walter White. In the Paris incident, the *Courier*, a black paper in distant Pennsylvania, conducted the most thorough and probing inquiry.[105]

In the archetypal example, the lynching of Emmett Till attracted a huge amount of attention from black and white newspapers and magazines across the country, from the NAACP, from ordinary Americans from all walks of life, and from observers around the world. As a consequence, it became indelibly etched into the national memory in a way that most, perhaps all, of the lynchings that took place in the previous century had not. As a result, black children around the country—not merely those in Mississippi—experienced the lynching of Till in an intimate way, as a terrifying episode that many of them later credited as a defining experience in their decisions to participate in the civil rights movement of the 1960s. "The murder of this Chicago youth—who whistled at a white woman at a crossroads grocery store in Money, Mississippi, in August 1955 and was lynched for it—catalyzed men and women into an irresistible movement for change," writes the scholar Elliott J. Gorn. "So many people roughly of Till's age when he was murdered look back at his death and the acquittal of his killers as a formative moment in their lives, from Anne Moody to Muhammad Ali, from Stokely Carmichael to Congressman John Lewis."[106]

Historians tend to view the late lynching period as the slow and ugly but inevitable *end* of lynchings, with closing chapter titles like "Judge Lynch's Demise" or the "Demise of Lynching."[107] This study does not dispute that lynching saw its demise in these years. It suggests, however, that the changes to this practice offer valuable insights that remain largely unarticulated as long as the acts themselves are regarded as significant only because they underscore the demise of this type of racist violence in America rather than as something that remained very real and vital in the lives of those continuing to perpetrate and to suffer its reality throughout the middle decades of the twentieth century.

Conclusion

Over the course of roughly 110 years, whites in the Midwest used various types of violence to establish and maintain control over blacks and to seize their property. From the 1830s to the early 1860s, and especially in the 1850s, they conducted slave hunts, capturing fugitive slaves to return them to their aggrieved masters for a bounty or kidnapping free blacks to sell into slavery for pure profit. On a number of occasions they killed their victims, either intentionally or through abuse, as they did when a group of slave catchers near Cedarville, Ohio, beat a free black man into submission, causing his death before they could sell him. In Nashville, Illinois, two slave hunters killed a fugitive slave in 1857 and then sawed his head off, pickled it in a jug of alcohol, and carried it to Missouri for a reward. The local histories written in counties across the Midwest in the late nineteenth and early twentieth centuries are littered with such stories, as are the contemporary newspapers. A comprehensive study of slave hunting there will surely yield significant new insights into midwestern history.

Although slave hunting disappeared with the collapse of slavery during and after the Civil War, racist violence of all types did not. Lynch mobs targeted black victims across all eleven of the decades examined in *Hostile Heartland*, from the grisly attacks in the Old Northwest before the Civil War to the underground lynchings of the late lynching period. They used unrestrained violence throughout the period, as exemplified by the castration and execution in Golconda in 1857, the hanging or dismemberment of five black men in Mt. Vernon, Indiana, in 1878, and the double hanging in Marion, Indiana, in 1930.

Whites often instigated race riots, assaulting black victims, stealing or destroying their property, and, not infrequently, driving large numbers of them from town. The rioters in Cincinnati essentially went to war against blacks in 1841, firing cannon blasts into the city's black quarters. More than three decades later, white miners opened fire indiscriminately on black passersby in Coal Creek, Indiana, leaving at least three dead. In one of the most notorious riots in the history of the Midwest, whites in Pierce City, Missouri, first hung a black prisoner, then raided the armory, and finally invaded the black neighborhood, killing two more blacks, burning several houses, and expelling the entire black population. During the World War I period, midwesterners engaged in some of the worst race riots in American history, including those in East St. Louis and Chicago.

Mobs regularly whipped blacks as punishment. In the Old Northwest in the antebellum years, they flogged their victims, sometimes to death, as part of what in that period they called lynching. They continued to use whipping thereafter, although its frequency apparently declined, at least as measured by its documentation in the primary sources. In addition, as the term *lynching* came to be identified exclusively with lethal violence during the Civil War, whites no longer associated whippings with it. In Little Dixie, where slavery was well-established until the early 1860s, whites continued to draw on that heritage for decades, conducting routine floggings against both men and women.

By the end of Reconstruction and increasingly thereafter, police officers menaced black communities, conducting indiscriminate raids on their homes and businesses, arresting anyone they regarded as suspicious-looking, and maiming and killing them, often on the slightest pretext. By the early twentieth century, these officers had supplanted mobs as the greatest threat to the black population of the Midwest. The *American Citizen*, a black newspaper, recognized the relation between the decline in lynching and the rise of police violence. "Another fleeing Negro killed in Kansas City Mo.," it reported in May 1897. "Scarcely a week rolls by now except a Negro is put to sleep in K.C." These trends were related, it added: "Lynching has not been attempted [in Kansas City] lately, but they find a way of hustling the Negro along almost as effectively. An officer in the discharge of his duty they say—well this is May—maybe he was."[1]

Individual white men murdered blacks capriciously, often on a whim. After one such homicide in Eureka, Indiana, on July 4, 1868, the white perpetrator self-righteously marched down to the park, stood on a bench, announced his deadly act, and encouraged his listeners to do the same. If white men, individually or in small groups, killed black men with impunity, they often groped, fondled, and raped black women with the same impunity, all the while hypocritically charging blacks with the same behavior against white women. When a black woman told of being gang raped during the 1841 Cincinnati riot, for instance, local whites ignored her claims because no white person could or would substantiate them. Yet when white men attacked Alton and Ella Pearl in Silex in 1906, they flogged *him* outdoors but for reasons unspecified flogged *her* in a warehouse.

Throughout the entire period, white midwesterners resorted to racist violence for a variety of reasons. Fundamentally, though, they aimed to defend white supremacy, to keep blacks in their appointed place on the bottom rung of the social ladder. When the end of the Civil War and the dissolution of slavery prompted a surge of black refugees into the Hoosier State in the summer of 1865, whites—led by Union veterans—attacked them viciously along the southern lip of the state in a series of incidents in Evansville, Boonville, New Albany, and Jeffersonville. Decades later, whites in Lawrence County, Ohio, responded with rage when they saw Luke Murray, a black butler, driving an expensive car, taking responsibility for the Davidson farm during the absence of the patriarch, and acting as a protector for a young white woman coveted by local men. To put Murray in his place, they hauled him from the South Point jail, hanged him, and threw his broken body into the Ohio River.

Under the auspices of white supremacy, however, whites were motivated to act violently against blacks for very specific reasons, real or imagined. Often, they objected to competition from blacks for jobs, as mobs demonstrated in places like Toledo, Ohio, where during the 1862 race riot they pummeled black dockworkers and stevedores, and Coal Creek and Knightsville, Indiana, where they targeted black miners with a series of riots in the 1870s.

Whites often feared black settlement in their all-white or mostly white towns. Consequently, they utilized violence of all types to curb popular black migration movements from the South or to control the migration of rural blacks to urban centers. Often they succeeded in redirecting unwanted blacks elsewhere, expelling them altogether, or relegating them to segregated neighborhoods. In the late 1840s white farmers in Ohio, including the Quakers at times, repeatedly expelled from Mercer, Shelby, Darke, and Miami Counties black settlers who had recently purchased land in the area. In the early decades of the twentieth century, whites in rural counties and urban centers in southwest Missouri undertook a cleansing of blacks in many of its counties, especially in the south-central part of the region.

In addition to their fears about these swelling black populations, whites felt threatened by the concomitant possibility that blacks would send their children to white schools or acquire additional political power, concerns that were often interrelated. With a series of race riots that rocked Ohio in 1841, whites challenged the efforts of blacks and white liberals in the legislature to integrate a school in Brown County. During the Exodus, Democrats in Indiana responded with explicitly political violence to their concern that the influx of black migrants would advantage the Republican Party. During a related riot in Rockport, a mob killed a black victim while chanting the name of the Democratic presidential candidate.

Frequently, white men simply used violence to defend what they considered their prerogatives. They punished blacks who, despite the obstacles placed in their way, still managed to achieve economic success. In Cairo, Illinois, Joseph Spencer earned the resentment and enmity of less successful whites with his attainments as the owner of a floating hotel and his skill as a gambler. In 1854 he lost his life to a lynch mob as a result. In Salina, Kansas, Wade Adams Sr. attracted the same kinds of negative attention from resentful whites because of his success as a farmer. In the mid-1890s he experienced the lynching of his son, Dana, the threatened lynching of two of his other sons, and the destruction of his farm buildings, his machinery, and his crops by mobs. In addition, white men sought to exert their control over interracial sexual relations by allowing whites to rape black women, "protect" white women from alleged black rapists, and subordinate black men by portraying them as sexual predators and then punishing them in terrible ways. In each instance, white men—the principal perpetrators of racist violence—used this violence to solidify their position atop the sexual hierarchy.

Throughout the entire period, the white majority volunteered its support for racist violence. In the case of mob violence, many thousands of ordinary whites participated in it, destroying black-owned churches, schools, businesses, and houses, and targeting black people with violence of every conceivable type. Bolstering the violence—and, in turn, drawing strength from it—were the racist laws and practices that governed race relations. From the early nineteenth century until the Civil War, whites in the free states of the Old Northwest passed Black Laws designed to subordinate blacks and to prevent them from even living in those states. Whites in the one midwestern slave state, Missouri, enforced human bondage during the same period. After the Civil War, white midwesterners maintained a handful of racist laws—primarily segregating schools—but introduced strict racist practices that assumed the power of law over time.

By the turn of the twentieth century, whites were expanding these practices and, in more than a few cases, attempting to expand them into the
system of racial discrimination known as Jim Crow, a system that survived
through World War II.

Just as significant, the vast majority of white community and state leaders—including newspaper editors, businessmen, police officers, governors,
legislators, and judges—supported the violence, either overtly or tacitly.
Even when some whites condemned racist violence, these leaders almost
always refused to investigate, prosecute, or convict perpetrators, no matter how indisputable the evidence against the accused. As exemplified in
the South Point, Ohio, lynching of 1932, white people were not willing
to convict local youths who, they insisted, were only doing what they
thought was right and proper. Furthermore, despite political pressure
from the NAACP and a direct appeal from its national secretary, Walter
White, during the summer of 1932, Governor White refused to intervene
in the case, a decision clearly reflecting both his racial predilections and
his political calculations in advance of an upcoming election. If a refusal
to punish racist violence suggests support for it, then white midwesterners
were very supportive, indeed.

Though often emphatically racist, the growing middle and upper classes
increasingly opposed mob violence because they feared the threat that it
posed to their economic and legal systems. Accordingly, they sought to
end it through legislation that would punish municipalities that failed to
control it, the deployment of state militias that would supplement local
resources when necessary, and the growth and professionalization of
police forces that would oppose racist mobs but simultaneously assume
their role in controlling blacks. Responding to a series of gruesome lynchings in the state at the turn of the century, for example, Indiana governor
Winfield T. Durbin dispatched troops to Evansville to prevent another
such killing in 1903. Shortly thereafter, they unleashed a deadly barrage
on an advancing mob.

Whites were particularly likely to practice racist violence on holidays
of various sorts, occasions when drunkenness and revelry among whites
and blacks brought together people of different social groups that might
not normally fraternize. The Godley family discovered this in 1902 when
a conflict with whites—and then with police officers—on Christmas Eve
quickly escalated into the lynching of Mumpford Godley and the flight
of his wounded brother Joe from the city. During the slavery period and
for years thereafter, whites often attacked blacks on the Fourth of July,
as typified by the previously mentioned beheading of the fugitive slave

in Nashville, Illinois, in 1857 or the murder of the black resident by the
enthusiastic white killer in Eureka, Indiana, in 1868. Frederick Douglass
recognized this predilection for violence on the Fourth when he lamented:
the Fourth "is *yours*, not *mine*. *You* may rejoice, I must mourn."

White Midwesterners were masters of the false narrative. From the
antebellum years through the turn of the century, they were fervent racists
who subscribed to popular stories about themselves as meritocratic and
racially liberal, and at the same time absolved themselves of responsibility for acts of racist violence by ascribing them to white interlopers from
more southerly locales. In the Old Northwest whites routinely blamed
acts of racist violence in their own states on southerners and on Kentuckians in particular. They accused them of stealing across the Ohio River to
commit these often heinous acts; they occasionally disguised themselves
as Kentuckians to obscure their own acts of racist violence; and to divert
attention from themselves they blamed southern settlers in the southern
reaches of their states for the purportedly higher levels of racial animus
there. For their part, white southerners recognized and widely publicized
this midwestern tendency to deny the racist impulses within themselves
and the hypocrisy that it revealed.

Similarly, whites were adept at creating and publicizing negative images
of blacks, crafting a narrative that emphasized their supposedly criminal
behavior, the aggressive sexual prowess of black men and their preference
for white women, their shiftless behavior, the promiscuity of black women,
and so forth. In creating these images, they justified the targeting of blacks
with violence, instilled and reinforced the fears of whites, and thereby
gave white men carte blanche to defend themselves and their families
with acts of extreme violence. Nowhere, perhaps, did they exemplify this
more clearly than in their interactions with the men of the Godley family in Southwest Missouri and Southeast Kansas, where they continually
gossiped about the ruthless and dissolute ways of these people and then
defended themselves by murdering, in rapid succession, Will, French,
Pete, and Mumpford. They created so negative an image of this family, in
fact, that when forced to concede that they had killed the wrong Godley in
Pittsburg, white townspeople dismissively asserted that the dead man had
gotten just what he deserved and promised to wreak the same vengeance
on his brother Joe when caught.

The black victims of racist violence included men and women, irrespective of age or class. Young-to-middle-aged men were the most likely
victims, particularly of lynch mobs and police officers, but all black
women lived in a racist rape culture that made them potential victims

of unpunished sexual abuse at any moment. Men, women, and children suffered at the hands of rioters and of the whipping mobs that menaced Little Dixie. Black property owners, especially the successful ones, were likely victims. Those who suffered the lash, the noose, or the policeman's pistol were not the only victims, however. The families who loved them and often depended on them lived for the rest of their lives with the emotional pain and humiliation, and often the economic costs foisted on them by whites. Furthermore, particularly resistant families who refused to submit to the strictures of the racist society in which they lived, earned far more than their fair share of such violence.

The white victims of racist violence, many of whom bore the label of race traitor, included in the antebellum-period abolitionists who argued in favor of immediate emancipation of all slaves and equal rights for free blacks. These included men such as Elijah Lovejoy, who was murdered by a mob in Alton, Illinois, in 1837, and Henry W. De Puy, who narrowly escaped a similar situation in Indianapolis in 1845. White victims also included women who, casting convention aside, rejected patriarchal protection and openly pursued consensual sexual relationships with black men, such as the woman in Indianapolis in 1840 who, for her courage, found herself hauled around the capital on a horse, nearly naked and suffering taunts and insults. In general, any white person who acted in a manner that other whites perceived as sympathetic toward blacks might find him- or herself victimized. One of these was Harry T. Loper, the restaurateur in Springfield, Illinois, who in 1908 assisted in spiriting from town two potential lynching victims and then saw a mob annihilate his business. On several occasions, police officers and soldiers who protected the lives of would-be black victims suffered insult or assault at the hands of fellow whites. In particular, the soldiers who gunned down mob members in places like Washington Court House, Urbana, Evansville, and Cairo learned that their support for the law over white supremacy won them few friends.

Many of the black and white victims of racist violence actively resisted and opposed white supremacy by a wide range of methods. Black midwesterners often took up arms to combat or to disperse white mobs, as evidenced during the race riot in Cincinnati in 1841, the race riot and expulsion in Pierce City, Missouri, in 1901, and the defense of southern cotton workers in Alexander County, Illinois, in 1924. With their preemptive raid to disarm the black community in Crestline, Ohio, during the racial tensions in Bucyrus in 1931, police officers indicated that the possibility of an armed black response was a risk that demanded action.

Blacks resisted as well through their steadfast determination to challenge the white supremacist practices of their oppressors by asserting their own dignity and humanity and by bucking the rules repeatedly. Although this strain of resistance runs throughout the study, Joseph Spencer and the unyielding black families identified in Kansas—such as the Godleys, the Vinegars, the Porters, the Tolivers, and the Adamses—best exemplified this spirit, often at tremendous cost to themselves.

Blacks challenged white supremacy as well through their concentration in black neighborhoods, often in larger urban areas where they could carve out some sense of autonomy and, as a result of their sheer numbers, could better defend themselves from attacks by whites and develop an embryonic middle class. In 1876 they successfully defended themselves in Indianapolis when a white mob, concerned that their numbers presented a political threat to white Democratic control, chose to intimidate them with violence. Even in the sundown Missouri Ozarks, blacks in the region fled to places like Joplin and Springfield where, despite acts of racist violence, they were too important to the local economy and too large in total numbers to expel entirely.

In the late nineteenth and, particularly, in the early twentieth century, blacks increasingly opposed racism and racist violence by establishing their own newspapers, which challenged white narratives, promoted black perspectives, and called for the arrest and prosecution of those responsible for attacks on blacks. Black newspapers in Kansas, for example, challenged stories by whites that were promulgated against the Godleys after the assaults against them in Missouri and Kansas in 1901–1902, enabling this book to patch together alternative and far more flattering stories about this family. Again in 1932, black newspapers, particularly the *Pittsburgh Courier*, provided an illuminating record of the events in Lawrence County, Ohio, that was very much at odds with the version published in the white press. As shown, too, in the Lawrence County incident, black organizations, such as the Lincoln Club at the local level and the NAACP at the state and national levels, organized the black population against discrimination and violence, pressed for prosecutions of the whites responsible for it, and lobbied influential officials to act on behalf of their black constituents. Finally, individual black midwesterners pursued remedies through the courts, even if the final outcomes were often disappointing to them. In Kansas, Alfred Toliver, Wade Adams Sr., and Henry Godley all filed charges or lawsuits against the lynch mobs and police officers responsible for the deaths of their sons. In Lawrence County blacks demanded an autopsy of the lynching victim, threatened to sue the county under the Ohio anti-mob law, and pressed for the prosecution of those responsible.

The white minority also resisted racist violence in a variety of ways. In the antebellum period, abolitionists in the Old Northwest appealed primarily to moral suasion. In Alton, Illinois, Elijah Lovejoy used his newspaper, the *Alton Observer*, to denounce discrimination and brutality; in Indianapolis Henry W. De Puy, editor of the *Indiana Freeman*, used his newspaper similarly but he also directly reproved bloodthirsty mobs on the streets of the city. In other cases, even whites disposed toward mob violence opposed its indiscriminate use against blacks who were regarded as too old, too frail, or too virtuous to suffer mob violence, as revealed by the mob members in Gallatin County, Illinois, who decided not to whip an "old and inoffensive negro" in 1842 or the whites in Ozark County, Missouri, who permitted "Aunt" Ann and "Uncle" Andy to live among them because they were old and unthreatening and lived some distance away from their white neighbors.

In the late nineteenth century and to a much greater extent in the first decades of the twentieth, police officers protected black people from racist mobs, and particularly from lynch mobs. They did so in a number of ways, including spiriting black prisoners out of town, confronting and dispersing crowds, and opening fire on mobs that defied them. In Danville, Illinois, in 1903 Hardy Whitlock used the least force necessary in the situation by simply spraying the hands of mob members with shotgun pellets to make them drop their battering ram. In Cairo, Illinois, in 1910 Sheriff Nellis did not. Acting three months after the highly publicized lynching of Will James there, he and his deputies let loose a deadly barrage of fire on the mob that had ignored their warning shots and stormed the jail. Bolstering the efforts of police officers at the turn of the twentieth century, state officials across the Midwest passed anti-mob legislation that gave officials in local communities new incentives designed to protect themselves from criminal prosecution or to shield taxpayers from costly lawsuits.

Hostile Heartland confirms some of the relatively recent findings related to the study of racist violence. First, with respect to lynching, it challenges the long-held understanding that a so-called lynching era existed during the period from 1880 to 1930 by showing that lynching was as common in the 1860s and 1870s and, ironically, was practiced in a period long associated with the triumph of enlightened racial attitudes among whites. The response of white Indianans to the influx of southern blacks immediately after the Civil War and during the Exodus of the late 1870s exemplifies both of these arguments. Second, this study confirms that lynching was a common practice in the Midwest as early as the 1830s and, as Waldrep determined, that the term *lynching* connoted both nonlethal and lethal acts of mob violence committed during that period. It also shows, however, that the line between the two types sometimes owed as much to chance as to the intent of the mob until the term finally assumed its current definition, that of always involving lethality, around the time of the Civil War.

The study also demonstrates that lynchings persisted in the Midwest until well into the 1940s, but they changed perceptibly in response to a loss of their popular legitimacy during what may be defined as the late lynching period. It identifies the latter type as underground lynchings and characterizes them as events that were targeted at blacks who were often strangers and that were conducted largely in rural areas by small groups of secretive white men who avoided publicity by acting in secluded places, usually at night, and disposed of the evidence as completely as possible. The study also reveals that, despite these changes, the perpetrators still retained the support of the local white community (even if that support was more muted) and usually escaped without punishment for their crimes. These attributes were all clearly in evidence in the lynching of Luke Murray in Lawrence County, Ohio.

This book presents three additional findings from its research on underground lynchings. First, just as previous studies have shown that black northerners who ventured into the South unaware of its unique racial etiquette could find themselves the victims of indignant local whites, this one demonstrates that the same could happen to black southerners who entered the Midwest, as Luke Murray and James Person learned in Ohio and Illinois in the 1930s and 1940s. In addition, *Hostile Heartland* challenges the validity of the conventional narrative of lynching that suggests in brief but sweeping terms that lynching inevitably disappeared as an increasingly cosmopolitan white population came to regard that tradition as, for a variety of reasons, wrong and inconsistent with the nation's values. Instead, it shows that the late lynching period was a distinct phase in the history of lynching, had its own unique characteristics, and should be considered no less seriously than should other periods. Finally, it suggests that in the Midwest the rise of underground lynchings predated a similar shift across the South a decade or two later.

In various respects, this book examines the significance of narrative traditions to the history of racist violence generally and of lynching particularly. Despite the evidence to the contrary, white midwesterners argued that they employed lynching to punish black lawbreakers and to defend an innocent and terrified white population, thereby placing the blame on the victims and absolving themselves for their acts of racist vengeance. Traditionally, they cloaked their argument in what Lisa Arellano has described as "a constellation of formulaic narrative practices" which, when applied to "a set of violent practices," made them recognizable as a lynching.[2] By the time of the Murray lynching in Lawrence County in 1932, however, whites were losing control of their narrative. In the face of the efforts of local black activists and members of the Ohio NAACP, as well as the growing skepticism of an increasingly cosmopolitan white audience, they failed to persuade the nation that they were merely defending themselves from a knife-wielding black brute.

Hostile Heartland also addresses in detail several other types of racist violence that whites deployed against blacks over the decades. Castration was a relatively conventional—and perhaps more openly discussed—aspect of lynching in the antebellum period, not a development that came in the late nineteenth century, as many have assumed. Furthermore, if castration, along with other types of violence, was deployed to punish alleged black rapists or those who engaged in consensual sexual relations across the color line in this early period, then this practice presents a challenge to the southern-based scholarship dating the emergence of the lynching-for-rape scare to the era after the Civil War. Whipping was another type of violence widely utilized throughout the Midwest but nowhere more frequently than in Little Dixie, where this relic of slavery's past was deployed against blacks regardless of their age or gender.

By addressing racist violence of all types, the study provides insights that the examination of lynchings and race riots alone cannot. Although the latter two practices often resulted in the expulsions that quickly created many of the sundown towns across the Midwest, other types of violence often served the same purpose. In Webb City, Missouri, which apparently experienced no lynchings or race riots in the first three decades of the twentieth century, other types of violence prompted the repeated expulsions of its small black population. In some of the smaller towns in Little Dixie whippings accomplished the same objective. In addition, many of these less prominent types of violence were routinely used to enforce white control in some of the larger towns and cities where blacks eventually collected and to encourage respect among blacks for the Jim Crow practices gradually introduced after the Civil War and accelerated after Reconstruction.

This study supports and furthers the recent scholarship on sundown towns by showing that whites across the Midwest established and maintained these exclusionary places in order to create "white man's heavens," prevent "nigger paradises," and seize black property in acts of generational theft that have had a lasting impact. However, it expands the concept of sundown towns beyond the notion of all-white towns. Generally, it agrees that these municipalities *could* be all white. Yet it shows that some of them could tolerate the return of some blacks until whites' concerns became too pronounced to ignore, prompting another "thinning" and the beginning of a similar cycle. In addition, the book asserts that some of these municipalities could expel large numbers of blacks but tolerate small numbers of trusted ones, restrict them to segregated residential neighborhoods, and subject them to nightly curfews and other restrictions as deemed necessary.

With respect to black resistance, *Hostile Heartland* demonstrates that the targeting of particular black families by whites in Kansas and adjacent states through the use of racist violence against them, the creation of largely negative narratives about them, and the bias of the criminal justice system against them can be interrogated in ways that shed new light on both the victims and the perpetrators. It asserts that the victimized families absolutely rejected the racist social order in which they lived and instilled in their children a spirited resistance that survived even after they had experienced some of the worst abuse that whites could impose on them. In this sense, the book undergirds the findings of Charles M. Payne, who, in his study of the black freedom struggle of the 1950s and 1960s, identified what he called "movement families" that in his view played a critical role in the success of that effort.[3] *Hostile Heartland* does not assert that the families addressed herein were "movement families" because there was in fact no movement at that time. It does, however, demonstrate the critical role of parental influence in instilling resistance to oppression in the children of these particularly resistant families so that a generation of activists was ready when a broad-based freedom struggle did emerge in the mid-twentieth century.

With this innovative approach to the study of black families, along with its emphasis on acts of armed black resistance stretching back to the antebellum period, this work challenges the proliferating scholarship concerning the so-called long civil rights movement that dates the modern black freedom struggle to the 1920s and 1930s. It also challenges the assertions of many historians who have claimed that blacks did not regularly pursue armed self-defense until returning veterans of World War I took up that effort. Instead, it shows that black people engaged in these same types of resistance for generations and, if they did not—indeed, could not—understand their local actions as part of a larger national movement, they certainly prepared their children decade after decade until national developments provided them with new and revolutionary opportunities in the years after World War I.

Whereas most works about racist violence focus narrowly on a single geographical area established by the researcher, be it a town, a county, a state, or a region, *Hostile Heartland* demonstrates one of the shortcomings of that approach. It shows that events within such an area can spill well beyond those artificially created boundaries and influence—and in turn be influenced by—similar events elsewhere. In this instance the events in the Missouri Ozarks clearly created a contagion that spread beyond that region and inspired similar events in places like Walnut, Kansas, and Sapulpa, Oklahoma. In addition, they demonstrate that the boundaries established for a singular academic purpose may be insufficient at times to capture the experiences endured by the real people who lived in these places.

After evaluating the role of new technology in racist violence and resistance, the study concludes that it has, as Amy Wood has suggested, a generally neutral impact. The introduction and increasingly widespread use of railways and automobiles, telegraphs and telephones, newspapers and photographs, could be utilized as readily to facilitate or to prevent either practice. The advantage offered, for example, by the rapid movement of mob members by train or automobile to participate in a lynching or an expulsion could be offset just as quickly by the rapid movement of the militia or the police to prevent or contain that event. The availability of lynching postcards could provide inspiration to racists and induce revulsion in those opposed to the practice.

This book suggests several intriguing lines for future inquiry. With respect to lynching, scholars need to focus much greater attention on the lynching of blacks in the antebellum period in both the South and the Midwest because this period appears to be as prone to lynching and as ripe for analysis as was the period immediately after the Civil War just a short time ago. Also, they need to identify additional underground lynchings and develop new methodologies for doing so, a task made much more difficult by the fact that the mobs conducting them cloaked their actions in secrecy. Nonetheless, some of those that received some press coverage may be posited, as I have done here, by a careful reading of these narratives and by an enhanced understanding of the common characteristics associated with such killings in this period.

With its concept of situational suicides, *Hostile Heartland* provides researchers with new ways of identifying and interrogating the lynchings of blacks and the responses of both blacks and whites to them. It suggests that in some cases blacks like Joseph Spencer in Illinois in 1854 and the unidentified drowning victim in Indiana in 1904 *chose* to kill themselves rather than take their chances with the mobs that had cornered them. It also suggests that in other cases, blacks like Louis Seeman in Nebraska in 1929 may or may not have chosen to kill themselves. If they did not, the evidence raises the suspicion that the white authorities and newspaper editors involved in these so-called suicide incidents as participants or defenders may have framed them as such to avoid the scrutiny and potential legal and financial consequences that could result from acts of mob violence, particularly by the twentieth century. Such suspicions are raised by incidents like the posse killing in Burlington, Kansas, in 1930. Given the situations in which these men found themselves—and the fact that none of them would have committed suicide had it not been for the mobs threatening them—it is difficult to regard them as anything other than uncounted victims of lynch mobs.

In his recent call for a revival of midwestern history, Jon K. Lauck resurrects a long tradition in the history of a region that seeks to sanitize the ugliest aspects of its history. Despite the evidence of their commitment to white supremacy, white midwesterners are often viewed as a forward-thinking people whose legacy is principally one of racial progressiveness. "The small number of blacks in the early Midwest faced racism and attempts at legal exclusion," Lauck writes, "but also benefited from the prohibition on slavery included in the Northwest Ordinance, the prevalence of free labor ideology, and the growth of abolitionist sentiment in the Midwest, which led to the creation of the midwestern-based antislavery Republican Party in the 1850s. Many midwesterners fought to keep slavery illegal in the region prior to the Civil War, and some historians believe that the 'main credit of the abolitionist crusade should go to the Middle West rather than to New England.'"[4] Although *Hostile Heartland* is a part of this trend toward reviving midwestern history, it identifies a long, ugly, and pervasive strain of racism at the core of midwestern society. While it certainly identifies some white resistance to racist violence, it roots much of it in the self-interest of its proponents rather than in their racial liberalism. For the blacks who lived in the region between 1835 and 1945, the Heartland was a hostile place, indeed.

Notes

Introduction

1. *Daily Review* (Decatur, IL), July 28, 1903, 2.
2. *Chicago Daily Tribune*, July 27, 1903, 1.
3. *Daily Review* (Decatur, IL), July 28, 1903, 2.
4. *Daily Review* (Decatur, IL), July 28, 1903, 1.
5. Bernard Bailyn, *The Peopling of British North America: An Introduction* (New York: Vintage Books, 1988), 3.
6. Charles M. Payne, *I've Got the Light of Freedom: The Organizing Tradition and the Mississippi Freedom Struggle* (Berkeley: University of California Press, 1995), 202.
7. Tameka Bradley Hobbs, *Democracy Abroad, Lynching at Home: Racial Violence in Florida* (Gainesville: University Press of Florida, 2015), 28, 29.
8. Amy Louise Wood, *Lynching and Spectacle: Witnessing Racial Violence in America, 1890–1940* (Chapel Hill: University of North Carolina Press, 2009), 5–6.
9. James W. Loewen, *Sundown Towns: A Hidden Dimension of American Racism* (New York: New Press, 2005).
10. Brent M. S. Campney, *This Is Not Dixie: Racist Violence in Kansas, 1861–1927* (Urbana: University of Illinois Press, 2015). See also Guy Lancaster, *Racial Cleansing in Arkansas, 1883–1924: Politics, Land, Labor, and Criminality* (Lanham, MD: Lexington Books, 2014); Kimberly Harper, *White Man's Heaven: The Lynching and Expulsion of Blacks in the Southern Ozarks, 1894–1909* (Fayetteville: University of Arkansas Press, 2010).
11. W. Fitzhugh Brundage, *Lynching in the New South: Georgia and Virginia, 1880–1930* (Urbana: University of Illinois Press, 1993), 17.
12. Christopher Waldrep, *The Many Faces of Judge Lynch: Extralegal Violence and Punishment in America* (New York: Palgrave Macmillan, 2002), 2.

13. Lisa Arellano, *Vigilantes and Lynch Mobs: Narratives of Community and Nation* (Philadelphia: Temple University Press, 2012), 16 (emphasis in the original).

14. Sundiata Keita Cha-Jua, "'The cry of the Negro should not be remember the Maine, but remember the hanging of Bush': African American Responses to Lynching in Decatur, Illinois, 1893," in *Lynching beyond Dixie: American Mob Violence outside the South*, ed. Michael J. Pfeifer (Urbana: University of Illinois Press, 2013), 167–168.

15. Shawn Leigh Alexander, *An Army of Lions: The Civil Rights Struggle before the NAACP* (Philadelphia: University of Pennsylvania Press, 2012); Paul Ortiz, *Emancipation Betrayed: The Hidden History of Black Organizing and White Violence in Florida from Reconstruction to the Bloody Election of 1920* (Berkeley: University of California Press, 2005), xix. See also Campney, *This Is Not Dixie.*

16. Campney, *This Is Not Dixie,* 116–131.

17. Paul Mokrzycki, "Introduction: A Revival and a Burial," *Middle West Review* 1:1 (Fall 2014), ix.

18. Campney, *This Is Not Dixie,* 215.

19. James R. Shortridge, *The Middle West: Its Meaning in American Culture* (Lawrence: University Press of Kansas, 1989), 3, 11.

Chapter 1. *The Antebellum Old Northwest*

1. *Clinton County (OH) Whig,* reprinted in *Albany (NY) Evening Journal,* August 31, 1839, 2.

2. *Clinton County (OH) Whig,* reprinted in *Albany (NY) Evening Journal,* August 31, 1839, 2. The reference to "Lynching" comes from *Hampshire Gazette* (Northampton, MA), September 4, 1839, 3. For other references to this incident as a lynching by newspapers across the country, see, e.g., *Sun* (Baltimore, MD), August 26, 1839, 2; *Columbian Centinel* (Boston, MA), August 31, 1839, 4; *Maumee City (OH) Express,* August 31, 1839, 2.

3. Waldrep, *Many Faces of Judge Lynch.* On lynching and its definition, see also Arellano, *Vigilantes and Lynch Mobs*; Ashraf H. A. Rushdy, *American Lynching* (New Haven: Yale University Press, 2012).

4. Waldrep, *Many Faces of Judge Lynch*; Michael J. Pfeifer, *Rough Justice: Lynching and American Society, 1874–1947* (Urbana: University of Illinois Press, 2004).

5. Eugene H. Berwanger, *The Frontier against Slavery: Western Anti-Negro Prejudice and the Slavery Extension Controversy* (Urbana: University of Illinois Press, 2002), 23. For more on the Black Laws in Ohio, see David A. Gerber, *Black Ohio and the Color Line, 1860–1915* (Urbana: University of Illinois Press, 1976), 3–24.

6. Leon F. Litwack, *North of Slavery: The Negro in the Free States, 1790–1860* (Chicago: University of Chicago Press, 1971), 74. On abolitionism in the Old Northwest and in surrounding states, see Dana Elizabeth Weiner, *Race and Rights: Fighting Slavery in the Old Northwest* (DeKalb: Northern Illinois University Press, 2013); Lowell J. Soike, *Busy in the Cause: Iowa, the Free-State Struggle*

in the West, and the Prelude to the Civil War (Lincoln: University of Nebraska Press, 2014).

7. Berwanger, *Frontier against Slavery*, 44.

8. Litwack, *North of Slavery*, 94.

9. W. H. McIntosh, *The History of Darke County, Ohio* (Chicago: W. H. Beers & Co., 1880), 220.

10. Gerber, *Black Ohio and the Color Line*, 18.

11. Litwack, *North of Slavery*, 72–73.

12. Alexis de Tocqueville, *Democracy in America*, trans. Henry Reeve (London: Longman, Green, Longman, and Roberts, 1862), 1:428.

13. *Brooklyn (NY) Eagle*, April 25, 1844, 2. For another account, see *Alton (IL) Telegraph & Democratic Review*, April 20, 1844, 3.

14. *Weekly Ohio Statesman* (Columbus), July 30, 1845, 3. On the events in Columbus, see also (Canton) *Ohio Repository*, August 7, 1845, 3; *Liberator* (Boston), September 5, 1845, 142.

15. (Canton) *Ohio Repository*, reprinted in *Emancipator* (New York), February 21, 1839, 173.

16. *Huron Reflector* (Norwalk, OH), March 12, 1839, 2.

17. *Liberator* (Boston), August 8, 1845, 125 (emphasis in the original).

18. *Adams County Democrat* (West Union, OH), November 28, 1856, 2.

19. Nelson W. Evans and Emmons B. Stivers, *A History of Adams County, Ohio: From Its Earliest Settlement to the Present Time* (West Union, Ohio: E. B. Stivers, 1900), 444.

20. *Marion (IL) Intelligencer*, reprinted in *Brooklyn (NY) Daily Eagle*, September 2, 1856, 2.

21. *Weekly Ohio Statesman* (Columbus), July 30, 1845, 3.

22. Mrs. P. T. Chapman, *A History of Johnson County, Illinois* (Herrin: Press of The Herrin News, 1925), 138. See also *Shawneetown (IL) Gazette*, summarized in *Liberator* (Boston), July 3, 1846, 108.

23. *Alton (IL) Weekly Courier*, December 14, 1854, 2.

24. *Liberator* (Boston), February 21, 1840, 3.

25. *New-Albany (IN) Argus*, January 16, 1840, 3.

26. Jacob Piatt Dunn, *Greater Indianapolis: The History, the Industries, the Institutions, and the People of a City of Homes* (Chicago: Lewis Publishing, 1910), 1:240.

27. *Liberator* (Boston), August 8, 1845, 125 (emphasis in the original).

28. *Indiana State Sentinel* (Indianapolis), July 10, 1845, 1.

29. *Wooster (OH) Republican*, July 16, 1857, 2. On the decapitation, see *Chicago Tribune*, reprinted in *Freeport (IL) Daily Journal*, July 24, 1857, 2.

30. Frederick Douglass, quoted in James A. Colaiaco, *Frederick Douglass and the Fourth of July* (New York: Palgrave Macmillan, 2006), 73, 52 (emphasis in the original). For an interesting discussion of racist violence and black celebrations, see W. Fitzhugh Brundage, *The Southern Past: A Clash of Race and Memory* (Cambridge: Belknap Press of Harvard University Press, 2005), 59–70.

31. *Daily Pantagraph* (Bloomington, IL), May 20, 1858, 3. See also p. 2 of that issue.

32. *Cincinnati Gazette*, reprinted in *Sandusky (OH) Clarion*, September 21, 1847, 2.

33. William Henry Perrin, ed., *History of Jefferson County* (Chicago: Globe Publishing, 1883), 270.

34. *Cincinnati Daily Enquirer*, September 6, 1841, 2. For a rebuttal of the claims about Kentuckians, see *Cincinnati Daily Enquirer*, September 7, 1841, 2.

35. *Weekly Ohio Statesman* (Columbus), July 30, 1845, 3.

36. *Daily Pantagraph* (Bloomington, IL), May 20, 1858, 3 (emphasis in the original).

37. *Cincinnati Daily Enquirer*, September 9, 1841, 2.

38. *Evansville (IN) Enquirer*, reprinted in *Sandusky (OH) Register*, July 31, 1857, 2.

39. *Evansville (IN) Daily Enquirer*, July 28, 1857, 2.

40. *Louisville (KY) Advertiser*, reprinted in *Wabash Enquirer* (Terre Haute, IN), July 29, 1840, 2. On armed black resistance in the North in the antebellum period, see Thomas P. Slaughter, *Bloody Dawn: The Christiana Riot and Racial Violence in the Antebellum North* (New York: Oxford University Press, 1991); Ella Forbes, *But We Have No Country: The 1851 Christiana, Pennsylvania, Resistance* (Cherry Hill, NJ: Africana Homestead Legacy, 1998).

41. *New Garden (IN) Protectionist*, March 1, 1841, 77.

42. Rev. A. W. Drury, *History of the City of Dayton and Montgomery County, Ohio* (Chicago-Dayton: S. J. Clarke Publishing, 1909), 166.

43. *Evansville (IN) Daily Enquirer*, August 2, 1857, 2.

44. *History of Gallatin, Saline, Hamilton, Franklin and Williamson Counties, Illinois: From the Earliest Time to the Present; Together with Sundry and Interesting Biographical Sketches, Notes, Reminiscences* (Chicago: Goodspeed Publishing, 1887), 35.

45. *Cincinnati Philanthropist*, reprinted in *Liberator* (Boston), October 8, 1841, 162.

46. *Cincinnati Daily Enquirer*, September 4, 1841, 2.

47. *New York Times*, September 27, 1852, 3.

48. *Nashville (IL) Democrat*, reprinted in *Alton (IL) Weekly Courier*, September 3, 1852, 2.

49. *New-York Commercial Advertiser*, March 4, 1837, 1.

50. *Shawneetown (IL) Republican*, summarized in *Adams Sentinel* (Gettysburg, PA), May 2, 1842, 3.

51. *History of Gallatin*, 35.

52. *Philanthropist*, reprinted in *Liberator* (Boston), May 14, 1841, 79.

53. *Wilmington (OH) Herald of Freedom*, reprinted in *Liberator* (Boston), July 21, 1854, 113.

54. *Chicago Tribune*, reprinted in *Freeport (IL) Daily Journal*, July 24, 1857, 2.

55. Andrew W. Young, *History of Young County, Indiana: From Its First Settlement to the Present Time* (Cincinnati: Robert Clarke & Co., 1872), 101–102.

56. Lewis C. Baird, *Baird's History of Clark County, Indiana* (Indianapolis: B. F. Bowen, 1909), 153.

57. *Indianapolis Locomotive*, August 5, 1848, reprinted in Dunn, *Greater Indianapolis*, 240.

58. *Columbian Centinel* (Boston), July 18, 1838, 6.

59. *Kentucky Star* (location unknown), reprinted in *Emancipator* (New York), August 2, 1838, 55.

60. *Cincinnati Daily Enquirer*, September 10, 1841, 2 (emphasis in the original).

61. *Philanthropist*, reprinted in *Liberator* (Boston), October 8, 1841, 162.

62. *Evansville (IN) Journal*, reprinted in *Liberator* (Boston), October 8, 1841, 162.

63. *Liberator* (Boston), August 8, 1845, 125. On the mob violence in Alton, see Paul Simon, *Freedom's Champion: Elijah Lovejoy* (Carbondale: Southern Illinois University Press, 1994).

64. *Anti-Slavery Bugle* (Salem, OH), August 21, 1846, 1.

65. *New York Daily Tribune*, August 4, 1846, 1.

66. *Cincinnati Herald*, reprinted in *Anti-Slavery Bugle* (Salem, OH), September 17, 1847, 3.

67. *Anti-Slavery Bugle* (Salem, OH), August 21, 1846, 1.

68. *Cincinnati Herald*, reprinted in *Anti-Slavery Bugle* (Salem, OH), September 17, 1847, 3. For another example of northern Quakers putting racial prejudice before religious principle, see Slaughter, *Bloody Dawn*, 25–26.

69. *Liberator* (Boston), August 8, 1845, 125.

70. Dunn, *Greater Indianapolis*, 240, 242. Dunn conceded that the 1840 lynchings created an atmosphere in which the 1845 lynching could occur. The first case, he wrote, "may have caused a revulsion of feeling which, as well as the influx of a disorderly class of settlers, made the sentiment of the community more hostile to the negro. At any rate it showed very badly on July 4, 1845, when a negro was beaten to death by a mob" (241).

71. *New York Herald*, August 10, 1860, 5.

72. *Anti-Slavery Bugle* (Salem, OH), August 21, 1858, 4.

73. *Xenia (OH) Torch Light*, reprinted in *Anti-Slavery Bugle* (Salem, OH), August 21, 1858, 4.

74. Quoted in *Anti-Slavery Bugle* (Salem, OH), September 22, 1860, 3.

75. *Cincinnati Daily Enquirer*, September 9, 1841, 2.

76. *Advertiser and Journal* (Cincinnati), January 21, 1841, 2 (emphasis in the original).

77. *Dayton (OH) Transcript*, reprinted in *Advertiser and Journal* (Cincinnati), January 30, 1841, 2.

78. *Ohio Statesman* (Columbus), January 27, 1841, 2.

79. *Philanthropist*, reprinted in *Liberator* (Boston), May 14, 1841, 79.

80. *Cincinnati Daily Enquirer*, September 10, 1841, 2.

81. *New-York Commercial Advertiser*, March 4, 1837, 1.

82. *Cleveland Herald*, reprinted in *New Garden (IN) Protectionist*, March 1, 1841, 77.

83. *Liberator* (Boston), February 21, 1840, 81.

84. *Louisville (KY) Democrat,* summarized in *Cincinnati Enquirer,* August 4, 1850, 2.

85. *Cleveland Herald,* reprinted in *New Garden (IN) Protectionist,* March 1, 1841, 77.

86. *Cincinnati Daily Enquirer,* September 10, 1841, 2.

87. *Liberator* (Boston), September 5, 1845, 142.

88. *Logansport (IN) Telegraph,* July 19, 1845, 2.

89. *Cincinnati Enquirer,* reprinted in *Coshocton (OH) Democrat,* March 9, 1859, 2.

90. *Daily Pantagraph* (Bloomington, IL), May 20, 1858, 3 (emphasis in the original).

91. *Huntington (IN) Democrat,* July 17, 1862, 2.

92. *Peoria (IL) Union,* reprinted in *Cincinnati Daily Enquirer,* July 26, 1862, 1.

93. *Fayetteville (NC) Observer,* August 4, 1862, 3.

94. *New Albany (IN) Ledger,* reprinted in (Richmond, VA) *Daily Dispatch,* August 16, 1862, 1.

95. Campney, *This Is Not Dixie.*

96. On the Dubuque lynching, see Robert R. Dykstra, *Bright Radical Star: Black Freedom and White Supremacy on the Hawkeye Frontier* (Cambridge: Harvard University Press, 1993), 10–11.

97. Noel Ignatiev, *How the Irish Became White* (New York: Routledge, 1995), 130.

98. *Indianapolis News,* December 13, 1880, 2.

99. Martha Hodes, *White Women, Black Men: Illicit Sex in the 19th Century South* (New Haven: Yale University Press, 1997). For studies corroborating and building on the findings of Hodes, see Joshua D. Rothman, *Notorious in the Neighborhood: Sex and Families across the Color Line in Virginia, 1787–1861* (Chapel Hill: University of North Carolina Press, 2003); Diane Miller Sommerville, *Rape and Race in the Nineteenth-Century South* (Chapel Hill: University of North Carolina Press, 2004). For another challenge to the conventional wisdom about rape and racist violence, see Lisa Lindquist Dorr, *White Women, Rape, and the Power of Race in Virginia, 1900–1960* (Chapel Hill: University of North Carolina Press, 2004).

100. For studies supporting the 1880–1930 periodization, see Brundage, *Lynching in the New South*; Stewart E. Tolnay and E. M. Beck, *A Festival of Violence: An Analysis of Southern Lynchings, 1882–1930* (Urbana: University of Illinois Press, 1995). For studies revising this periodization, see George C. Wright, *Racial Violence in Kentucky, 1865–1940: Lynchings, Mob Rule, and "Legal Lynchings,"* Louisiana Paperback ed. (Baton Rouge: Louisiana State University Press, 1996); William D. Carrigan, *The Making of a Lynching Culture: Violence and Vigilantism in Central Texas, 1836–1916* (Urbana: University of Illinois Press, 2004); Campney, *This Is Not Dixie,* 86–87.

101. Waldrep, *Many Faces of Judge Lynch,* 13–66; Michael J. Pfeifer, *The Roots of Rough Justice: Origins of American Lynching* (Urbana: University of Illinois

Press, 2011). For other recent studies that contribute to this debate on antebellum lynching, see Manfred Berg, *Popular Justice: A History of Lynching in America* (Chicago: Ivan R. Dee, 2011), 23–44; Sarah L. Silkey, *Black Woman Reformer: Ida B. Wells, Lynching, and Transatlantic Activism* (Athens: University of Georgia Press, 2015), 6–44.

102. Pfeifer, *Roots of Rough Justice*, 34. For another study of antiblack lynching in a slave state, see Thomas G. Dyer, "A Most Unexampled Exhibition of Madness and Brutality: Judge Lynch in Saline County, Missouri, 1859," in *Under Sentence of Death: Lynching in the South*, ed. W. Fitzhugh Brundage (Chapel Hill: University of North Carolina Press, 1997), 81–108.

103. Pfeifer, *Roots of Rough Justice*, 70.

Chapter 2. Illinois and the Legacy of Antebellum Racist Violence

1. Edward Willett, *Cleveland Daily Plain Dealer*, November 19, 1863, 1. Unless otherwise noted, all newspapers cited in this chapter originate in Illinois, except papers in large and well-known cities like St. Louis, Missouri, or Cincinnati, Ohio.

2. For the local account, which mirrored versions published in other places, see *Cairo City Times*, November 29, 1854, 3; *Cairo City Times*, December 13, 1854, 3. On Willett's profession, see *Alton Weekly Courier*, December 14, 1854, 2. Founded in 1837, Cairo grew quickly after 1853, spurred by the sale of lots and by the completion of the Illinois Central Railroad. By 1860 the city claimed 2,188 residents. See John M. Lansden, *A History of the City of Cairo, Illinois* (Chicago: R. R. Donnelley & Sons, 1910), 58–62, 128; Roger Biles, *Illinois: A History of the Land and Its People* (DeKalb: Northern Illinois University Press, 2005), 117. Biles notes that Cairo was initially founded and incorporated in 1818 by a Baltimore businessman. "When he died a year later," however, "the site reverted to the government. In the late 1830s, the Cairo City and Canal Company acquired the property and began to build levees, warehouses, stores, and other facilities in expectation of its becoming the southern terminus of the Illinois Central Railroad. When economic depression forced the halt to railroad construction in 1840, the community sank swiftly into decline, and in one year the population fell from about two thousand to one hundred." Cairo stagnated until the completion of the Illinois Central Railroad. "Its reputation as a lawless haven for drifters, vagrants, and criminals minimized population growth as well." Biles, *Illinois*, 117. Over a century later, officials for the National Association for the Advancement of Colored People produced a timeline of black history in Cairo. They found that in 1823 "about twenty slaves, the earliest black inhabitants, are brought by the Brid families to build the first buildings on the site of what is now Cairo, Illinois." "A Cairo Chronology," [1973], TMs, 10 pp., in David Ibata Collection of Cairo Racial Strife (1969–1975), box 1, ser. 1, folder 1/2.

3. Willett, *Cleveland Daily Plain Dealer*, November 19, 1863, 1.

4. *St. Louis Intelligencer*, reprinted in *Mount Carmel Register*, December 13, 1854, 1.

5. Willett, *Cleveland Daily Plain Dealer*, November 19, 1863, 1. For a later account that deviates significantly from contemporary reports, see H. C. Bradsby, "Part I. History of Cairo," in William Henry Perrin, ed., *History of Alexander, Union and Pulaski Counties, Illinois* (Chicago: O. L. Baskin, 1883), 50–53. Although it referred to the trespassing charge, its outlandish version of events portrayed Spencer as a serial murderer and whites in Cairo as slow to be riled but understandably pressed into self-defense by the sheer danger posed by the black victim.

6. Willett, *Cleveland Daily Plain Dealer*, November 19, 1863, 1. According to Willett, Spencer did not kill any of the white men whom he shot, although one of them required the amputation of an arm.

7. *Alton Weekly Courier*, December 14, 1854, 2. On the number of mob members, see *St. Louis Intelligencer*, reprinted in *Mount Carmel Register*, December 13, 1854, 1.

8. Willett, *Cleveland Daily Plain Dealer*, November 19, 1863, 1.

9. *Missouri Republican*, reprinted in *Daily Alton Telegraph*, December 2, 1854, 3.

10. *St. Louis Intelligencer*, reprinted in *Mount Carmel Register*, December 13, 1854, 1.

11. Bradsby in Perrin, *History of Alexander, Union and Pulaski Counties*, 52–53.

12. Willett, *Cleveland Daily Plain Dealer*, November 19, 1863, 1.

13. Tolnay and Beck, *Festival of Violence*), 25 (emphasis in original).

14. *Louisville (KY) Courier*, reprinted in *Standard* (Clarksville, TX), January 27, 1855, 1.

15. (Newburgh, IN) *Warrick Democrat*, December 19, 1854, 2.

16. Willett, *Cleveland Daily Plain Dealer*, November 19, 1863, 1.

17. Bradsby in Perrin, *History of Alexander, Union and Pulaski Counties*, 50, 51.

18. Bradsby in Perrin, *History of Alexander, Union and Pulaski Counties*, 51–52.

19. Bradsby in Perrin, *History of Alexander, Union and Pulaski Counties*, 52.

20. Lansden, *History of the City of Cairo, Illinois*, 278.

21. Arellano, *Vigilantes and Lynch Mobs*, 16.

22. Berwanger, *Frontier against Slavery*, 7–18.

23. Berwanger, *Frontier against Slavery*, 21.

24. William Henry Perrin, ed. *History of Effingham County, Illinois* (Chicago: O. L. Baskin & Co., 1883), "Appendix. Early History of Illinois," 58–59.

25. "Black Bottom," in John Willis Allen Papers, box 18, folder 34: "Counties in Illinois, General Information; Perry-Pope," Southern Illinois University, University Archives. In the same folder, see also "Pope County Notes: 3. Black Bottom."

26. *History of Wayne and Clay Counties, Illinois* (Chicago: Globe Publishing Co., 1884), 424.

27. Johnetta L. Jones, "Negroes in Jackson County, 1850–1910," (master's thesis, Southern Illinois University, 1971), 9–10, Special Collections Research Center, Morris Library, Southern Illinois University.

28. Litwack, *North of Slavery*, 71.

29. Berwanger, *Frontier against Slavery*, 49.

30. Berwanger, *Frontier against Slavery*, 49.

31. Berwanger, *Frontier against Slavery*, 50. On the population figures, see 51.

32. *Daily Illinois State Journal* (Springfield), August 4, 1857, 2 (emphasis in the original).

33. Biles, *Illinois*, 85. Similarly, Litwack found relatively lax enforcement of this draconian law. "The Illinois act remained on the statute books until 1865 and was upheld by the state supreme court, but few efforts were made to invoke it, and one Negro called it 'a dead letter.'" Litwack, *North of Slavery*, 71.

34. Richard J. Jensen, *Illinois: A History* (Urbana: University of Illinois Press, 2001), 8, 3.

35. Biles, *Illinois*, 83; Berwanger, *Frontier against Slavery*, 7–29.

36. Berwanger, *Frontier against Slavery*, 44, 39, 46.

37. *New York Evangelist*, reprinted in *Liberator* (Boston), April 29, 1853, 65.

38. Jones, "Negroes in Jackson County, 1850–1910," 18.

39. *Jonesboro Gazette*, reprinted in *Daily Illinois State Journal* (Springfield), August 25, 1857, 2.

40. Jensen, *Illinois*, 53.

41. *Jonesboro Gazette*, reprinted in *Daily Illinois State Journal* (Springfield), August 25, 1857, 2.

42. *Alton Weekly Courier*, September 3, 1852, 2.

43. *Mound City Emporium*, reprinted in *Daily Illinois State Journal* (Springfield), August 17, 1857, 2 (emphasis in the original).

44. Abraham Lincoln, "The Perpetuation of Our Political Institutions: Address before the Young Men's Lyceum of Springfield, Illinois," January 27, 1838. Abraham Lincoln Online: Speeches & Writings, http://www.abrahamlincolnonline.org/lincoln/speeches/lyceum.htm (accessed June 13, 2018). On Lovejoy, Simon, *Freedom's Champion*.

45. *Cairo Times and Delta*, reprinted in *Illinois State Chronicle* (Decatur), August 13, 1857, 2.

46. Roger B. Taney, quoted in Brian McGinty, *Lincoln and the Court* (Cambridge: Harvard University Press, 2008), 52.

47. *Illinois State Chronicle* (Decatur), August 13, 1857, 2.

48. *Wooster (OH) Republican*, July 16, 1857, 2.

49. *Cairo Times and Delta*, reprinted in *Illinois State Chronicle* (Decatur), August 13, 1857, 2.

50. *Cincinnati Times*, reprinted in *Philadelphia Inquirer*, August 3, 1857, 1.

51. *Cairo Times and Delta*, reprinted in *Illinois State Chronicle* (Decatur), August 13, 1857, 2.

52. *Chicago Tribune*, reprinted in *Daily Illinois State Journal* (Springfield), August 4, 1857, 2. An observer affirmed that this application of the Black Law was unusual. "The law," he noted, "long ago [became] a dead letter out of Cairo." See *Cincinnati Times*, reprinted in *Philadelphia Inquirer*, August 3, 1857, 1.

53. All quotations in the paragraph are from *Cincinnati Times*, reprinted in *Philadelphia Inquirer*, August 3, 1857, 1.

54. *Cairo Daily Democrat*, December 3, 1865, 4.

55. *Chicago Republican*, November 17, 1865, 1. For another clash, see *Daily National Intelligencer* (Washington, DC), August 10, 1865, 1.

56. On the northern retreat from Reconstruction, see David W. Blight, *Race and Reunion: The Civil War in American Memory* (Cambridge: Belknap Press of Harvard University Press, 2001); Edward J. Blum, *Reforging the White Republic: Race, Religion, and American Nationalism, 1865–1898* (Baton Rouge: Louisiana State University Press, 2005); Christopher Waldrep, *African Americans Confront Lynching: Strategies of Resistance from the Civil War to the Civil Rights Era* (New York: Rowman & Littlefield, 2009), 16–19. On the retreat in the Midwest, see Leslie A. Schwalm, *Emancipation's Diaspora: Race and Reconstruction in the Upper Midwest* (Chapel Hill: University of North Carolina Press, 2009); Campney, *This Is Not Dixie*.

57. Biles, *Illinois*, 142–143.

58. Wanda A. Hendricks, *Gender, Race, and Politics in the Midwest: Black Club Women in Illinois* (Bloomington: Indiana University Press, 1998), xiv; Biles, *Illinois*, 143.

59. "Appendix: Lynchings in the Northeast, Midwest, and West, 1840–1877," in Pfeifer, *Roots of Rough Justice, n.p.*; Dykstra, *Bright Radical Star*, 10–11.

60. *St. Louis Intelligencer*, reprinted in *Mount Carmel Register*, December 13, 1854, 1.

61. Willett, *Cleveland Daily Plain Dealer*, November 19, 1863, 1.

62. Philip Dray, *At the Hands of Persons Unknown: The Lynching of Black America* (New York: Random House, 2002), 174. After lynching James, notes Dray, the mob was "in such a frenzied state it set off in search of other black 'suspects.' The town's entire black population having, for the moment, vanished, a pack of shouting men and boys invaded the jail, seized a white man named Henry Salzner awaiting trial for murdering his wife, and hanged him in a courtyard." On a 1910 race riot, see Dray, *At the Hands of Persons Unknown*, 176.

63. Joanne Wheeler, "Together in Egypt: A Pattern of Race Relations in Cairo, Illinois, 1865–1915," in *Toward a New South? Studies in Post–Civil War Southern Communities*, ed. Orville Vernon Burton and Robert C. McMath Jr. (Westport, CT: Greenwood, 1982), 105. See Loewen, *Sundown Towns*, and James Allen, *Without Sanctuary: Lynching Photography in America* (Santa Fe, NM: Twin Palms, 2000), plates 45–52; *Without Sanctuary*, http://withoutsanctuary.org/ (accessed May 30, 2018).

64. *St. Louis Democrat*, reprinted in (Indianapolis) *Evening News*, September 9, 1873, 2. On the legal execution of William Campbell, see *Chicago Daily Tribune*, August 30, 1873, 5.

65. Mark Twain, *The Adventures of Huckleberry Finn* (New York: Harper & Brothers, 1918), 121–122.

66. Biles, *Illinois*, 143, 144; Hendricks, *Gender, Race, and Politics*, 62.

67. *Springfield (MA) Daily Republican*, October 2, 1902, 6.

68. Dray, *At the Hands of Persons Unknown*, 176.

69. *Daily Journal-Gazette* (Mattoon), November 8, 1915, 1.

70. *Mattoon Commercial-Star*, November 9, 1915, 1.

71. *Chicago Daily Tribune*, October 9, 1924, 1. In both the Taylorville and the Chicago lynchings, some of the most prominent mob members were European immigrants. In Chicago, most of the mob members were Jewish residents of the Maxwell Street district.

72. *Edwardsville Intelligencer*, March 3, 1870, 1. For more details on the 1867 lynching, see *Chicago Tribune*, December 17, 1867, 2.

73. *Cairo Bulletin*, reprinted in *Cincinnati Enquirer*, February 1, 1875, 10.

74. *Cairo Daily Bulletin*, July 7, 1883, 4.

75. "Lynching of Negro at E-Town," [manuscript], John Willis Allen Papers, box 8: "Counties in Illinois, General Information; Hardin (E-M)," folder, "Hardin Co., Elizabethtown," University Archives, Southern Illinois University. On the Elizabethtown lynching, see also *Cairo Daily Bulletin*, June 28, 1882, 4.

76. See Berwanger, *Frontier against Slavery*, 45–46.

77. Lansden, *History of the City of Cairo*, 278.

78. *St. Louis Intelligencer*, reprinted in *Mount Carmel Register*, December 13, 1854, 1.

79. Willett, *Cleveland Daily Plain Dealer*, November 19, 1863, 1.

Chapter 3. Indiana during Reconstruction

1. *Crisis* (Columbus, OH), October 22, 1862, 308. Unless otherwise noted, all newspapers cited in this chapter were published in Indiana, except papers in large and well-known cities like Chicago, Illinois, Louisville, Kentucky, or Cincinnati and Cleveland, Ohio.

2. Gregory S. Rose, "The Distribution of Indiana's Ethnic and Racial Minorities in 1850," *Indiana Magazine of History* 87 (September 1991): 248.

3. James H. Madison, *The Indiana Way: A State History* (Bloomington: Indiana University Press, 1986), 107.

4. Quoted in Berwanger, *Frontier against Slavery*, 30.

5. Quoted in Litwack, *North of Slavery*, 69.

6. *Evansville Daily Enquirer*, July 28, 1857, 2.

7. Madison, *Indiana Way*, 107. On the outlawing of voting and interracial marriage, see also Berwanger, *Frontier against Slavery*, 36.

8. *History of Pike and DuBois Counties, Indiana: From the Earliest Times to the Present* (Chicago: Goodspeed Bros., 1885), 206.

9. Berwanger, *Frontier against Slavery*, 34.

10. Madison, *Indiana Way*, 169.

11. On the New Albany riot, see, e.g., *Louisville Daily Democrat*, July 23, 1862, 2.

12. *Sun* (Baltimore), July 19, 1865, 1.

13. *Plain Dealer* (Cleveland), July 28, 1865, 2.

14. For the population figures, see Emma Lou Thornbrough, "African Americans," in *Peopling Indiana: The Ethnic Experience*, ed. Robert M. Taylor Jr. and

Connie A. McBirney (Indianapolis: Indiana Historical Society, 1996), 12–37. See also Department of the Interior, Census Office, Statistics of the Population of the United States at the Tenth Census (June 1, 1880) (Washington, DC: Government Printing Office, 1883) 388.

15. *Plain Dealer* (Cleveland), July 28, 1865, 2.

16. *Jasper Weekly Courier*, August 5, 1865, 2.

17. *Vincennes Sun*, reprinted in *Sullivan Democrat*, August 3, 1865, 2.

18. *Boonville Enquirer*, reprinted in *Jasper Weekly Courier*, July 8, 1865, 3.

19. *Vincennes Sun*, reprinted in *Sullivan Democrat*, August 17, 1865, 2.

20. *New Albany Daily Commercial*, September 7, 1865, 4.

21. *Louisville Democrat*, reprinted in *Daily Age* (Philadelphia), August 23, 1865, 2.

22. *Vincennes Sun*, quoted in *Sullivan Democrat*, August 17, 1865, 3 (both quotations).

23. *Cincinnati Daily Gazette*, March 15, 1866, 4.

24. *Seymour Times*, May 9, 1867, 3.

25. *Warrick Herald*, reprinted in *New Albany Daily Commercial*, July 12, 1868, 4.

26. *Grandview Monitor*, reprinted in *New Albany Daily Commercial*, July 14, 1868, 4.

27. *Cincinnati Daily Gazette*, January 20, 1870, 3. See also *Cincinnati Daily Gazette*, September 7, 1869, 3.

28. *History of Warrick, Spencer and Perry Counties, Indiana: From the Earliest Time to the Present, Together with Interesting Biographical Sketches, Reminiscences, Notes, Etc.* (Chicago: Goodspeed Bros., 1885), 69.

29. *New Albany Daily Standard*, November 17, 1871, 4.

30. *Indianapolis News*, October 12, 1878, 1.

31. *Jasper Weekly Courier*, October 18, 1878, 5.

32. *Chicago Daily Tribune*, May 5, 1876, 2, 5.

33. *Warren Republican* (Williamsport), April 25, 1878, 1.

34. *Indianapolis News*, June 22, 1878, 4. On the second episode at Coal Creek, see also *Indianapolis Sentinel*, reprinted in *Huntington Democrat*, June 20, 1878, 2.

35. *Rockport Journal*, October 14, 1880, 3.

36. *Louisville Democrat*, reprinted in *Daily Age* (Philadelphia), September 16, 1865, 2.

37. *Daily Constitutional Union* (Washington, DC), August 23, 1865, 2.

38. *Cincinnati Daily Times*, May 12, 1876, 3.

39. William Cohen, *At Freedom's Edge: Black Mobility and the Southern White Quest for Racial Control, 1861–1915* (Baton Rouge: Louisiana State University Press, 1991), 194.

40. *Rockford (IL) Weekly Gazette*, February 11, 1880, 2.

41. *Indianapolis Daily Sentinel*, December 19, 1879, 1.

42. *Cincinnati Daily Gazette*, April 16, 1880, 2.

43. *Fort Wayne Weekly Sentinel*, December 15, 1880, 1.

44. *Alexandria (VA) Gazette*, reprinted in *Macon (GA) Telegraph and Messenger*, January 18, 1880, 2.

45. Cohen, *At Freedom's Edge*, 194.

46. General Rob[er]t M. Evans, *History of Vanderburgh County, Indiana, from the Earliest Times to the Present, with Biographical Sketches, Reminiscences, Etc.* (Madison, WI: Brant & Fuller, 1889), 188.

47. *Indianapolis News*, October 11, 1878, 1.

48. *Sullivan Democrat*, April 23, 1873, 2.

49. *New York Tribune*, April 19, 1878, 1.

50. *Inter Ocean* (Chicago), April 23, 1878, 4.

51. *Chicago Daily Tribune*, May 5, 1876, 2.

52. *Cincinnati Daily Times*, May 12, 1876, 3.

53. Cohen, *At Freedom's Edge*, 187.

54. *Cincinnati Commercial*, June 17, 1880, 6.

55. *Cincinnati Daily Gazette*, August 12, 1880, 4.

56. *Cincinnati Daily Gazette*, August 12, 1880, 4.

57. *Indianapolis Sentinel*, September 24, 1880, 1.

58. *Rockport Journal*, October 14, 1880, 3. See also *Indianapolis Journal*, October 12, 1880, 1.

59. *Louisville Democrat*, reprinted in *Daily Age* (Philadelphia), August 10, 1865, 2.

60. On these settlement patterns, see Gregory S. Rose, "Upland Southerners: The County Origins of Southern Migrants to Indiana by 1850," *Indiana Magazine of History* 82 (September 1986): 242–263.

61. *Rochester Standard*, December 12, 1867, 2.

62. *Northern Indianian* (Warsaw), December 5, 1867, 2.

63. *Rochester Standard*, December 12, 1867, 2.

64. Thornbrough, "African Americans," 15.

65. *Richmond (VA) Whig and Public Advertiser*, August 11, 1865, 3.

66. *Indianapolis Journal*, reprinted in *Cambridge City Tribune*, July 1, 1875, 2.

67. *Sullivan Democrat*, October 2, 1872, 2.

68. Warder W. Stevens, *Centennial History of Washington County: Its People, Industries, and Institutions* (Indianapolis: B. F. Bowen & Company, 1916), 435. See also *New Albany Daily Commercial*, September 24, 1867, 1.

69. *Dearborn Independent* (Aurora), October 16, 1879, 2.

70. *Dearborn Independent* (Aurora), April 29, 1880, 2.

71. *Summit County Beacon* (Akron, OH), April 28, 1880, 1.

72. *Indianapolis Journal*, August 7, 1880, 4.

73. *Louisville Courier-Journal*, reprinted in *Marietta (GA) Journal*, December 6, 1900, 2.

74. *News-Sentinel* (Fort Wayne), March 22, 1922, 16.

75. These population statistics are found in or derived from *Statistics of the Population of the United States at the Tenth Census*, June 1, 1880, 388–89. The

Camden Expositor remarked on three of these twenty-two counties in 1881, noting that the county in Indiana "having the least population is Starke, with 5,105, all whites. There are two other counties—Brown and Jasper—with no colored people." See *Camden Expositor*, February 17, 1881.

76. In 1860 only Indianapolis, New Albany, and Richmond had more than 250 blacks; by 1870 Evansville, Jeffersonville, Madison, and Terre Haute had also reached this threshold; by 1880 so too had Crawfordsville and Vincennes. These population statistics are found in or derived from Department of the Interior, *Ninth Census*, vol. 1, *The Statistics of the Population of the United States*, June 1, 1870 (Washington, DC: Government Printing Office, 1872), 122–131; *Statistics of the Population of the United States at the Tenth Census*, June 1, 1880, 388, 417–418.

77. An unidentified observer, quoted in James H. Madison, *A Lynching in the Heartland: Race and Memory in America* (New York: Palgrave, 2001), 72.

78. Madison, *Indiana Way*, 171. For a study that problematizes the distinction between so-called de jure and de facto racism, see Matthew D. Lassiter, "De Jure/De Facto Segregation: The Long Shadow of a National Myth," in Matthew D. Lassiter and Joseph Crespino, eds., *The Myth of Southern Exceptionalism* (New York: Oxford University Press, 2010), 25–48.

79. Ray Stannard Baker, *Following the Color Line: American Negro Citizenship in the Progressive Era* (Doubleday, Page & Company, 1908 [repr.: New York: Harper Torchbooks, 1964]), 124.

80. *Indiana State Sentinel* (Indianapolis), January 20, 1886, 1.

81. *Wheeling (WV) Register*, June 4, 1890, 2. On the lynching of Eli Ladd, see, e.g., *Muncie Herald*, reprinted in *Daily Democrat* (Huntington), June 5, 1890, 4.

82. *Indianapolis Sentinel*, reprinted in *Daily Picayune* (New Orleans), January 29, 1901, 1.

83. *Louisville Courier-Journal*, reprinted in *Marietta (GA) Journal*, December 6, 1900, 2.

84. *Marion Chronicle*, reprinted in *Bluffton Banner*, February 18, 1903, 7.

85. *Negro Star* (Wichita, KS), October 2, 1925, 1.

86. *Evansville Courier*, December 18, 1900, 1.

87. Robert P. Swierenga, "The Settlement of the Old Northwest: Ethnic Pluralism in a Featureless Plain," *Journal of the Early Republic* 9 (Spring 1989): 85.

88. Madison, *Indiana Way*, 170.

89. Writing of settlement patterns in Indiana after the War of 1812, Madison wrote: "Three major streams of migration can be identified. The smallest in size was that from the New England states. Considerably larger was the stream from the Mid-Atlantic states, principally New York and Pennsylvania. Largest of all was the population movement from the southern states. These three streams tended to settle in a pattern that reflected their geographic origins, with southerners most heavily congregated in the southern part of the state, Mid-Atlantic peoples in the central part, and New Englanders in the northern part." Providing a useful summary, he added: "The 1850 census showed that of

Indiana's American-born residents who had migrated to the state, 2.7 percent had come from the New England states, 19.9 percent from the Mid-Atlantic states, 31.4 percent from Ohio, and 44.0 percent from the southern states." Madison, *Indiana Way*, 58–59, 62.

90. On the vote for the 1851 exclusion measure, see Richard F. Nation, "Violence and the Rights of African Americans in Civil War–Era Indiana: The Case of James Hays," *Indiana Magazine of History* 100 (September 2004): 216.

91. *Evansville Courier*, July 22, 1899, 1.

92. Campney, *This Is Not Dixie*, appendix 1, 220–238.

93. *Sun* (Baltimore), July 26, 1862, 2.

94. *New Hampshire Patriot and Gazette* (Concord), August 9, 1865, 2. In *This Is Not Dixie*, 25–26, I identified a similar outbreak of racist violence in Kansas in 1865.

95. Campney, *This Is Not Dixie*, 37–40, 42–43, 72–74.

96. Campney, *This Is Not Dixie*, 42–43.

97. Rose, "Upland Southerners," 242. For a similar articulation of this notion, see Swierenga, "Settlement of the Old Northwest," 85.

98. For the Kansas figures, see Campney, *This Is Not Dixie*, 63–115, 132–155, 220–238.

99. On racism and racist violence in the Midwest, see, e.g., Cha-Jua, *America's First Black Town*; Hendricks, *Gender, Race, and Politics*; Roberta Senechal de la Roche, *In Lincoln's Shadow: The 1908 Race Riot in Springfield, Illinois* (Urbana: University of Illinois Press, 1990).

100. W. Fitzhugh Brundage, "Introduction," in *Under Sentence of Death: Lynching in the South*, ed. W. Fitzhugh Brundage (Chapel Hill: University of North Carolina Press, 1997), 4. On the roughly ninety lynchings in those four states, see chaps. Two, Three, Seven, and Eight in this book; Campney, *This is Not Dixie*; Pfeifer, *Rough Justice*; Pfeifer, *Roots of Rough Justice*, appendix, n.p.; Michael J. Pfeifer, ed., *Lynching beyond Dixie: American Mob Violence Outside the South* (Urbana: University of Illinois Press, 2013), 261–317.

101. See Pfeifer, *Lynching beyond Dixie*, appendix, 261–317.

102. *Mobile (AL) Register*, reprinted in *Daily Illinois State Register* (Springfield), September 22, 1877, 2.

103. *Augusta (GA) Chronicle*, October 17, 1878, 2.

104. *Cincinnati Daily Gazette*, August 12, 1880, 4.

105. Ashraf H. A. Rushdy, *End of American Lynching* (New Brunswick: Rutgers University Press, 2012), 60, 61.

106. James Cameron, *A Time of Terror* (Milwaukee: T/D Publications, 1982); Madison, *Lynching in the Heartland*; Cynthia Carr, *Our Town: A Heartland Lynching, a Haunted Town, and the Hidden History of White America* (New York: Crown, 2006); Dray, *At the Hands of Persons Unknown*.

107. The Marion hanging is characterized here as perhaps the final lynching in Indiana because scholars may yet find other episodes that took place in the state after 1930. Recently, Pfeifer documented several clandestine and largely

unpublicized lynchings in Illinois and Ohio in the 1930s and 1940s. See Pfeifer, *Lynching beyond Dixie*, appendix.

108. For an examination of the role of spectacle—including photographs—in the enforcement of white supremacy in the twentieth century, see Wood, *Lynching and Spectacle*.

Chapter 4. Black Families and Resistance in Kansas, 1880–1905

1. *Atchison Daily Champion*, September 23, 1880, 4. Unless otherwise noted, all newspapers cited in this chapter originated in Kansas.

2. *Atchison Daily Champion*, September 24, 1880, 4.

3. According to the historian Kimberly Harper, the name of this town was spelled initially as "Peirce City" but was later changed to "Pierce City." Harper, *White Man's Heaven*, 2–3. Because the current spelling—Pierce City—is commonly used in the scholarship (and was often used incorrectly among contemporaries), it will be used here as well.

4. Unidentified observer, quoted in Harper, *White Man's Heaven*, 23.

5. *Carthage (MO) Democrat*, reprinted in *Galena (KS) Evening Times*, August 20, 1901, 1.

6. Unidentified white woman, quoted in Harper, *White Man's Heaven*, 27.

7. *Pittsburg Daily Headlight*, August 23, 1901, 5.

8. *Pittsburg Daily Headlight*, December 26, 1902, 3, 4.

9. The various newspaper reports about the Pittsburg lynching victim most commonly list his name as Montgomery. The 1900 census and a lawsuit filed by the victim's father after the lynching, however, both suggest that his name was Mumpford. I have continued to use "Montgomery" in the quoted passages but have used "Mumpford" otherwise. See Missouri, Lawrence County, Pierce Township, Pierce City, Ward 1, Supervisor's District no. 13, Enumeration District no. 84, *Twelfth Census of the United States, Schedule no. 1*, Population (Form 7-224), June 6, 1900, sheet 7A; *Pittsburg Kansan*, March 19, 1903, 1.

10. *Topeka Plaindealer*, January 2, 1903, 1.

11. *Pittsburg Daily Headlight*, December 26, 1902, 3.

12. *Topeka Daily Capital*, December 28, 1902, 2.

13. *Lawrence Daily Journal-World*, December 27, 1902, 1.

14. *Topeka Daily Capital*, December 28, 1902, 2.

15. *Lawrence Daily Journal-World*, December 26, 1902, 2.

16. *Pittsburg Kansan*, December 25, 1902, 1.

17. *Lawrence Chieftain*, quoted in Harriet C. Frazier, *Lynchings in Missouri, 1803–1981* (Jefferson, NC: McFarland, 2009), 138.

18. *Pittsburg Kansan*, November 2, 1905, 1. On the arrest of Joe Godley, see *Pittsburg Daily Headlight*, April 14, 1904, 5; *Evening News* (San Jose, CA), April 13, 1904, 8. The *Evening News* reported that on his arrest Joe expressed to a reporter his fear that mob violence remained a very real possibility: "I know they will never let me live long enough to be tried."

19. *Pittsburg Daily Headlight*, February 25, 1905, 2.

20. *Springfield (MO) Republican*, August 7, 1902, 8. On the name of the widow, America, see Harper, *White Man's Heaven*, 29.

21. *Salina Daily Republican-Journal*, December 27, 1902, 1. On the name of Katy Godley, see Missouri, Lawrence County, Pierce Township, Pierce City, Ward 1, Supervisor's District no. 13, Enumeration District no. 84, *Twelfth Census of the United States, Schedule no. 1*, Population (Form 7-224), June 6, 1900, sheet 7A.

22. *Pittsburg Kansan*, November 2, 1905, 1. On the suit, see *Pittsburg Kansan*, March 19, 1903, 1.

23. *Lawrence Daily Journal*, June 8, 1882, 2.

24. *Daily Kansas Tribune* (Lawrence), June 8, 1882, 2. On the fate of Margaret, see William M. Tuttle Jr., "Separate but Not Equal: African Americans and the 100-year Struggle for Equality," in *Embattled Lawrence*, ed. Dennis Domer and Barbara Watkins (Lawrence: University of Kansas Continuing Education, 2001), 142.

25. *Chicago Daily Tribune*, June 11, 1882, 3.

26. *Topeka Daily Capital*, April 12, 1883, 1.

27. Tuttle, "Separate but Not Equal," 142.

28. *Salina Union*, April 21, 1893, 5.

29. *Salina Daily Republican*, April 20, 1893, 4.

30. *Salina Herald*, April 21, 1893, 4.

31. *Topeka Daily Capital*, October 8, 1898, 3.

32. *Salina Daily Republican-Journal*, October 6, 1898, 4.

33. *Tonganoxie Mirror*, December 30, 1897, 8.

34. *Tonganoxie Mirror*, February 16, 1899, 8.

35. *Tonganoxie Mirror*, March 2, 1899, 8.

36. *Tonganoxie Mirror*, June 8, 1899, 8.

37. *Tonganoxie Mirror*, February 16, 1899, 8. On the name of Vina Toliver and for other information on the Toliver family, see Kansas, Leavenworth County, Tonganoxie Township, Tonganoxie, Ward "x," Supervisor's District no. [illegible], Enumeration District no. 107, *Twelfth Census of the United States, Schedule no. 1*, Population (Form 7-224), June 5 (?), 1900, sheet 4A.

38. *Tonganoxie Mirror*, August 7, 1902, 1.

39. *Leavenworth Times*, August 7, 1902, 4.

40. *Leavenworth Times*, August 22, 1902, 4.

41. *Lawrence Daily Journal*, August 23, 1898, 4.

42. *Lawrence Daily World*, August 23, 1898, 3.

43. Stephen J. Leonard, *Lynching in Colorado, 1859–1919* (Boulder: University Press of Colorado, 2002), 125.

44. *Lawrence Daily Journal*, November 17, 1900, 4.

45. *New York Times*, November 18, 1900, 4.

46. *Parsons Weekly Blade*, May 20, 1893, 2.

47. *New York Times*, November 17, 1900, 1.

48. *Lawrence Daily Journal*, June 11, 1882, 1.

49. *Daily Kansas Tribune* (Lawrence), July 3, 1882, 2.

50. *Topeka Sunday Capital*, June 11, 1882, 1.

51. *New York Times*, November 17, 1900, 1.

52. *Tonganoxie Mirror*, February 16, 1899, 8.

53. *Salina Daily Republican*, April 21, 1893, 4.

54. *Lawrence Daily Journal*, January 12, 1894, 1.

55. *Chicago Herald*, reprinted in *Atchison Daily Champion*, December 14, 1884, 2.

56. *Tonganoxie Mirror*, February 16, 1899, 8.

57. See Brent M. S. Campney, "W. B. Townsend and the Struggle against Racist Violence in Leavenworth," *Kansas History* (Fall–Winter 2008–2009): 260–273.

58. *Leavenworth Times*, February 15, 1899, 4.

59. Payne, *I've Got the Light of Freedom*, 207–208, 235 (emphasis in the original).

60. Mike Belt, "Book Chronicles Lawrence Lynching," *Lawrence Journal-World*, June 19, 2005, http://www2.ljworld.com/news/2005/jun/19/lynching/ (accessed June 11, 2018).

61. City of Pittsburg, Police Department History, https://www.pittks.org/wp-content/uploads/2017/06/The-Pittsburg-Police-Departments-History-2017.pdf (accessed May 30, 2018).

62. Harper, *White Man's Heaven*, 40.

63. "Harriet C. Frazier's response to Brent M. S. Campney's review of her *Lynchings in Kansas: 1850s–1932* in July 2015," *H-Law*, October 14, 2015, https://networks.h-net.org/node/16794/reviews/74306/campney-frazier-lynchings-kansas-1850s-1932 (accessed May 30, 2018).

64. Kidada E. Williams, "Regarding the Aftermaths of Lynching," *Journal of American History* (December 14, 2014): 858. For a moving example of how scholars may reconstruct the personal relationships of lynching victims, see Amy Kate Bailey and Stewart E. Tolnay, *Lynched: The Victims of Southern Mob Violence* (Chapel Hill: University of North Carolina Press, 2015), 36–39.

65. Harper, *White Man's Heaven*, xv–xvi.

66. Michael J. Pfeifer, "Final Thoughts on the State of the Field of Lynching Scholarship," *Journal of American History* (December 2014): 859–860.

Chapter 5. Missouri's Little Dixie, 1899–1921

1. *Paris Mercury*, reprinted in *Mexico Missouri Message*, December 14, 1899, 3; *Monroe City Democrat*, December 7, 1899, 1. Unless otherwise noted, all newspapers cited in this chapter originate in Missouri.

2. *Paris Mercury*, reprinted in *Mexico Missouri Message*, December 14, 1899, 3; *Monroe City Democrat*, December 7, 1899, 1.

3. *Stoutsville Banner*, reprinted in *Marion County Herald* (Palmyra), May 14, 1903, 8.

4. *Marion County Herald* (Palmyra), June 27, 1901, 1.

5. Three of these seven definitions differentiated between core and peripheral counties, and one of them confused the matter further by identifying not only core and peripheral counties but also portions of several others. The seven definitions identified a combined total of all or parts of twenty-seven different counties. See R. Douglas Hurt, *Agriculture and Slavery in Missouri's Little Dixie* (Columbia: University of Missouri Press, 1992), ix–xiv.

6. Department of the Interior, *Population of the United States in 1860*; Compiled from the Original Returns of the Eighth Census (Washington, DC: Government Printing Office, 1864), 280–283.

7. *Mexico Missouri Message*, August 1, 1907, 1.

8. See Diane Mutti Burke, *On Slavery's Border: Missouri's Small-Slaveholding Households, 1815–1865* (Athens: University of Georgia Press, 2010).

9. On this lynching, see Dyer, "A Most Unexampled Exhibition."

10. *New York Tribune*, reprinted in *Liberator* (Boston), August 22, 1856, 137.

11. Michael Fellman, *Inside War: The Guerrilla Conflict in Missouri during the American Civil War* (New York: Oxford University Press, 1989). See also Clay Mountcastle, *Punitive War: Confederate Guerrillas and Union Reprisals* (Lawrence: University Press of Kansas, 2009); Jeremy Neely, *The Border between Them: Violence and Reconciliation on the Kansas-Missouri Line* (Columbia: University of Missouri Press, 2011).

12. Burke, *On Slavery's Border*, 281, 283, 282.

13. John W. McKerley, "'We Promise to Use the Ballot as We Did the Bayonet': Black Suffrage Activism and the Limits of Loyalty in Reconstruction Missouri," in *Bleeding Kansas, Bleeding Missouri: The Long Civil War on the Border*, ed. Jonathan Halperin Earle and Diane Mutti Burke (Lawrence: University Press of Kansas, 2013), 205–224.

14. *St. Louis Democrat*, reprinted in *New York Tribune*, September 9, 1869, 2.

15. Fellman, *Inside War*, 70. On the challenges facing black Missourians after the Civil War, see Neely, *Border between Them*; Aaron Astor, "The *Lexington Weekly Caucasian*: White Supremacist Discourse in Post–Civil War Western Missouri," and McKerley, "'We Promise to Use the Ballot,'" both in *Bleeding Kansas, Bleeding Missouri*, 189–203, 205–224.

16. *Weekly Graphic* (Kirksville), August 9, 1889, 2.

17. *La Plata Home Press*, August 24, 1905, 1.

18. [undecipherable], William Moore, G. P. Law, John Henderson, and W. C. Payne to Governor A. M. Hyde, May 16, 1921, 1, 2, 3, in Arthur Mastick Hyde, Papers, folders 365–369 (C0007), State Historical Society of Missouri Manuscript Collection, Columbia.

19. Governor A. M. Hyde to W. C. Payne, May 20, 1921, in Arthur Mastick Hyde, Papers, folders 365–369.

20. *Rising Son* (Kansas City), March 2, 1907, 1.

21. *Freeman* (Indianapolis), February 4, 1899, 4.

22. *St. Louis Globe-Democrat*, reprinted in *Kansas City Star*, December 17, 1906, 11.

23. *St. Louis Palladium*, July 13, 1907, 1.

24. *Moberly Weekly Monitor*, July 27, 1899, 4.

25. *St. Louis Post-Dispatch*, March 18, 1914, 12.

26. Selden P. Spencer to A. M. Hyde, May 28, 1921, in Arthur Mastick Hyde, Papers, folders 365–369.

27. Green Tree Negro Republican Club to A. M. Hyde, May 8, 1921, in Arthur Mastick Hyde, Papers, folders 365–369.

28. Walter White to A. M. Hyde, May 26, 1921, in Arthur Mastick Hyde, Papers, folders 365–369.

29. John F. Williams to The Commanding General [of the] Missouri National Guard, "Report on lynching of James Scott, negro, Columbia, Apr. 29," 2, in Arthur Mastick Hyde, Papers, folders 365–369.

30. Du Bois quoted in Dray, *At the Hands of Persons Unknown*, 294.

31. Ida M. Becks and Dora M. Harris to A. M. Hyde, April 30, 1923, in Arthur Mastick Hyde, Papers, folders 365–369.

32. *Kansas City Call*, May 4, 1928, news clippings file, microfilm 225, frame 0795, Tuskegee Institute Archives, Tuskegee, AL. In another case, this time in 1903, whites in Columbia attempted a lynching: "A negro employe[e] of a circus [in Columbia] was obliged to flee from a tent at a performance last night to escape lynching by Missouri university students." See *Lawrence* (Kansas) *Daily Journal*, May 12, 1903, 1.

33. *Shelby County Herald*, reprinted in *Monroe City Democrat*, June 13, 1901, 4.

34. *Sedalia Weekly Democrat*, February 8, 1903, 2.

35. *Moberly Evening Democrat*, June 15, 1903, 1.

36. *Sedalia Evening Democrat*, April 5, 1901, 1.

37. *Sedalia Evening Democrat*, August 25, 1902, 2.

38. *Mexico Missouri Message*, August 1, 1907, 1.

39. *Weekly Monitor* (Moberly), July 19, 1907, 1.

40. *Paris Appeal*, reprinted in *Monroe City Democrat*, July 25, 1907, 4.

41. *Mexico Missouri Message*, August 1, 1907, 1.

42. *Monroe City Democrat*, July 25, 1907, 1.

43. *St. Louis Post-Dispatch*, August 11, 1907, 16.

44. *Moberly Weekly Democrat*, August 9, 1907, 1.

45. *Monroe City Democrat*, July 25, 1907, 1.

46. *Monroe City Democrat*, June 6, 1901, 1.

47. *St. Louis Republic*, March 20, 1901, 6.

48. Missouri, Lincoln County, Hurricane Township, Elsberry Village, Ward 2, Supervisor's District no. 9, Enumeration District no. 50, *Twelfth Census of the United States,* schedule no. 1, *Population (Form 7-224)*, June 6–7, 1900, sheets 6B and 7A. The census material also indicates that there were several other babies

or toddlers living in the household, ranging in age from a few weeks old to three years old.

49. *St. Louis Post-Dispatch*, February 10, 1903, 5.

50. *Moberly Evening Democrat*, March 6, 1903, 3.

51. *St. Louis Post-Dispatch*, February 10, 1903, 5.

52. *Mexico Missouri Message*, August 1, 1907, 1.

53. *St. Louis Post-Dispatch*, August 11, 1907, 16.

54. *Mexico Missouri Message*, August 1, 1907, 1.

55. *St. Louis Post-Dispatch*, August 16, 1906, 11.

56. *Mexico Missouri Message*, December 13, 1900, 1.

57. *Sunday Morning Democrat* (Moberly), September 15, 1901, 8.

58. *Mexico Missouri Message*, January 31, 1901, 2.

59. *Moberly Weekly Monitor*, July 27, 1899, 4.

60. See photos in Frazier, *Lynchings in Missouri.*

61. *Chillicothe Constitution*, March 24, 1902, 12.

62. *Paris Appeal*, reprinted in *Monroe City Democrat*, August 15, 1907, 7.

63. *Chillicothe Constitution*, January 23, 1915, 1.

64. *Chillicothe Constitution*, July 18, 1914, 1. On the initial incident, see *Chillicothe Constitution*, April 21, 1914, 4.

65. *Chillicothe Constitution*, January 27, 1915, 2.

66. *St. Louis Post-Dispatch*, August 11, 1907, 16.

67. *Moberly Weekly Democrat*, August 9, 1907, 1. For further evidence of the antiblack policy in Stoutsville, see *Mexico Missouri Message*, August 1, 1907, 1.

68. *Stoutsville Banner*, reprinted in *Marion County Democrat* (Palmyra), August 8, 1901, 3.

69. *St. Louis Post-Dispatch*, August 16, 1906, 11.

70. *St. Louis Post-Dispatch*, August 15, 1906, 1.

71. *St. Louis Republic*, March 20, 1901, 6.

72. *Sedalia Evening Democrat*, April 5, 1901, 1.

73. *Sedalia Evening Democrat*, February 10, 1903, 1.

74. *Moberly Weekly Democrat*, August 9, 1907, 1.

75. *Monroe City Democrat*, August 26, 1915, 1.

76. *Monroe City Democrat*, September 7, 1916, 1.

77. *Marion County Herald* (Palmyra), May 14, 1903, 4.

78. *Monroe City Democrat*, July 30, 1903, 5.

79. *Stoutsville Banner*, reprinted in *Marion County Herald* (Palmyra), May 14, 1903, 4.

80. *Monroe City Democrat*, July 1, 1915, 3.

*81. *Monroe City Democrat*, July 1, 1915, 2.

82. *Monroe City Democrat*, August 26, 1915, 1; *Monroe City Democrat*, September 2, 1915, 1.

83. *Monroe City Democrat*, July 8, 1915, 2.

84. *Monroe City Democrat*, September 14, 1916, 1.

85. *Moberly Weekly Monitor*, December 20, 1912, 2.

86. Elliott Rudwick, *Race Riot at East St. Louis, July 2, 1917* (Urbana: University of Illinois Press, 1982).

87. *Macon Daily Chronicle-Herald*, November 26, 1919, 1.

88. *Moberly Weekly Democrat*, April 14, 1908, 5.

89. Campney, *This Is Not Dixie*.

90. *La Plata Home Press*, September 8, 1938, 2.

91. Quoted in Crystal N. Feimster, *Southern Horrors: Women and the Politics of Rape and Lynching* (Cambridge: Harvard University Press, 2009), 174. Feimster also showed, however, that white mobs lynched black women far more often than previously recognized.

92. Wright, *Racial Violence in Kentucky, 1865–1940*, 10–11.

93. Geoff Ward, "Microclimates of Racial Meaning: Historical Racial Violence and Environmental Impacts," *Wisconsin Law Review* (2016): 576–577.

94. Feimster, *Southern Horrors*, 159.

95. Loewen, *Sundown Towns*.

96. Lancaster, *Racial Cleansing in Arkansas*, 140.

Chapter 6. *The Missouri Ozarks and Beyond, 1894–1930*

1. *Springfield Democrat*, January 25, 1894, 8. Unless otherwise noted, all newspapers cited in this chapter were published in Missouri.

2. *St. Louis Post-Dispatch*, January 22, 1894, 1.

3. *St. Louis Post-Dispatch*, August 25, 1901, 1.

4. *Springfield Democrat* (weekly ed.), May 31, 1894, 3.

5. *Pittsburg (KS) Daily Headlight*, June 29, 1894, 4.

6. *Monett Leader*, reprinted in *Springfield Democrat*, May 24, 1895, 2.

7. *St. Louis Post-Dispatch*, August 25, 1901, 1.

8. *Leader-Democrat* (Springfield), November 25, 1901, 3.

9. *Springfield Republican*, September 7, 1904, 1.

10. *Joplin Globe*, June 8, 1922, 1.

11. *Springfield Republican*, March 11, 1903, 4.

12. *Webb City Daily Register*, August 24, 1904, 1. See also *Springfield Republican*, May 23, 1902, 1.

13. *Missouri Sharp Shooter* (Rolla), August 21, 1903, 4.

14. *Webb City Daily Register*, August 23, 1904, 1.

15. *Webb City Daily Register*, April 13, 1904, 1.

16. *Post-Dispatch Sunday Magazine* (St. Louis), September 20, 1903, 8.

17. *Post-Dispatch Sunday Magazine* (St. Louis), September 20, 1903, 8.

18. *St. Louis Post-Dispatch*, August 25, 1901, 1.

19. Elliot Jaspin, *Buried in the Bitter Waters: The Hidden History of Racial Cleansing in America* (New York: Basic Books, 2007), 78.

20. *St. Louis Post-Dispatch*, August 25, 1901, 1.

21. *Aurora Argus* reprinted in *St. Louis Post-Dispatch*, August 25, 1901, 1.

22. *Pittsburg (KS) Daily Headlight*, August 23, 1901, 5.

23. *St. Louis Post-Dispatch*, August 25, 1901, 1.

24. *St. Louis Post-Dispatch*, August 25, 1901, 1.

25. *St. Louis Post-Dispatch*, April 16, 1903, 3.

26. *Sedalia Evening Democrat*, April 17, 1903, 5.

27. *St. Louis Post-Dispatch*, April 16, 1906, 2.

28. *St. Louis Post-Dispatch*, April 16, 1906, 2.

29. *Springfield Leader*, October 17, 1930, 30. Kimberly Harper also discusses the rise and fall of black influence in Springfield. See Harper, *White Man's Heaven*, 109–124.

30. *Parsons (KS) Daily Sun*, October 7, 1907, 1. See also *Springfield Republican*, October 2, 1907, 7; *Springfield Republican*, October 6, 1907, 1, 4.

31. *St. Louis Post-Dispatch*, August 25, 1901, 1.

32. *St. Louis Post-Dispatch*, August 25, 1901, 1.

33. *St. Louis Post-Dispatch*, April 16, 1903, 3.

34. Harper, *White Man's Heaven*, 84.

35. *St. Louis Post-Dispatch*, August 25, 1901, 1.

36. *Kansas City Star*, July 14, 1920, 6.

37. *Current Local* (Van Buren), July 15, 1920, 1.

38. *Post-Dispatch Sunday Magazine (St. Louis)*, September 20, 1903, 8.

39. *Webb City Register*, April 16, 1907, 4.

40. *Webb City Register*, October 26, 1914, 1.

41. *Enterprise-Register* (Palatine, IL), February 21, 1903, 6.

42. *Webb City Register*, February 14, 1916, 1.

43. *Cassville Republican*, reprinted in *Neosho Times*, June 28, 1917, 2.

44. *Aurora Advertiser*, reprinted in *Springfield Leader*, November 12, 1930, 10.

45. P. W. Burden to Secretary of State, December 14, 1922, in Arthur Mastick Hyde, Papers, folders 365–369, (COOO7), The State Historical Society of Missouri Manuscript Collection, Columbia.

46. Willow Springs Klan to A. M. Hyde, January 26, 1923, in Arthur Mastick Hyde, Papers, folders 365–369.

47. Neosho, Granby, and Diamond Klans to A. M. Hyde, January 28, 1923, in Arthur Mastick Hyde, Papers, folders 365–369.

48. Mrs. A Desmedt to A. M. Hyde, January 23, 1924, in Arthur Mastick Hyde, Papers, folders 365–369.

49. Secretary to the Governor to Mrs. A. Desmedt, February 6, 1924, in Arthur Mastick Hyde, Papers, folders 365–369.

50. Pleasant Hill Klan to A. M. Hyde, January 28, 1923, in Arthur Mastick Hyde, Papers, folders 365–369.

51. T. S. Hardy to A. M. Hyde, April 26, 1921, in Arthur Mastick Hyde, Papers, folders 365–369.

52. "Ku Klux Klan Is Established Here," *Springfield Republican*, April 26, 1921, news clipping in Arthur Mastick Hyde, Papers, folders 365–369.

53. Department of the Interior, Census Office, *Twelfth Census of the United States, Taken in the Year 1900*, vol. 1, *Population*, pt. 1 (Washington, D.C: United States Census Office, 1901), 590–591; Department of Commerce, Bureau of the Census, *Fifteenth Census of the United States: 1930, Population*, vol. 3, pt. 1, *Alabama–Missouri* (Washington, DC: Government Printing Office, 1932), 1372–1384.

54. *Pittsburg (KS) Headlight*, November 2, 1899, 1.

55. *Pittsburg (KS) Daily Tribune*, October 31, 1899, 4. See also *Pittsburg (KS) Daily Headlight*, October 31, 1899, 1.

56. *Pittsburg (KS) Plain Dealer*, November 4, 1899, 2.

57. *Pittsburg (KS) Daily Tribune*, November 3, 1899, 4.

58. Campney, *This Is Not Dixie*, 98.

59. *Walnut (KS) Advance*, August 23, 1901, 4.

60. Harper, *White Man's Heaven*, 84.

61. *Pittsburg (KS) Daily Headlight*, August 23, 1901, 5.

62. *Daily Ardmoreite* (Ardmore, OK), August 27, 1901, 3.

63. *Muskogee (OK) Daily Phoenix*, August 27, 1901, 1.

64. *Muskogee (OK) Daily Phoenix*, August 27, 1901, 1.

65. *St. Louis Post-Dispatch*, August 25, 1901, 1.

66. *Arkansas Gazette* (Little Rock), March 26, 1914, 6.

67. *Arkansas Gazette* (Little Rock), August 4, 1922, 2.

68. Lancaster, *Racial Cleansing in Arkansas*, 92.

69. *Arkansas Gazette* (Little Rock), October 6, 1905, 1.

70. *Arkansas Democrat* (Little Rock), January 30, 1909, 4. On the 1909 expulsion, see *Arkansas Gazette* (Little Rock), January 29, 1909, 1.

71. *Arkansas Gazette*, quoted in Lancaster, *Racial Cleansing in Arkansas*, 94–95.

72. *St. Louis Post-Dispatch*, August 25, 1901, 1.

73. Jaspin, *Buried in the Bitter Waters*, 73.

74. *St. Louis Post-Dispatch*, August 25, 1901, 1.

75. *Evening Star* (Independence, KS), April 17, 1903, 2.

76. *Sedalia Evening Democrat*, April 17, 1903, 5. As noted in chapter 4, the spellings Peirce City and Pierce City often appeared in contemporary accounts. The former spelling, the correct one, was less commonly used well into the twentieth century.

77. *Guthrie (OK) Daily Leader*, August 26, 1901, 1.

78. Jaspin, *Buried in the Bitter Waters*, 79.

79. *Guthrie (OK) Daily Leader*, August 26, 1901, 1.

80. Harper, *White Man's Heaven*, 162.

81. *Sun* (Chanute, KS), June 30, 1906, 2.

82. Jaspin, *Buried in the Bitter Waters*, 70.

83. *Neosho Daily News*, September 8, 1954, 1.

84. *St. Louis Post-Dispatch*, July 7, 1963, 1B, 8B.

85. For brief but instructive discussions of antiblack violence in the Missouri Ozarks, see Michael J. Pfeifer, "The Ritual of Lynching: Extralegal Justice in Missouri, 1890–1942," *Gateway Heritage* (Winter 1993), 22–33; Loewen, *Sundown Towns*, 71–74, 95–96; Jaspin, *Buried in the Bitter Waters*, 66–85.

86. Loewen, *Sundown Towns*, 95–96.

87. Loewen, *Sundown Towns*, 96.

88. Harper, *White Man's Heaven*, 235–249.

89. Jaspin, *Buried in the Bitter Waters*, 79.

90. Lancaster, *Racial Cleansing in Arkansas*.

91. Loewen, *Sundown Towns*, 95.

92. *Joplin Globe*, February 14, 1954, 7E.

93. Jonathan Fairbanks and Clyde Edwin Tuck, *Past and Present of Greene County, Missouri: Early and Recent History and Genealogical Records of Many Representative Citizens* (Indianapolis: A. W. Bowen & Company, 1915), https://thelibrary.org/lochist/history/paspres/ch10.html (accessed May 18, 2018).

94. *Kansas City Star*, May 28, 1907, 8.

95. Charles Neider, ed., *The Complete Essays of Mark Twain* (Garden City, NY: Doubleday, 1963), 673.

96. Neider, *Complete Essays of Mark Twain*, 673.

Chapter 7. The Old Northwest, 1890s–1930s

1. *Chicago Daily Tribune*, July 27, 1903, 1.

2. *Decatur (IL) Herald*, July 26, 1903, 1.

3. *Daily Review* (Decatur, IL), July 28, 1903, 2.

4. *Coshocton (OH) Age*, June 27, 1885, 1.

5. *Cincinnati Daily Gazette*, December 4, 1882, 2.

6. *Daily Inter Ocean* (Chicago), December 4, 1882, 5.

7. *Daily Inter Ocean* (Chicago), December 4, 1882, 5.

8. *Daily Inter Ocean* (Chicago), December 4, 1882, 5.

9. *Bloomington Daily Pantagraph*, December 4, 1882, 1.

10. *Chicago Daily Tribune*, December 4, 1882, 8.

11. *Daily Inter Ocean* (Chicago), December 4, 1882, 5.

12. Baker, *Following the Color Line*, 206, 208 (emphasis in the original).

13. *Piqua (OH) Daily Call*, August 8, 1903, 1.

14. *Lima (OH) Times-Democrat*, October 30, 1906, 1.

15. *Daily Independent* (Murphysboro, IL), July 22, 1924, 1.

16. *Daily Review* (Decatur, IL), July 28, 1903, 2.

17. *Chicago Daily Tribune*, July 27, 1903, 1.

18. *Jacksonville (IL) Daily Journal*, July 23, 1924, 1.

19. *Chicago Daily Tribune*, September 9, 1903, 1.

20. *Indianapolis Star*, July 15, 1907, 5.

21. *St. Louis Post-Dispatch*, September 1, 1902, 7.

22. *Cook County Herald* (Arlington Heights, IL), August 10, 1906, 5.

23. *Alton (IL) Evening Telegraph*, July 31, 1906, 2.

24. *Daily Independent* (Murphysboro, IL), January 10, 1924, 1.

25. *Cincinnati Enquirer*, January 25, 1931, 1.

26. *Indianapolis News*, May 25, 1906, 15.

27. *Inter Ocean* (Chicago), January 12, 1910, 1.

28. *Chicago Daily Tribune*, July 27, 1903, 1.

29. *Chicago Daily Tribune*, August 30, 1915, 1.

30. *Hamilton (OH) Daily Democrat*, April 16, 1894, 1.

31. *Newark (OH) Daily Advocate*, April 18, 1894, 4.

32. *Daily Review* (Decatur, IL), July 28, 1903, 2.

33. *Indianapolis News*, February 18, 1910, 1.

34. *Daily Review* (Decatur, IL), February 18, 1910, 1.

35. *Weekly Sentinel* (Fort Wayne, IN), February 23, 1910, 6.

36. *New York Times*, October 18, 1894, 1. See also *Cincinnati Enquirer*, October 18, 1894, 1; *Cincinnati Enquirer*, October 19, 1894, 1.

37. Brian Butler, *An Undergrowth of Folly: Public Order, Race Anxiety, and the 1903 Evansville, Indiana, Riot* (New York: Garland, 2000), 193–194.

38. *Evansville (IN) Courier*, July 8, 1903, 1.

39. Quoted in *Daily Review* (Decatur, IL), July 28, 1903, 2.

40. *Piqua (OH) Daily Call*, June 5, 1897, 11.

41. *Chicago Daily Tribune*, July 27, 1903, 1.

42. *Carbondale (IL) Free Press*, December 26, 1930, 1.

43. *Indianapolis Star*, September 2, 1903, 1.

44. *Inter Ocean* (Chicago), September 3, 1903, 3.

45. *Alton (IL) Evening Telegraph*, October 22, 1906, 3. See also *Inter Ocean* (Chicago), October 21, 1906, 11.

46. *Democratic Standard* (Coshocton, OH), June 18, 1897, 14.

47. *Cincinnati Enquirer*, June 6, 1897, 1.

48. *Akron (OH) Daily Democrat*, August 23, 1900, 2.

49. *Lima (OH) Times-Democrat*, August 31, 1916, 1.

50. *Lima (OH) Times-Democrat*, August 31, 1916, 2.

51. *Inter Ocean* (Chicago), August 16, 1908, 7. For a detailed discussion of Loper's actions, his suffering at the hands of the mob, and the Springfield race riot generally, see de la Roche, *In Lincoln's Shadow*, 27–30, 93–103.

52. *Columbus (IN) Republican*, August 6, 1903, 2.

53. *Bremen (IN) Enquirer*, August 13, 1903, 8.

54. *Inter Ocean* (Chicago), August 16, 1908, 7.

55. *Chicago Daily Tribune*, July 27, 1903, 1.

56. *Daily Free Press* (Carbondale, IL), July 29, 1903, 8.

57. *Rockford (IL) Republic*, August 6, 1913, 3.

58. *Inter Ocean* (Chicago), August 17, 1913, 2. See also *Inter Ocean* (Chicago), August 10, 1913, 3.

59. *Indianapolis News*, June 9, 1902, 13.

60. *Fort Wayne (IN) Daily News*, June 19, 1902, 3.

61. *Dixon (IL) Evening Telegraph*, July 11, 1913, 1.

62. *Evansville (IN) Courier and Press*, April 27, 1904, 1.

63. Winfield T. Durbin to the Members of Company E, First Regiment I.N.G., at the Annual Camp of Instruction, Indiana National Guard, Indianapolis, August 2, 1903, in *Papers and Addresses of Winfield T. Durbin* (Marion, IN: Chronicle Company, n.d.), 2.

64. *Columbus (IN) Republican*, July 9, 1903, 5.

65. *Biennial message of Gov. James A. Mount of Indiana 1899*, 9, 10, James A. Mount collection. S996. Rare Books and Manuscripts, Indiana State Library, Indianapolis.

66. *Journal of the House of Representatives of the State of Indiana, Sixty-Fourth Session of the General Assembly* (Indianapolis: Wm. S. Burford, 1906), 57, https://babel.hathitrust.org/cgi/pt?id=nyp.33433082089305;view=1up;seq=63 (accessed May 28, 2018).

67. Theodore Roosevelt to Winfield T. Durbin, August 6, 1903, Theodore Roosevelt Center at Dickinson State University, http://theodorerooseveltcenter.org/Research/Digital-Library/Record/ImageViewer?libID=0185599&imageNo=1 (accessed May 29, 2018).

68. Winfield T. Durbin to Theodore Roosevelt, August 10, 1903, Theodore Roosevelt Center at Dickinson State University, http://theodorerooseveltcenter.org/Research/Digital-Library/Record/ImageViewer?libID=041716&imageNo=1 (accessed on May 28, 2018).

69. *Cincinnati Enquirer*, June 5, 1897, 5.

70. *Miami Helmet* (Piqua, OH), November 17, 1898, 2.

71. *Daily Herald* (Delphos, OH), January 28, 1899, 1.

72. *City Item* (Massillon, OH), April 20, 1898, 2.

73. *Inter Ocean* (Chicago), May 17, 1905, 2.

74. Dray, *At the Hands of Persons Unknown*, 175, 176. Indiana had a similar law, as Governor Durbin noted during his 1905 address. See *Journal of the House of Representatives of the State of Indiana*, 58.

75. Baker, *Following the Color Line*, 213 (emphasis in the original).

76. *Indianapolis Morning Star and Journal*, September 13, 1904, 1.

77. *Dixon (IL) Evening Telegraph*, October 16, 1915, 1.

78. *Chicago Daily Tribune*, July 19, 1916, 2.

79. *Indianapolis News*, July 28, 1922, 10.

80. *Daily Republican* (Rushville, IN), July 28, 1922, 1.

81. *Cincinnati Enquirer*, January 25, 1931, 1, 2.

82. Pfeifer, *Rough Justice*.

83. Richard Wright, *Native Son* (1940; reprint, New York: Harper & Row, 1966), 228, 229.

84. Gordon Parks, *The Learning Tree* (1963; Greenwich, CT: Fawcett Crest, 1969), 26.

85. Parks, *Learning Tree*, 239. On the threatened lynching, see 205–207.

86. Keneth Kinnamon, "How *Native Son* Was Born," in *Richard Wright: Critical Perspectives Past and Present*, ed. Henry Louis Gates Jr. and K. A. Appiah (New York: Amistad, 1993), 113.

Chapter 8. *The Midwest in the Late Lynching Period*

1. "The body of . . ." in *Ironton Evening Tribune*, June 10, 1932, 10; Theodore M. Berry, "Sordid Story of Ironton Lynch Orgy is Re-Told," *Pittsburgh (PA) Courier*, August 6, 1932, sec. 2, p. 9. Unless otherwise noted, all newspapers cited in this chapter were published in Ohio.

2. *Ironton Evening Tribune*, June 10, 1932, 10.

3. William W. Giffin, *African Americans and the Color Line in Ohio, 1915–1930* (Columbus: Ohio State University, 2005), 110–111.

4. Giffin, *African Americans and the Color Line*, 118.

5. Giffin, *African Americans and the Color Line*, 66, 67.

6. U.S. Department of Commerce, *Fifteenth Census of the United States: 1930, Population*, vol.3, pt. 2, *Montana–Wyoming* (Washington, DC: Government Printing Office, 1932), 469, 475.

7. On racist violence in Lawrence County, see *Cincinnati Enquirer*, reprinted in *Plain Dealer* (Cleveland), May 12, 1859, 2; on the 1901 threatened lynching, see *Ironton News*, July 22, 1932, 1.

8. *Ironton Evening Tribune*, July 25, 1932, 2.

9. *Pittsburgh (PA) Courier*, August 6, 1932, sec. 2, p. 9; *Pittsburgh (PA) Courier*, June 25, 1932, 2.

10. *Ohio State Journal*, reprinted in *Plain Dealer* (Cleveland), July 30, 1850, 2.

11. *Ironton News*, July 22, 1932, 1.

12. *Plain Dealer* (Cleveland), July 6, 1901, 2.

13. Berry, *Pittsburgh (PA) Courier*, August 6, 1932, 19. On the length of Murray's tenure with the Davidson family, see *Ironton Evening Tribune*, July 25, 1932, 2.

14. *Ironton Sunday Tribune*, June 12, 1932, 12.

15. *Ironton Evening Tribune*, July 27, 1932, 2.

16. *Ironton Evening Tribune*, July 28, 1932, 2.

17. Berry, *Pittsburgh (PA) Courier*, August 6, 1932, sec. 2, p. 9.

18. *Ironton Evening Tribune*, June 11, 1932, 2.

19. *Ironton Evening Tribune*, July 28, 1932, 3.

20. *Ironton Evening Tribune*, June 16, 1932, 10.

21. *Ironton Evening Tribune*, July 26, 1932, 2.

22. *Ironton News*, July 18, 1932, 8.

23. *Ironton Sunday Tribune*, June 12, 1932, 12.

24. *Ironton Evening Tribune*, July 28, 1932, 2, 3.

25. *Ironton Evening Tribune*, July 28, 1932, 2.

26. *Pittsburgh (PA) Courier*, June 25, 1932, 2.

27. Berry, *Pittsburgh (PA) Courier*, August 6, 1932, sec. 2, p. 9.

28. *Ironton Sunday Tribune*, July 17, 1932, 3.

29. *Ironton Evening Tribune*, July 25, 1932, 2.

30. *Pittsburgh (PA) Courier*, June 25, 1932, 2.

31. *Ironton Evening Tribune*, July 25, 1932, 2.

32. Berry, *Pittsburgh (PA) Courier*, August 6, 1932, sec. 2, p. 9. Although some newspapers claimed that Mrs. Davidson and Nancy were mother and daughter, they were in fact aunt and niece.

33. MSS 13 B05 F07, Ohio NAACP Collection, Minutes of the 3rd Annual Ohio NAACP Branches Convention, September 1932, [5], Archives & Library at the Ohio History Center, Ohio History Connection, Columbus, OH.

34. *Ironton Evening Tribune*, June 13, 1932, 2.

35. *Ironton Evening Tribune*, June 15, 1932, 10.

36. *Ironton Evening Tribune*, June 16, 1932, 2.

37. *Ironton Evening Tribune*, June 21, 1932, 2.

38. *Ironton Sunday Tribune*, July 17, 1932, 3.

39. *Ironton News*, July 18, 1932, 8.

40. *Ironton News*, July 22, 1932, 1.

41. *Ironton Evening Tribune*, July 28, 1932, 2.

42. *Ironton Evening Tribune*, June 22, 1932, 3.

43. *Ironton Evening Tribune*, June 24, 1932, 2; *Ironton Evening Tribune*, June 27, 1932, 8.

44. *Ironton Evening Tribune*, July 22, 1932, 3.

45. *Ironton Evening Tribune*, July 24, 1932, 3.

46. *Ironton Evening Tribune*, July 28, 1932, 3.

47. Berry, *Pittsburgh (PA) Courier*, August 6, 1932, sec. 2, p. 9.

48. *Ironton Evening Tribune*, July 28, 1932, 2.

49. *Ironton Evening Tribune*, July 28, 1932, 2.

50. *Ironton Evening Tribune*, July 26, 1932, 2, 8.

51. *Ironton Evening Tribune*, July 28, 1932, 2.

52. See Campney, *This Is Not Dixie*, esp. 99–101.

53. *Ironton Evening Tribune*, July 28, 1932, 2.

54. *Ironton Evening Tribune*, July 27, 1932, 2. See also *Ironton News*, July 27, 1932, 1.

55. *Ironton Evening Tribune*, July 28, 1932, 2.

56. *Ironton Evening Tribune*, July 27, 1932, 2.

57. *Ironton Evening Tribune*, July 28, 1932, 2.

58. MSS 13 B05 F07, Ohio NAACP Collection, Minutes of the 3rd Annual Ohio NAACP Branches Convention, September 1932, [5].

59. *Ironton News*, July 27, 1932, 1.

60. *Ironton Evening Tribune*, July 25, 1932, 2.

61. *Ironton Evening Tribune*, July 26, 1932, 2. See also *Ironton Evening Tribune*, July 27, 1932, 7.

62. *Ironton Sunday Tribune*, July 31, 1932, 4.

63. *Ironton Evening Tribune*, August 13, 1932, 2.

64. Berry, *Pittsburgh (PA) Courier*, August 6, 1932, sec. 2, p. 9.

65. *Ironton Evening Tribune*, July 27, 1932, 2.

66. *Ironton Evening Tribune*, August 3, 1932, 3.

67. *Ironton Evening Tribune*, August 16, 1932, 8.

68. *Ironton Sunday Tribune*, August 14, 1932, 3.

69. *Negro Star* (Wichita), August 19, 1932, 2.

70. *Negro Star* (Wichita), August 19, 1932, 2.

71. MSS 13 Bo5 Fo7, Ohio NAACP Collection, Minutes of the 3rd Annual Ohio NAACP Branches Convention, September 1932, [18–19].

72. *Ironton Evening Tribune*, October 13, 1932, 2.

73. *Ironton Evening Tribune*, August 8, 1932, 8.

74. *Broad Ax* (Chicago), December 25, 1926, 2. For more on the role of policemen in stifling mob violence and in assuming the role of the mob, see Campney, *This Is Not Dixie*, 116–131, 133, 135–137.

75. On the significance of the Marion lynching, see, e.g., Madison, *Lynching in the Heartland*; Rushdy, *End of American Lynching*, 60–61, 73.

76. *Repository* (Canton), August 9, 1930, 5.

77. *Springfield (MA) Republican*, August 14, 1930, 2.

78. On the increasing tendency among urban midwesterners to regard their rural counterparts as rubes and hicks, see Shortridge, *Middle West*, 8–9, 39–66.

79. *Freeport (IL) Journal-Standard*, December 9, 1946, 1. See also *Decatur (IL) Herald*, July 14, 1943, 1.

80. Marjorie McKenzie, "Rumor Caused Mob to Lynch Man," *Pittsburgh (PA) Courier*, July 24, 1943, 4. In 1942 a black newspaper published a notice from Person's family, which was anxiously searching for James. Writing from Somerville, Tennessee, a family member, Columbus Person, wrote that James was "mentally defected," required hospitalization for "mental treatments," and supposedly was on his way to Chicago. See *Plaindealer* (Kansas City, KS), October 9, 1942, 2.

81. McKenzie, *Pittsburgh (PA) Courier*, July 24, 1943, 4.

82. McKenzie, *Pittsburgh (PA) Courier*, July 24, 1943, 4.

83. *Decatur (IL) Daily Review*, December 9, 1946, 13. See also *Daily Illinois State Journal* (Springfield), November 9, 1943, 8.

84. *Chicago Daily Tribune*, November 9, 1943, 1.

85. Loewen, *Sundown Towns*, 286.

86. *Chicago Daily Tribune*, November 9, 1943, 1.

87. Amy Louise Wood, "Rethinking the Geography of Lynching," *Southern Spaces*, December 4, 2013, http://southernspaces.org/2013/rethinking-geography-lynching (accessed December 22, 2018). See also Mary L. Dudziak, *Cold War*

Civil Rights: Race and the Image of American Democracy (Princeton: Princeton University Press, 2000); and Sarah L. Silkey, "British Public Debates and the 'Americanization' of Lynching," Fumiko Sakashita, "Lynching across the Pacific: Japanese Views and African American Responses in the Wartime Antilynching Campaign," and Meredith L. Roman, "U.S. Lynch Law and the Fate of the Soviet Union: The Soviet Uses of American Racial Violence," all in *Swift to Wrath: Lynching in Global Historical Perspective*, ed. William D. Carrigan and Christopher Waldrep, 160–180; 181–214; 215–236 (Charlottesville: University of Virginia Press, 2013).

88. *Lincoln (NE) State Journal*, July 16, 1929, 7.

89. *Lincoln (NE) Star*, July 22, 1929, 2. See also *Nebraska State Journal*, July 15, 1929, 1; *Evening State Journal* (Lincoln, NE), August 8, 1929, 2.

90. *Daily Journal-Gazette and Commercial-Star* (Mattoon, IL), July 15, 1929, 1.

91. *Idaho Statesman* (Boise), May 8, 1930, 3.

92. *Emporia (KS) Weekly Gazette*, May 15, 1930, [issue incomplete and not paginated].

93. *Daily Republican* (Burlington, KS), May 9, 1930, 1. See also issues of this newspaper for May 7, 1930, 1; May 8, 1930, 1.

94. Question 20 in "Interview with William Bradford Huie," *Eyes on the Prize Interviews: The Complete Series* (Washington University Digital Gateway), http://digital.wustl.edu/cgi/t/text/text-idx?c=eop;cc=eop;rgn=main;view=text;idno=hui0015.1034.050 (accessed May 13, 2018).

95. Stephen J. Whitfield, *A Death in the Delta: The Story of Emmett Till* (Baltimore: Johns Hopkins University Press, 1991), 16.

96. McKenzie, *Pittsburgh (PA) Courier*, July 24, 1943, 4.

97. Clarence Lang, "Locating the Civil Rights Movement: An Essay on the Deep South, Midwest, and Border South in Black Freedom Studies," *Journal of Social History* 47: 2 (Winter 2013): 373.

98. "Lynching Goes Underground," cited in Manfred Berg, *Popular Justice: A History of Lynching in America* (Lanham, MD: Ivan R. Dee, 2011), 165.

99. *Alton (IL) Evening Telegraph*, June 2, 1955, 6.

100. *Southern Illinoisan* (Carbondale), May 17, 1970, 8.

101. McKenzie, *Pittsburgh (PA) Courier*, July 24, 1943, 1.

102. Berg, *Popular Justice*, 165.

103. Payne, *I've Got the Light of Freedom*, 13.

104. Hobbs, *Democracy Abroad*, 27–28.

105. On "lynching's fraught connection to modernity," see Wood, *Lynching and Spectacle*, 5.

106. Elliott J. Gorn, "Unquiet Emmett Till," *Southern Spaces*, January 30, 2015, http://southernspaces.org/2015/unquiet-emmett-till (accessed December 22, 2018).

107. Pfeifer, *Rough Justice*, 122; Tolnay and Beck, *Festival of Violence*, 202. See also Brundage, *Lynching in the New South*, 245.

Conclusion

1. *American Citizen* (Kansas City, KS), May 21, 1897, 2.
2. Arellano, *Vigilantes and Lynch Mobs*, 16.
3. Payne, *I've Got the Light of Freedom*, 207–235.
4. Jon K. Lauck, *The Lost Region: Toward a Revival of Midwestern History* (Iowa City: University of Iowa Press, 2013), 27.

Bibliography

Primary Sources

The primary materials used for this book derive from the extensive microfilm newspaper collections and manuscript collections at the Kansas State Historical Society in Topeka, the Kenneth Spencer Research Library at the University of Kansas in Lawrence, the Special Collections Research Center of the Morris Library at Southern Illinois University in Carbondale, the State Historical Society of Missouri in Columbia, the Special Collections and University Archives at Pittsburg (Kansas) State University, and the Ohio History Center in Columbus. They also derive from newspapers compiled in for-profit online databases including geneaologybank.com, newspapers.com, and newspaperarchive.com.

Secondary Sources

In the course of researching this book, I consulted a large body of scholarly literature on racist violence, the black freedom struggle, and the Midwest. Far from comprehensive, what follows is a bibliography of those studies that I regard as the most influential for my own work.

Alexander, Shawn Leigh. *An Army of Lions: The Civil Rights Struggle before the NAACP*. Philadelphia: University of Pennsylvania Press, 2012.

Bailey, Amy Kate, and Stewart E. Tolnay. *Lynched: The Victims of Southern Mob Violence*. Chapel Hill: University of North Carolina Press, 2015.

Berwanger, Eugene H. *The Frontier against Slavery: Western Anti-Negro Prejudice and the Slavery Extension Controversy*. Urbana: University of Illinois Press, 2002.

Brundage, W. Fitzhugh. *Lynching in the New South: Georgia and Virginia, 1880–1930*. Urbana: University of Illinois Press, 1993.

Campney, Brent M. S. *This Is Not Dixie: Racist Violence in Kansas, 1861–1927*. Urbana: University of Illinois Press, 2015.

Capeci, Dominic J., Jr. *The Lynching of Cleo Wright*. Lexington: University Press of Kentucky, 1998.

Carrigan, William D. *The Making of a Lynching Culture: Violence and Vigilantism in Central Texas, 1836–1916*. Urbana: University of Illinois Press, 2004.

de la Roche, Roberta Senechal. *In Lincoln's Shadow: The 1908 Race Riot in Springfield, Illinois*. Carbondale: Southern Illinois University Press, 2008.

Dray, Philip. *At the Hands of Persons Unknown: The Lynching of Black America*. New York: Random House, 2002.

Feimster, Crystal N. *Southern Horrors: Women and the Politics of Rape and Lynching*. Cambridge: Harvard University Press, 2009.

Gerber, David A. *Black Ohio and the Color Line, 1860–1915*. Urbana: University of Illinois Press, 1976.

Hendricks, Wanda A. *Gender, Race, and Politics in the Midwest: Black Club Women in Illinois*. Bloomington: Indiana University Press, 1998.

Hobbs, Tameka Bradley. *Democracy Abroad, Lynching at Home: Racial Violence in Florida*. Gainesville: University Press of Florida, 2015.

Lancaster, Guy. *Racial Cleansing in Arkansas, 1883–1924: Politics, Land, Labor, and Criminality*. Lanham, MD: Lexington Books, 2014.

Litwack, Leon F. *North of Slavery: The Negro in the Free States, 1790–1860*. Chicago: University of Chicago Press, 1971.

Loewen, James W. *Sundown Towns: A Hidden Dimension of American Racism*. New York: New Press, 2005.

Ortiz, Paul. *Emancipation Betrayed: The Hidden History of Black Organizing and White Violence in Florida from Reconstruction to the Bloody Election of 1920*. Berkeley: University of California Press, 2005.

Pfeifer, Michael J. *The Roots of Rough Justice: Origins of American Lynching*. Urbana: University of Illinois Press, 2011.

———. *Rough Justice: Lynching and American Society, 1874–1947*. Urbana: University of Illinois Press, 2004.

Silkey, Sarah L. *Black Woman Reformer: Ida B. Wells, Lynching, and Transatlantic Activism*. Athens: University of Georgia Press, 2015.

Tolnay, Stewart E., and E. M. Beck. *A Festival of Violence: An Analysis of Southern Lynchings, 1882–1930*. Urbana: University of Illinois Press, 1995.

Waldrep, Christopher. *The Many Faces of Judge Lynch: Extralegal Violence and Punishment in America*. New York: Palgrave Macmillan, 2002.

Ward, Geoff K. *The Black Child-Savers: Racial Democracy and Juvenile Justice*. Chicago: University of Chicago Press, 2012.

Williams, Kidada E. *They Left Great Marks on Me: African American Testimonies of Racial Violence from Emancipation to World War I*. New York: New York University Press, 2012.

Wood, Amy Louise. *Lynching and Spectacle: Witnessing Racial Violence in America, 1890–1940*. Chapel Hill: University of North Carolina Press, 2009.

Wright, George C. *Racial Violence in Kentucky, 1865–1940: Lynchings, Mob Rule, and "Legal Lynchings."* Louisiana Paperback ed. Baton Rouge: Louisiana State University Press, 1996.

Index

segregation: residential, 109, 117, 123, 162, 189, 198; school, 48, 96, 162, 190. *See also* Jim Crow practices; sundown towns and counties

Shawneetown, IL, 23, 147

Shelbina, MO, 100, 103, 104–105

Shelbyville, IN, 59–60, 62, 65

Shortridge, James R., 8, 230n78

Silex, MO, 103, 105, 108, 110, 189

slave-hunting and slave-catching, 18, 23, 24, 41, 45–46, 187, 190

slavery: attitudes toward, in Indiana, 55; in Illinois, 40–41; legacy of, in Missouri, 99, 109, 188, 197

Sneed, Ike, threatened lynching of, 74

Sneed family, 87

soldiers: black, 57, 59, 178–179; in guerrilla conflict in Missouri, 94; resistance to mobs, 143–145, 193; violence against blacks by, 47, 54. *See also* militias

southern white critique of Midwest, 31, 60, 67–69, 169, 181–182, 192, 196

South Point, OH, 161–169, 175–176, 178–179, 184, 189, 191

Spencer, Joseph, lynching of, 17, 35–39, 48–49, 52–53, 190, 194, 200, 208n5, 208n6

Spencer, Selden P., 98

Springfield, IL, 45, 193, 226n51

Springfield, MO, 114, 119–121, 123–124, 129–135

Springfield, OH, 138–139, 162

St. Louis, MO, 45, 98, 106, 108, 130, 131

Stoutsville, MO, 105, 107, 108

suicide, circumstantial. *See* circumstantial suicide

sundown towns and counties, 4–5, 10, 194, 197–198; in Arkansas, 128–129, 132, 133; in Illinois, 146; in Indiana, 65–66, 68; in Missouri Ozarks, 93, 95, 105–114, 119, 121–125, 127, 129; in Ohio, 162–163, 165–166, 176–177, 179, 181–183; in Oklahoma, 129–130, 130–134

Taney, Roger B., 45

Taylorville, IL, 50, 211n71

Terre Haute, IN, 140–141, 142, 214n76

Terry, Bill, lynching of, 16, 34

This Is Not Dixie (book), 2, 5, 7, 71, 111

Thornbrough, Emma Lou, 64

threatened lynching, 7, 18, 32, 88, 114, 122–123, 132; in Cairo, IL, 145; in Chicago,

140; in Evansville, IN, 145; in Ironton, OH, 162; in Jefferson County, IL, 19; in Jeffersonville, IN, 20; in Lawrence, KS, 83; in Salina, KS, 81; in Tonganoxie, KS, 83; in Vienna, IL, 142; in Webb City, MO, 116

Till, Emmett, lynching of, 3, 181, 184

Toledo, OH, 31, 70, 189

Toliver family, 82–83, 84, 86, 87, 194, 217n37

Tolnay, Stewart E., 37

Tonganoxie, KS, 82–83, 86–87

Townsend, W. B., 87

Tucker, John, lynching of, 16, 18

Twain, Mark, 49–50, 134–135

Urbana, OH, 146, 153, 154, 193

Vanderburgh County, IN, 20, 151

Vienna, IL, 17, 32, 142

Vinegar, Margaret, 80, 81, 87, 89, 217n24

Vinegar, Pete, lynching of, 80–81

Waldrep, Christopher, 5–6, 14, 34, 196

Ward, Geoff, 111

Warren County, OH, 13, 30

Washington, Marvin, whipping of, 101, 110

Washington County, IL, 42–43, 45

Washington Court House, OH, 145, 193

Weaver, L. M., 166, 167, 172

Webb, Uriah, death in riot, 62

Webb City, MO, 116, 119, 122–123, 132, 197

Wells-Barnett, Ida B., 154

Wheeler, Joanne, 49

whippings and floggings, 2, 113, 116, 127, 132; in the antebellum period, 16–17, 21, 29, 32, 188; in Little Dixie, 92–112, 193, 197

White, George, 167, 173, 191

White, Walter, 98, 173, 184, 191

Whitfield, Stephen J., 182

Whitlock, Hardy, 136, 139–140, 144–146, 154–155, 195

Williams, Kidada E., 91

Willis, Hollie, lynching of, 178–179, 184

Wood, Amy Louise, 4, 9, 199

Wright, George C., 110–111, 155

Wright, Oliver, lynching of, 104

Wright, Richard, 159–160

Wyatt, David, lynching of, 1

Xenia, OH, 27, 30

BRENT M. S. CAMPNEY is an associate professor of history at the University of Texas Rio Grande Valley. He is the author of *This Is Not Dixie: Racist Violence in Kansas, 1861–1927*.

The University of Illinois Press
is a founding member of the
Association of American Presses.

———————————————

Composed in 10.5/13 Minion Pro
by Kirsten Dennison
at the University of Illinois Press
Cover illustration: Illustration of man from
St. Louis Post-Dispatch, September 20, 1903;
background illustration ©iStock.com/andipantz.
Cover designed by Jason Gabbert

University of Illinois Press
1325 South Oak Street
Champaign, IL 61820-6903
www.press.uillinois.edu